The English Language in Nova Scotia

Essays on Past and Present Developments in English across the Province

Edited, with introductions, by
Lilian Falk & Margaret Harry

Roseway Publishing
Lockeport, Nova Scotia

'The Vowel Phonemes of Halifax and General Canadian English' by A. Murray Kinloch was originally published in *Papers from the 3rd Annual Meeting of the Atlantic Provinces Linguistic Association,* 1980.

'The Dialect of Lunenburg' by M.B. Emeneau was originally published in *Language 11* (1935). It is reprinted with permission.

'Between Emphasis and Exaggeration' by Lilian Falk was previously published in *Papers from the Annual Meeting of the Atlantic Provinces Linguistic Association*, 14, 1990.

'The Use of Nicknames in Cape Breton' by William Davey & Richard MacKinnon was originally published in *The Centre of the World at the Edge of a Continent: Cultural Studies of Cape Breton Island*, edited by Carol Corbin & Judith A. Rolls, by the University College of Cape Breton Press, Sydney, Nova Scotia, in 1996.

Cover illustration: "Bruce's Boat," hooked rug by Brenda Conroy, reproduced by permission of Bruce Tudor.
Cover and book design: Brenda Conroy
Printed and bound in Canada by Hignell Printing.

Published by Roseway Publishing Co. Ltd.
Lockeport, Nova Scotia B0T 1L0
phone/fax (902) 656-2223
email ktudor@atcon.com
www.outdoorns.com/~roseway

Canadian Cataloguing in Publication Data
Main entry under Title:

The English Language in Nova Scotia
ISBN 1-896496-07-5

1. English Language — Nova Scotia. 2. Linguistics — Nova Scotia.
I. Falk, Lilian, 1933- II. Harry, Margaret, 1943-

PE3241.A1E53 1998 427.971 C98- 950223-6

Contents

Contributors

Lindsey Arnold is a doctoral candidate in the Philosophy of Education at OISE/University of Toronto. She is working in the fields of aesthetics, semiotics, literary theory, feminism, and postmodernism, with a specific interest in the risks and possibilities of subversive modes of textual engagement.

George Elliott Clarke teaches English at Duke University, Durham, NC. A well known poet and playwright, he has done much to encourage Black literature in his native Nova Scotia, and is currently completing a study of African Canadian literature.

William Davey teaches Medieval Literature at the University College of Cape Breton, Sydney. He has been studying local variations of English for some time and is a co-founder, with Richard MacKinnon, of the *Dictionary of Cape Breton English* project.

John Edwards is a professor of Psychology at St. Francis Xavier University, Antigonish. He specializes in the relationship between language and group identity, and particularly its social implications. He is editor of the *Journal of Multilingual and Multicultural Development.*

M. B. Emeneau had a long and distinguished career teaching Linguistics at Yale University and later at the University of California at Berkeley, becoming a Professor Emeritus in 1971. Much of his work deals with Dravidian (Tamil) linguistics. He now lives in retirement in California.

Karin Flikeid teaches French and Linguistics at Saint Mary's University, Halifax. A researcher in the field of Acadian linguistics, she is working on a comprehensive study of Acadian French in Nova Scotia.

Stephanie Inglis teaches Mi'kmaq Studies at the University College of Cape Breton, Sydney. Her fields of research include language contact and language death, as well as modality and morphology in Mi'kmaq.

A. Murray Kinloch taught English for many years at the University of New Brunswick, Fredericton. A specialist in Phonetics/Phonology, he made many studies of the pronunciation of Canadian English. He died in 1993.

Richard MacKinnon teaches Folklore in the Department of Heritage, Culture, and Leisure Studies at the University College of Cape Breton, Sydney. He is a co-founder, with William Davey, of the *Dictionary of Cape Breton English* project.

Deborah Poff is Vice-President (Academic) and a professor of Political Science at the University of Northern British Columbia, Prince George. She was formerly Director of the Institute for the Study of Women at Mount Saint Vincent University, Halifax. She is working in the field of Applied Ethics, and is co-editor of the journal *Business Ethics in Canada.*

Lewis J. Poteet teaches English at Concordia University, Montreal. He is interested in both regional and occupational dialects, and his research in these fields has resulted in the publication of several specialized dictionaries and lexicons.

John G. Reid teaches History and Atlantic Canada Studies at Saint Mary's University, Halifax. He specializes in the history of northeastern North America with particular interest in seventeenth century history.

Preface

As teachers in the Department of English at Saint Mary's University in Halifax, we have been conscious of the fact that it has always been easier to look up answers to questions about the English language in general than about the English language in Nova Scotia in particular. Books dealing with the history, structure, and varieties of English worldwide are easily available, but reference works dealing with the varieties of English in Nova Scotia have been very few. As a result, we have found ourselves encouraging our students to describe and analyse for themselves the way they speak. We have asked, for instance, whether such expressions as *anyways*, *down home*, *great big*, and *slow as cold molasses* are specific to Nova Scotia, or more general. In the course of such exercises, it soon became evident to all of us, students and professors alike, that Nova Scotian speech offers a rich field for exploration. Together, we compiled glossaries of regional expressions, wrote grammatical paradigms, and tried to pin down syntactic structures. Our work gradually led us to a realization that English in Nova Scotia, with its roots in Great Britain, Ireland, and the United States, and considerably influenced by many other groups, is both complex in itself and sometimes fascinatingly unlike General Canadian English. Out of our class discussions, and discussions with colleagues who are themselves engaged in various aspects of research on Maritime English, there arose the idea of assembling a number of essays on different topics dealing with the English language in Nova Scotia. The present collection is the result.

We hope that by bringing the following studies together in one volume we will be able to provide general readers, as well as students, with a book which will answer some of their questions about English in the province. In addition, we would also like it to encourage them to think about the distinctive features of their own language and speech habits, whether as speakers of Nova Scotian English, or of other varieties of English or other languages, with a new interest and appreciation.

We are grateful to those colleagues who have allowed us to include their papers, both those previously published, and those prepared especially for this collection; we are also grateful for their help in locating some older material, which we reprint here. We were particularly aware of the need to include here several chapters which have hitherto been available only in specialized periodicals or collections. We would also like to thank all the specialists and staff members of research libraries for their help, especially Douglas Vaisey and the staff of the Patrick Power Library at Saint Mary's University. Finally, our thanks to our colleagues and friends at Saint Mary's University for their steady support, to Kathleen Tudor and Brenda Conroy of Roseway Publishing for their invaluable assistance, and to our own family members for sustaining us with their good cheer and faith in our project.

Lilian Falk
Margaret Harry

Historical Introduction

John G. Reid

The term 'Nova Scotia' has had a variety of meanings over a period of almost four centuries. It originated from the colonial claim advanced by Scotland in 1621 to a territory corresponding to today's Maritime Provinces of Canada and the Gaspé peninsula. A small Scottish presence in 'New Scotland' was maintained from 1629 to 1632, with the sustenance of a trading relationship with Mi'kmaw and Wuastukwiuk (Maliseet) aboriginal peoples, but the Scottish withdrawal under the terms of the Treaty of Saint-Germain-en-Laye (1632) prepared the way for the modest expansion of the French settlement in the region that had first been attempted in 1604 and had been continuous on a small scale since 1610. The Scottish claim and the use of its Latin title — *Nova Scotia* — as a geographical term, persisted intermittently among New Englanders who had trading or fishing interests along the coastline. After British and New England forces had captured the French colonial headquarters of Port Royal in 1710, and renamed it Annapolis Royal, the consequence of the sustaining of the conquest in the Treaty of Utrecht was the establishment of a new British colony of Nova Scotia. Its boundaries were disputed both by France and by aboriginal inhabitants. The treaty's vague definition according to 'ancient limits' led the British to maintain that Nova Scotia covered all of today's Maritime region except for the islands of Cape Breton and Ile Saint-Jean (Prince Edward Island), which were specifically attributed to France in the treaty, and a portion of what later became the State of Maine. France, however, preferred a more restrictive definition by which Nova Scotia was confined to today's Nova Scotian peninsula. The Mi'kmaq and Wuastukwiuk, not parties to the Treaty of Utrecht, sought by diplomatic means and at times by armed force to confine the British residential presence, at most, to Annapolis Royal itself.

The fragile existence of Nova Scotia, its tiny military garrison heavily outnumbered both by aboriginal inhabitants and by French-speaking Acadian inhabitants, gained more substance with the establishment of a new military and settlement centre at Halifax in 1749. This aggressive expansion of British interests prompted a new round of diplomatic and military activity by the aboriginal peoples of the region, while the renewed outbreak of armed conflict between Britain and France in North America in 1754 further complicated matters for the ensuing nine years. Treaties between the British and the aboriginal peoples, and between the British and the French, led by 1763 to a general recognition of the British presence and to French withdrawal from all territorial claims in mainland North America. The term *Nova Scotia* was now applied by Great Britain to the entire area covered by the later Maritime provinces. Then came retrenchments. In 1769, the Island of St. John (Prince Edward Island) became a colony in itself. In 1784, following the immigration of Loyalist refugees from the newly recognized United States, New Brunswick and Cape Breton Island were similarly hived off, leaving peninsular Nova Scotia as a much reduced colony. The imperial government re-integrated Cape Breton with Nova Scotia in 1820, however, and it was with its modern boundaries that Nova Scotia became one of the four original provinces of the Dominion of Canada in 1867 (for details of these developments see Buckner & Reid, 1994).

While an outline of the evolution of 'Nova Scotia' as a politically defined entity has its uses as a framework within which to fit socio-cultural developments, it also has its limitations as a starting point for setting the context of linguistic configurations. For one thing, ethno-cultural and linguistic groupings defy classification according to political boundaries. Even more seriously, the European term *Nova Scotia* does nothing to convey the continuity of the aboriginal experience, which can be measured in millennia rather than in centuries. The first firm archaeological evidence of human habitation within the bounds of the modern province of Nova Scotia can be dated to approximately 10 600 years ago. The early hunters who occupied sites at Debert and Belmont in that era inhabited a territory that had a colder climate and a greater land area than would exist in later millennia, following the retreat of the glaciers. By 5000 years ago, through a process that remains poorly understood both in its chronology and in regard to the relationship between immigrations and the cultural evolution of existing peoples, cultural traditions had emerged that are defined by archaeologists as 'archaic.' Relying for subsistence on hunting, fishing, and gathering, these societies were based on frequent migration in a purposeful harvesting of natural resources according to the season, and were characterized by the use of ground and polished stone tools. In terms of material culture the ending of this phase, and the emergence some 2500 years ago of the direct cultural ancestors of the modern aboriginal inhabitants of the region, was marked by the appearance of ceramic technology. More generally, the Algonkian-speaking peoples — within the bounds of the present Nova Scotia, the Mi'kmaq — who were present before and at the time of first European contact lived principally by fishing, hunting, and gathering within a society and a polity that was based on substantial village occupancy as well as seasonal migration (see Davis, 1994).

Population estimates for the Mi'kmaq prior to European contact have varied widely. The figure of some 3000-3500 advanced in 1616 by the Jesuit missionary Pierre Biard was for many years accepted by scholars who were content to overlook the evidence that European disease had already diminished the Mi'kmaw population by that time. Much higher estimates followed when this omission was recognized, ranging up to 50 000, but a recent evaluation has suggested approximately 12 000 as a reasonable inference from the historical and environmental evidence (Pastore, 1994, pp. 34-5). This population extended over a territory that encompassed not only today's Nova Scotia but also eastern and northern New Brunswick, the Gaspé, and islands in the Gulf of St. Lawrence. Two of the most populous Mi'kmaw areas, however, were Kmitkinag (corresponding to mainland Nova Scotia) and Unimaki (Cape Breton Island). Of the aboriginal peoples of northeastern North America, the Mi'kmaq were among the first — probably about the turn of the sixteenth century — to encounter a European presence. The Mi'kmaq who signalled in 1534 to the French voyager Jacques Cartier that they wished to trade furs clearly already had experience with earlier visitors (Biggar, 1924, pp. 49-50). From that time, however, another century would pass before European colonial attempts — which had their small beginnings in Mi'kmaw territory in 1605 — would show any signs of leading to extensive residential settlement. Even then, it would take until the early eighteenth century before the Acadian French colonial population exceeded that of the Mi'kmaq, and until the invasion of Loyalist refugees in the 1780s before devastating changes took place in the human and physical environment. None of this is to underestimate the enormous earlier impact of European disease or the scope of adjustments made to accommodate such other manifestations of the European presence as the fur trade and imperial military rivalries. Nevertheless, the ability of the Mi'kmaq to maintain self-direction over the first three centuries of European contact formed a critical foundation for the feat of cultural and linguistic survival that followed in the ensuing 200 years (Wicken, 1994).

Cultural and linguistic survival would also come into question in the historical experience of the Acadians — and would also be attained in the face of repeated difficulties that in this case included the expulsion of 1755-62. Although French colonial attempts began in the Maritime region in 1604, and within the modern confines of Nova Scotia in 1605, the first substantial number of settlers came to Acadia in the 1630s and 1640s. While first-generation Acadians were drawn from a variety of French provinces — and they were joined over the years by a few from elsewhere altogether — a substantial proportion came from the Loudunais region of south-western France. Arriving largely in family groups, these early Acadians made Port Royal a village of some 300 inhabitants by 1650 (Clark, 1968, pp. 99-103; Griffiths, 1994, p. 57). The results of French-English military tensions were already exerting an influence on Acadian societal development, and a loose English occupation between 1654 and 1670 was a forerunner of the British regime that would follow the seizure of Port Royal in 1710 and the Treaty of Utrecht three years later. In the meantime, however, Acadians lived in a relationship of co-existence with the Mi'kmaq, and also forged trading ties with New England merchants. Acadian settlement expanded, with the establishment of new villages — continuing the marshland agricultural orientation of Port Royal — at Beaubassin (on the Isthmus of Chignecto) in the early 1670s, and a decade later on the Minas Basin. By the time of the Treaty of Utrecht, there were some 2500 Acadians, and by the middle of the eighteenth century their number had doubled at least twice (Clark, 1968, pp. 200-1; see also Daigle, 1993; Griffiths, 1992).

Rapid population growth among the Acadians was supported by agricultural expansion, and thriving trades not only with New England but also — illegally, from a British perspective — with the fortified town of Louisbourg. Built by the French during the years following the Treaty of Utrecht, Louisbourg became an important commercial centre on the basis of its extensive export trade in dried cod, as well as fulfilling its military and naval roles. Its population reached some 4000 prior to its final seizure by British forces in 1758 (Moore, 1979). Yet, while trade in agricultural products to Louisbourg was a significant contributor to Acadian economic growth, the persistence of French-British imperial rivalries was a source of instability for the Acadian communities. Many Acadian leaders opted for a strategy of neutrality, in an effort to gain a degree of insulation from these conflicts, although there were others who took a pro-French or pro-British stance. By the 1750s, with the founding of Halifax having given the British a powerful counterweight to Louisbourg, the Acadian dilemma had become acute. Following the British capture in 1755 of Fort Beauséjour, the French stronghold on the Isthmus of Chignecto, the Nova Scotia military council felt sufficiently strong to demand from Acadians an unqualified oath of allegiance to the British crown under threat that refusal would bring dire consequences. Acadian leaders hesitated and then declined. The British response was the expulsion of the Acadians that was carried out over a period of some seven years, and extended to Cape Breton Island and the Island of St. John when they were captured in 1758. Of an Acadian population of at least 13 000, all but some 1500 were deported to destinations in North America, western Europe, and elsewhere. Some returned in later years, so that by 1800 the Acadian population of the Maritime region has been estimated at 8400 (Griffiths, 1992, pp. 89-90; LeBlanc, 1970-71). The old Acadian communities around the Bay of Fundy were permanently destroyed, however, and a new configuration of Acadian settlements emerged. While the majority of Acadians now lived within what was to be designated in 1784 as New Brunswick, there was a substantial concentration in the Baie Ste-Marie area of Nova Scotia, and smaller centres elsewhere on the Nova Scotian peninsula and on Cape Breton Island (see Ross & Deveau, 1992). The Acadian experience in Nova Scotia would henceforth be that of a linguistic minority, but one of tenacity and proven durability.

The lands around the Bay of Fundy that had been the sites of the major

Acadian communities were soon re-occupied by settlers drawn primarily from New England. Some 8000 Planters — the word simply denoted, in the eighteenth century, colonists — arrived between 1759 and 1768. The decade prior to the beginning of this migration, however, had seen other British efforts to bring new populations to Nova Scotia result in only limited success. The foundation of Halifax had been carried out in 1749 by an expedition that brought some 2500 settlers from England, and they were soon joined by New Englanders and by Irish migrants from Newfoundland. Yet intermittent military pressure by the Mi'kmaq, who did not accept the legitimacy of British territorial expansion, played a major role in confining the would-be colonists to Halifax, and the population there soon shrank drastically. The recruitment of 'Foreign Protestants' — Swiss, German, and French settlers — did not altogether balance the abandonment of Halifax by many of the original immigrants of 1749-50. Moreover, the presence of the Foreign Protestants created for colonial authorities the problem of how to support a group eventually numbering some 2700, in the face of the clear unfeasibility of plans that involved distributing them around the province in smaller clusters of several hundred. The establishment of the initially fragile town of Lunenburg in 1753 was the stopgap solution found for just over half of these colonists — others ultimately settled elsewhere, or simply left Nova Scotia — but only gradually did Lunenburg go on to develop its agricultural and fishing economy (see McNutt, 1965, pp. 53-6; Bell, 1990).

The Planter migration took place in different circumstances. Most importantly, the expulsion of most of the Acadians had opened up for re-occupation lands of proven agricultural worth. The effective elimination of the French imperial presence from the region, through the fall of Louisbourg in 1758, created an impression among potential New England settlers that British territorial encroachments in Nova Scotia were now militarily unchallenged. While this was an oversimplification with regard to the Mi'kmaw inhabitants, even after the conclusion of a series of Mi'kmaq-British treaties in 1760-61, it was a comforting accompaniment to the sometimes misleading promises concurrently being made by Nova Scotian authorities of land grants and New England-style political structures (see Reid, 1991, pp. 47-9; and more generally, Conrad, 1988; 1991; 1995; Candow, 1995). The migration of Planters from Massachusetts, Rhode Island, and eastern Connecticut resulted in the settlement of a series of townships that had agricultural economies and encompassed former Acadian lands. Annapolis and Granville were located in the lower reaches of the Annapolis Valley. Others, such as Horton and Falmouth, were on the Minas Basin, while Cumberland was established on the Isthmus of Chignecto. There were also Planter townships scattered around the coastlines of the extreme southwest of peninsular Nova Scotia — Yarmouth and Liverpool are examples — that were economically oriented towards fishing and in some cases would later emerge as important trading ports. Long retaining their New England cultural flavour, even when new populations were added at the time of the Loyalist migration, the Planter communities saw debates and divergences at the time of the American Revolution and a series of religious revivals then and thereafter that resulted in the eclipse of New England Congregationalism in favour of the more experiential faith of the Newlights and Baptists (see Moody, 1994).

Yet there was more to religious diversity in the Nova Scotia of the Planter era than a simple evolution away from the formalities of Congregationalism. Among the Planters themselves, there were Quakers and — from the 1780s onwards — an increasing number of Methodist converts (see Robertson, 1988; 1991). More generally, Roman Catholicism persisted among the Acadians and, in forms influenced by traditional spirituality, among the Mi'kmaq. In Halifax, the Church of England co-existed with nonconformist congregations. Lutheranism was strong among the German-speakers of the Lunenburg area. Further variations were brought by a series of smaller, but distinct and significant, immigrations that also occurred during the Planter era and over the intervening years prior to the American Revolution. Several hundred Ulster Presbyterians arrived in the early 1760s from New Hampshire — some had been born in Ireland itself, others were Ulster descendants longer-established in New England — to populate the townships of Truro, Onslow, and Londonderry (see Campbell, 1991). Yorkshire Methodists recruited in 1772 by the lieutenant-governor of the day, Michael Francklin, were established for short periods in a variety of locations before settling in substantial numbers on the Isthmus of Chignecto during the mid-1770s. Although many were on the New Brunswick side of the 1784 dividing line, their cultural influence was seen in both that province and Nova Scotia through their role in the expansion of Wesleyan Methodism (see Latta, 1988; Robertson, 1988). Finally, starting on a noticeable scale in Nova Scotia in 1773, although preceded by some years on the Island of St. John, was the immigration of Highland Scots. Forerunners of Scottish migrations to Nova Scotia that would total many thousands by the mid-nineteenth century, those who disembarked from the early vessels to arrive at Pictou were both Catholic and Presbyterian — although the Catholics tended to settle further east, towards Antigonish and then in Cape Breton. Overwhelmingly Gaelic-speaking, they contributed to the linguistic as well as the religious diversity of the colony (Bumstead, 1982, pp. 61-9).

Diversity was also the hallmark of the Loyalist immigration of the 1780s. To be sure, there were some common threads of the Loyalist experience, most obviously in that all Loyalist refugees had in some way and for some reason opposed the creation of the United States of America, and had found it necessary or prudent to leave the United States in the aftermath of the Revolution. Even political principles among the Loyalists, however, defied easy generalizations, as Governor John Parr of Nova Scotia — ironically if perhaps unconsciously — recognized in excoriating the 'levelling republican principles' of Loyalists who by 1790 had become his political opponents (Parr,

1790). A further reality towards which Parr's outburst pointed was that the arrival of some 35 000 Loyalists in the Maritime region, of whom some 20 000 were settled within the reduced area of Nova Scotia and in Cape Breton following the boundary revisions of 1784, had greatly reinforced cultural affinities with the United States. This was a reversal of the trend that had been evident during the early 1770s, when the Planter population was being gradually overhauled by the growing numbers of arrivals from the British Isles (Bumstead, 1994, pp. 167-8). In social and cultural terms, however, the Loyalists formed a heterogeneous group. Their geographical origins could be found in most parts of the former Thirteen Colonies, but with especially large contingents from New York, New Jersey, and the Carolinas. Others were disbanded regular troops, not American in origin. Their occupations also ranged widely, with farmers and artisans predominating (MacKinnon, 1986, pp. 53-66). In terms of ethnicity, the Loyalists reflected the variations of the population of Anglo-America and, in the case of the disbanded soldiers, of the armies that had fought against the revolutionaries. Celts, both Scottish and Irish, were represented. Most notable of all, however, was the presence of some 3500 free Black Loyalists, as well as perhaps another 2000 who came as 'servants' (Walker, 1976, p. 12).

The Black Loyalists did not represent the beginning of the Afro-Nova Scotian presence. Fragmentary evidence reveals that some Black individuals resided in seventeenth-century Acadian communities. There were significant Black populations at Louisbourg and among the Planters (see Donovan, 1993, pp. 1, 8-11; Reid, 1994, pp. 96-7; Hartlen, 1991, pp. 123-8). The relatively large numbers in the Loyalist migration, however — even considering that some 1100 found Nova Scotia sufficiently unwelcoming that they left in 1792 for Sierra Leone — led to the foundation of Black communities on an unprecedented scale. Upon their arrival the Black Loyalists soon found that they could not expect fulfilment of British officials' promises of rewards for their loyalty on anything like the scale routinely demanded and received by other Loyalists. While the racially-based violence that led at Shelburne to the emergence of Birchtown as a distinct Black community did not set any simple pattern to be repeated elsewhere, the Black Loyalists there and in the other communities — in the Digby area, at Little Tracadie in Guysborough County, and at Preston — shared in greater or lesser degree the disadvantage of being left landless or having only small and poor quality land allocations (Walker, 1976, pp. 18-32, 94-5, 134-5). Following the outmigration to Sierra Leone in 1792, which left Preston virtually unoccupied and took major parts of the population also from the Birchtown and Digby settlements, the Black presence was temporarily reinforced by some 550 Maroons — Jamaican descendants of escaped slaves — who were deported to Nova Scotia in 1796, but were then removed to Sierra Leone four years later. More lasting was the immigration of about 2000 Black refugees from the War of 1812, who reoccupied Preston and founded the community of Hammonds Plains. Others settled in Halifax, where Africville later emerged as the main Black community (see Condon, 1994, pp. 200-1; Walker, 1976, p. 368). The destruction of Africville in the late 1960s, in the interests of urban renewal as it was then interpreted, became a symbol of more than a century and a half characterized by the related ills of racial discrimination and economic disadvantage. Nevertheless, the mobilization of Black organizations from the late 1960s onward has given reason to believe that cultural strength and community coherence can and will prevail (Stanley, 1993, pp. 450-1).

Considered overall, the Loyalist migration represented one of the crucial turning-points in the socio-cultural, and the environmental, history of Nova Scotia. Often at the expense of the non-British peoples of the region, the Loyalists occupied many places that had never before seen British colonial settlement. Towns such as Shelburne, Guysborough, and Sydney were established. Less conspicuous on the map, but more significant in terms of numbers, was the impact on rural areas. The processes of urban expansion and rural population growth continued in the early decades of the nineteenth century, fuelled by economic diversification and by large-scale immigration from the British Isles. Large numbers of the immigrants were English and Lowland Scots, who settled in both urban and rural settings, frequently blending in quickly with existing communities. More visibly distinct were the Celts. Welsh immigration to Nova Scotia was on a small scale, fewer than 50 people settling in 1818 the only thoroughly Welsh community — New Cambria, near Shelburne — and largely abandoning it within twenty years (Thomas, 1986, pp. 109-16, 254-5). The Irish and the Highland Scots were much more numerous. Between 1815 and 1830, over 8000 Irish were recorded as arriving in Nova Scotia, most directly from Ireland and some by way of Newfoundland. The actual numbers may have been higher still, although they were counterbalanced by some outmigration to New England. Irish immigration continued to be substantial in the 1830s, with a large urban concentration in Halifax, and was in the main complete before the era of the Great Famine in 1846-7 (see Punch, 1988, p. 224; 1981, pp. 10-11). The Highland Scots, meanwhile, continued to populate eastern Nova Scotia. Pictou and Antigonish were the principal mainland counties of Highland settlement, while Cape Breton Island — politically re-integrated with Nova Scotia in 1820 — received 10 000 Highland immigrants even within the short period from 1827 to 1832 (Ommer, 1994, pp. 285-6).

By the time of the 1861 census, the last before the formation of the Dominion of Canada in 1867, Nova Scotia had a population of almost 339 000. This was roughly ten times the number at the close of the Loyalist migration, and not quite three times what it had been in 1827 (Brookes, 1976, p. 30; Ommer, 1994, pp. 268-9). The population was culturally and linguistically diverse, with Mi'kmaq, French, German, Gaelic, and Irish as living languages along with English. Despite the cultural influence of Halifax — which would grow as railways extended the range of newspapers and other forms of cultural production in the later nineteenth century — the province remained overwhelmingly rural, and there was limited contact among the various ethnic and linguistic communities. The era of large-scale immigration had come to an end by 1861. Halifax continued to be a major port of entry for immigrants to Canada, but most now stayed only long enough to begin their travels to ultimate destinations further west. To be sure, there were new ethnicities added frequently to the Nova Scotian population throughout the late nineteenth century and the twentieth. Chinese, Lebanese, and European Jewish populations were located in Halifax by the turn of the twentieth century. Industrial expansion in Cape Breton began shortly thereafter to attract immigrant workers not only from the British Isles but also from eastern and southern Europe. Following the Second World War, South Asian, Dutch, West Indian, and Vietnamese populations — and others — grew in Nova Scotia as an element of the more general diversification of the Canadian population as a whole. Yet, in the context of the uneven economic history of the province, the numbers of new arrivals remained relatively small. Of those Nova Scotians who declared a single ethnic origin to the 1991 census — by which time the overall Nova Scotia population had reached 890 950 — 73.5 percent defined it as British. French ethnic origin accounted for 10.4 percent, other European 9.0 percent, Black 2.0 percent, African/Asian 1.7 percent, and Aboriginal 1.4 percent (pp. 12-26). Of the total population those who declared single ethnic origins numbered 532 850.

Thus, Nova Scotia in the post-Confederation era — in sharp contrast with the situation during the first half of the nineteenth century — was characterized by modest population growth based largely on the increase of an existing population. At certain times, notably during the 1880s, 1890s, 1920s, 1950s, 1960s, and 1970s, outmigration reached high enough levels to counteract natural increase significantly. Yet cultural complexities continued to be evident. Ethnic distinctions, so clear in mid-nineteenth century Nova Scotia — not only in the persistence of established non-British populations, but also in the profound ethnic distinctions among those whose origins were in distinct cultural and linguistic groups within the British Isles — continued to exert a strong influence. They were compounded by an increasingly complex series of relationships based on social class, which evolved along with developments in the regional economy. In part, the economic shifts were associated with the industrialization and urbanization of the later decades of the nineteenth century. Rural areas, however, also experienced substantial change. The nineteenth-century settlement of agricultural communities had not led to the creation of egalitarian commonwealths. Rather, factors such as the chronological ordering of settlement — who arrived first and acquired the most productive land — and the acquisitive ability of wealthy individuals, had led to the creation of wide disparities in wealth and power. These were complicated by declining population during periods of outmigration, by technological changes such as the availability of rail transportation for agricultural and fish products, and by the volatility of markets for natural resource commodities. By the eve of the First World War, rural areas that were close enough to urban centres to market food products effectively and had the necessary rail connections — as in the case of Truro and surrounding areas of Colchester County — were able to find a secure prosperity, as did those with a specialized product such as Annapolis Valley apples. For more remote areas, and for their inhabitants who were landless or worked only marginal lands, the prospects were much bleaker. Multiple occupation — the making of a living through seasonal combinations of male and female labour in occupations such as small-scale farming, fishing, working in the woods, other forms of wage labour, and selling craft or food products in neighbouring centres — can legitimately be seen as a cultural trait of rural Nova Scotia. As a cultural trait, however, it was and remains a response to economic necessity, a necessity often manifested in harsh forms (see Bittermann, 1988; Bittermann, MacKinnon & Wynn, 1993; Gwyn, 1992; Hornsby, 1992; Samson, 1994; McCann, 1993).

The urban and industrial history of Nova Scotia also gave rise to social and cultural complexities. The capital accumulation that was the basis for the growth of heavy industrial complexes in areas such as Pictou County and Cape Breton County in the late nineteenth century — as well as related port and manufacturing activities in Halifax, and industrial development in individual towns such as Amherst and Yarmouth — came largely from earlier merchant involvement in shipbuilding, lumbering, and overseas shipping trades. While the concept of a 'Golden Age' of wood, wind, and water in the mid-nineteenth century has had deservedly rough treatment from recent historians, the significance of the water-borne trading economy in many important local contexts remains clear. The transition to mining and heavy manufacturing — though some port communities continued successfully with wooden shipping and shipbuilding into the early twentieth century — was stimulated both by the completion of the Intercolonial Railway link to Montreal in 1879 and by the introduction of the protectionist 'National Policy' by the John A. Macdonald federal government in the same year. The resulting growth was rapid, passing its peak by the turn of the century. The First World War provided a temporary boom, but then came virtual collapse in the 1920s. Historians continue to debate the causes of this profound economic setback for Nova Scotia, allocating weight in varying proportions to factors such as capital instability, increasing outside ownership, unwelcome shifts in federal economic and transportation policy, resource deficiencies, and the disruption of international markets following the First World War. What is beyond dispute is the hardship visited upon working-class people who confronted unemployment, wage reductions, and short-time working in the 1920s, and then found no comfort whatever in the depressed 1930s (see Acheson, Frank, & Frost, 1985; Forbes, 1989; Inwood, 1993; Sager & Panting, 1990). The age of industrialization produced remarkable cultural convergences, as in the interaction of Highland Catholic traditions with Eastern European immigration in industrial Cape Breton. It also affected women and men in distinct ways, as in the tendency of rural young women to migrate to urban centres in Nova Scotia and New England to find employment in domestic and clerical occupations as well as in factory work. In both urban and rural settings, the factors of social class and gender interacted with those of ethnicity to produce new socio-cultural configurations (see Frank, 1985; 1983; Conrad, Laidlaw, & Smyth, 1988, pp. 6-24).

Although the Second World War provided conditions of full employment, the end of wartime production and transportation activities re-introduced Nova Scotians to the underlying structural problems that had been temporarily obscured but never resolved. Indeed, federal policies during the war that had favoured the development of an exclusive industrial heartland in central Canada had aggravated the potential difficulties, for example, of the aging Sydney steel mill in its postwar task of competing with central Canadian plants that had been modernized at government expense (Forbes, 1986). It was true that increasing federal and provincial revenues through the 1950s and 1960s facilitated government spending in areas such as health, education, and the delivery of other services, but the impact was uneven. The Halifax-Dartmouth metropolitan area benefited disproportionately, while smaller urban centres and the less prosperous rural areas were left to grapple more directly with entrenched economic weaknesses. A new wave of outmigration was a conspicuous result, Ontario being the favoured destination until the early 1970s, and from then on oil-producing Alberta. Regional development programs helped to shore up local economies in some places, but failed to produce the kind of general economic upturn that their most committed proponents had expected (Conrad, 1993; Stanley, 1993; Reid, 1993). By the late 1980s, new threats had emerged that persisted in the 1990s. The nature of Canadian federalism was clearly changing. The failure in the early 1990s of successive constitutional reform efforts — the Meech Lake Accord in 1990 and the Charlottetown Accord in 1992 — stalemated the possibility of decentralization by constitutional means, but the growth of public debt and the ceding of key responsibilities from Ottawa to the provinces in the federal budget of February 1995 worked in that direction. Where that left the principle of inter-regional economic partnership in Confederation was unclear. A further threat to Nova Scotia — albeit not as devastating as in the case of Newfoundland — was the environmental disaster that proceeded from several decades of industrially-modelled approaches to the fisheries, and the exhaustion of groundfish stocks. A strong case could be made in retrospect, without indulging in simplistic allocations of blame, that it was the community-based practices of inshore fishers that could have pointed the way towards a sustainable fishery. But retrospective views, by definition, came too late to be helpful (see Forbes, 1993; 1989b; Williams, 1995; Matthews & Phyne, 1988; Ommer, 1994).

Does all of this mean that a historical sketch of Nova Scotia and its cultures must end in pessimism? Not necessarily. Resilience is a recurrent theme in the experience of ordinary people in Nova Scotia. If examples are needed of its continuing currency, they can be found in the recent histories of peoples who have had the longer-term experience of marginalization: in the increasingly confident articulation of Mi'kmaw cultural and linguistic distinctiveness (see Inglis, Mannette, & Sulewski, 1991); in the numerous cultural and educational initiatives stimulated by the Fédération acadienne de la Nouvelle-Ecosse since its establishment in 1968 (see Ross & Deveau, 1992, pp. 159-89); and in the attainments over a similar period of the Black United Front and related organizations (see Pachai, 1987-91, II, pp. 245-89). The relationship between cultural integrity and social action is clear in each case. The cause of cultural integrity is not served, however, by the generation of romanticized views of an imaginary past. For reasons that have ranged from an ideologically-based nostalgia to the promotion among potential tourists of an image of quaintness, Nova Scotia's history has been viewed in various contexts in the present century through the distorted lens of a preoccupation with a lost — or partially preserved — age of rugged simplicity. It was no accident that the concept of the nineteenth-century Golden Age of sail was developed during the troubled interwar years. So — and all of these constructs retained their appeal in the post-1945 era — were the beliefs that Nova Scotian folklore was the product and the embodiment of untutored innocence, and that Nova Scotian culture as a whole could be tied to the ethnic stereotypes of 'tartanism' (Frank, 1993, pp. 264-6; MacKay, 1994; 1992; 1988; Macdonald, 1988).

Scepticism of such notions — and concern over the damage they may inflict by giving an impression of backwardness and bucolic indolence — does not imply a destructive cynicism. Of course, the importance of shipping and shipbuilding in the nineteenth century deserves serious attention, as does the study of folklore as the expression of popular artistry and hard-won experience, and the existence of a genuinely Highland heritage that the excesses of tartanism do nothing to illuminate. Scepticism, on the contrary, provides the essential link between academic study of the past and the possibility that an informed and nuanced popular understanding of the past can be enlisted in the making of reasoned decisions about the present and future. Over the past quarter of a century, the scholarly study of Nova Scotia, and of Atlantic Canada as a whole, has developed markedly in scale and sophistication (see Reid, 1989, pp. 1, 5-6). With the publication of this volume, the already established importance of linguistic analysis in the study of Nova Scotian culture and society is further demonstrated. The complexities of Nova Scotia's history, and the linguistic variations of Nova Scotians, are not only expressions of a past worth understanding but also pointers towards a present and future worth living.

References

Acheson, T. W., Frank, D., & Frost, J. D. (1985). *Industrialization and underdevelopment in the Maritimes, 1880-1930*. Toronto: Garamond Press.

Bell, W. P. (1990). *The 'Foreign Protestants' and the settlement of Nova Scotia: The history of a piece of arrested British colonial policy in the eighteenth century*. 2nd ed. Sackville, NB: Mount Allison University, Centre for Canadian Studies.

Biggar, H. P., (Ed.) (1924). *The voyages of Jacques Cartier*. Ottawa: Public Archives of Canada.

Bittermann, R. (Autumn 1988). The hierarchy of the soil: Land and labour in a 19th century Cape Breton community. *Acadiensis 18 (1)*, 33-55.

Bittermann, R., MacKinnon, R. A., & Wynn, G. (1993). Of inequality and interdependence in the Nova Scotian countryside, 1850-1870. *Canadian Historical Review 74*, 1-43.

Brookes, A. A. (Spring 1976). Out-migration from the Maritime provinces, 1860-1900: Some preliminary considerations. *Acadiensis 5 (2)*, 26-55.

Buckner, P. A. (1994). The 1860s: An end and a beginning. In P. A. Buckner, & J. G. Reid, (Eds.), *The Atlantic Region to Confederation: A history*. Toronto & Fredericton: University of Toronto Press & Acadiensis Press, 360-386.

Buckner P. A., & Reid, J. G., (Eds.) (1994). *The Atlantic Region to Confederation: A history*. Toronto & Fredericton: University of Toronto Press & Acadiensis Press.

Bumstead, J. M. (1994). 1763-1783: Resettlement and rebellion. In P. A. Buckner, & J. G. Reid, (Eds.) *The Atlantic Region to Confederation: A history*. Toronto & Fredericton: University of Toronto Press & Acadiensis Press, 156-183.

———. (1982). *The people's clearance: Highland emigration to British North America*. Edinburgh: Edinburgh University Press.

Campbell, C. (1991). A Scots-Irish plantation in Nova Scotia: Truro, 1760-1775. In M. Conrad, (Ed.), *Making adjustments: Change and continuity in Planter Nova Scotia, 1759-1800*. Fredericton, Acadiensis Press, 153-64.

Canada. Statistics Canada. *Census of Canada, 1991*. Ottawa: Statistics Canada.

Candow, J. (April 1995). The New England Planters in Nova Scotia. *Planter Notes 6 (2)*, 1-5.

Clark, A. H. (1968). *The geography of early Nova Scotia to 1760*. Madison: University of Wisconsin Press.

Condon, A. G. (1994). 1783-1800: Loyalist arrival, Acadian return, imperial reform. In P. A. Buckner, & J. G. Reid, (Eds.) *The Atlantic Region to Confederation: A history*. Toronto & Fredericton: University of Toronto Press & Acadiensis Press, 184-209.

Conrad, M. (1993). The 1950s: Decade of development. In E. R. Forbes & D. A. Muise, (Eds.), *The Atlantic provinces in Confederation*. Toronto & Fredericton: University of Toronto Press & Acadiensis Press, 382-420.

Conrad, M., (Ed.). (1995). *Intimate relations: Family and community in Planter Nova Scotia*. Fredericton: Acadiensis Press.

———. (1991). *Making adjustments: Change and continuity in Planter Nova Scotia, 1759- 1800*. Fredericton, Acadiensis Press.

Conrad, M., Laidlaw, T., & Smyth, D. (1988). *No place like home: Diaries and letters of Nova Scotia women, 1771-1938*. Halifax, Formac Publishing.

———. (1988). *They planted well: New England Planters in maritime Canada*. Fredericton: Acadiensis Press.

Daigle, J. (1980). L'Acadie, 1604-1763: Synthèse historique. In J. Daigle, (Ed.), *Les*

Acadiens des Maritimes: Etudes thématiques. Moncton: Université de Moncton, Chaire d'études acadiennes, 17-48.

Davis, S. A. (1994). Early societies: Sequences of change. In P. A. Buckner, & J. G. Reid, (Eds.), *The Atlantic Region to Confederation: A history*. Toronto & Fredericton: University of Toronto Press & Acadiensis Press, 3-21.

Donovan, K. (March 1993). Emblems of conspicuous consumption: Slaves in Ile Royale, 1713-1760. Paper delivered at the Southeastern American Society for Eighteenth Century Studies, Birmingham, AL.

Forbes, E. R. (1993). Epilogue: The 1980s. In E. R. Forbes & D. A. Muise, (Eds.), *The Atlantic provinces in Confederation*. Toronto & Fredericton: University of Toronto Press & Acadiensis Press, 505-515.

———. (1989a). *Challenging the regional stereotype: Essays on the 20th century Maritimes*. Fredericton: Acadiensis Press.

———. (1989b). Atlantic provinces, free trade and the Canadian Constitution. In E. R. Forbes, *Challenging the regional stereotype: Essays on the 20th century Maritimes*. Fredericton: Acadiensis Press, 200-216.

———. (Spring 1986). Consolidating disparity: The Maritimes and the industrialization of Canada during the Second World War. *Acadiensis 15 (2)*, 3-27.

Frank, D. (1993). The 1920s: Class and region, resistance and accommodation. In E. R. Forbes & D. A. Muise, (Eds.), *The Atlantic provinces in Confederation*. Toronto & Fredericton: University of Toronto Press & Acadiensis Press, 233-271.

———. (1985). Tradition and culture in the Cape Breton mining community. In K. Donovan, (Ed.), *Cape Breton at 200: Historical essays in honour of the Island's bicentennial, 1785-1985*. Sydney: University College of Cape Breton Press, 203-218.

———. (Spring 1983). The miner's financier: Women in the Cape Breton coal towns, 1917. *Atlantis 8*, 137-143.

Griffiths, N. E. S. (1994). 1600-1650: Fish, fur, and folk. In P. A. Buckner, & J. G. Reid, (Eds.), *The Atlantic Region to Confederation: A history*. Toronto & Fredericton: University of Toronto Press & Acadiensis Press, 40-60.

———. (1992). *The contexts of Acadian history, 1686-1784*. Montreal & Kingston: McGill- Queen's University Press.

Gwyn, J. (1992). Golden age or bronze moment? Wealth and poverty in Nova Scotia: The 1850s and 1860s. *Canadian Papers in Rural History 8*, 192-230.

Hartlen, G. C. (1991). Bound for Nova Scotia: Slaves in the Planter migration. In M. Conrad, (Ed.), *Making adjustments: Change and continuity in Planter Nova Scotia, 1759-1800*. Fredericton, Acadiensis Press, 123-8.

Hornsby, S. (1992). *Nineteenth century Cape Breton: A historical geography*. Kingston & Montreal: McGill-Queen's University Press.

Inglis, S., Mannette, J., & Sulewski, S., (Eds.). (1991), *Pagtatek*. Halifax: Garamond Press.

Inwood, K., (Ed.). (1993). *Farm, factory, and fortune: New studies in the economic history of the Maritime provinces*. Fredericton: Acadiensis Press.

Latta, P. (Fall 1988). Eighteenth century immigrants to Nova Scotia: The Yorkshire settlers. *Material History Bulletin 28*, 46-61.

Leblanc, R. G. (1970-71). The Acadian migrations. *Canadian Geographical Journal 81 (1)*, 10- 19.

Macdonald, N. (1988). Putting on the kilt: The Scottish stereotype and ethnic community survival in Cape Breton. *Canadian Ethnic Studies 20 (3)*, 132-146.

MacKay, I. (1994). *The quest of the folk: Antimodernism and cultural selection in twentieth- century Nova Scotia*. Kingston & Montreal: McGill-Queen's University Press.

———. (Spring 1992). Tartanism triumphant: The construction of Scottishness in Nova Scotia, 1933-1954. *Acadiensis 21 (2)*, 5-47.

———. (Spring/Summer 1988). Among the fisherfolk: J. F. B. Livesay and the invention of Peggy's Cove. *Journal of Canadian Studies 23 (1 & 2)*, 23-45.

MacKinnon, N. (1986). *This unfriendly soil: The Loyalist experience in Nova Scotia*. Kingston & Montreal: McGill-Queen's University Press.

MacNutt, W. S. (1965). *The Atlantic provinces: The emergence of colonial society*. Toronto: McClelland and Stewart.

Matthews, R., & Phyne, J. (Spring/Summer 1988). Regulating the Newfoundland inshore fishery: Traditional values versus state control in the regulation of a common property resource. *Journal of Canadian Studies 23 (1 & 2)*, 158-176.

McCann, L. D. (1993). The 1890s: Fragmentation and the new social order. In E. R. Forbes & D. A. Muise, (Eds.), *The Atlantic provinces in Confederation*. Toronto & Fredericton: University of Toronto Press & Acadiensis Press, 133-43.

Moody, B. (1994). Acadia and old Nova Scotia to 1784. In M. B. Taylor, (Ed.), *Canadian history: A reader's guide*. Vol. 1, Beginnings to Confederation. Toronto: University of Toronto Press, 108-11.

Moore. C. (May 1979). The other Louisbourg: Trade and merchant enterprise in Ile Royale, 1713-1758. *Histoire sociale-Social History 12 (23)*, 79-96.

Ommer, R. (1994). The 1830s: Adapting their institutions to their desires. In P. A. Buckner, & J. G. Reid, (Eds.), *The Atlantic Region to Confederation: A history*. Toronto & Fredericton: University of Toronto Press & Acadiensis Press, 284-306.

———. (Spring 1994). One hundred years of fishery crises in Newfoundland. *Acadiensis 23 (2)*, 5-20.

Pachai, B. (1987-91). *Beneath the clouds of the promised land: The survival of Nova Scotia Blacks*. 2 vols. Halifax: Black Educators Association of Nova Scotia.

Parr, John. (1790). Speech, 9 April. Qtd. in N. MacKinnon, (1986), *This unfriendly soil: The Loyalist experience in Nova Scotia*. Kingston & Montreal: McGill-Queen's University Press, 132.

Pastore, R. (1994). The sixteenth century: Aboriginal peoples and European contact. In P. A. Buckner, & J. G. Reid, (Eds.), *The Atlantic Region to Confederation: A history*. Toronto & Fredericton: University of Toronto Press & Acadiensis Press, 22-39.

Punch, T. M. (1988). 'Gentle as the snow on a rooftop': The Irish in Nova Scotia to 1830. In R. O'Driscoll & L. Reynolds, (Eds.), *The untold story: The Irish in Canada*. 2 vols. Toronto: Celtic Arts of Canada, I, 215-229.

———. (1981). *Irish Halifax: The immigrant generation, 1815-1859*. Halifax: Saint Mary's University, International Education Centre.

Reid, J. G. (1994). 1686-1720: Imperial intrusions. In P. A. Buckner, & J. G. Reid, (Eds.) *The Atlantic Region to Confederation: A history*. Toronto & Fredericton: University of Toronto Press & Acadiensis Press, 78-103.

———. (1993). The 1970s: Sharpening the sceptical edge. In E. R. Forbes & D. A. Muise, (Eds.), *The Atlantic provinces in Confederation*. Toronto & Fredericton: University of Toronto Press & Acadiensis Press, 460-504.

———. (1991). Change and continuity in Nova Scotia, 1758-1775. In M. Conrad,

(Ed.), *Making adjustments: Change and continuity in Planter Nova Scotia, 1759-1800*. Fredericton, Acadiensis Press, 45-59.

———. (Spring 1989). Canadian studies in Atlantic Canada: Some reflections. *Association for Canadian Studies Newsletter 11 (1).*

Robertson, A. B. (1991). To declare and affirm: Quaker contributions to Planter Nova Scotia. In M. Conrad, (Ed.), *Making adjustments: Change and continuity in Planter Nova Scotia, 1759-1800*. Fredericton, Acadiensis Press, 129-39.

———. (1988). Methodism among Nova Scotia's Yankee Planters. In M. Conrad, (Ed.), *They planted well: New England Planters in maritime Canada*. Fredericton: Acadiensis Press, 178-89.

Ross, S., & Deveau, A. (1992). *The Acadians of Nova Scotia, past and present*. Halifax: Nimbus.

Sager, E. W., with Panting, G. E. (1990). *Maritime capital: The shipping industry in Atlantic Canada, 1820-1914*. Kingston & Montreal: McGill-Queen's University Press.

Samson, D., (Ed.). (1994). *Contested countryside; Rural workers and modern society in Atlantic Canada, 1899-1950*. Fredericton: Acadiensis Press.

Stanley, D. (1993). The 1960s: The illusions and realities of progress. In E. R. Forbes & D. A. Muise, (Eds.), *The Atlantic provinces in Confederation*. Toronto & Fredericton: University of Toronto Press & Acadiensis Press, 421-459.

Thomas, P. (1986). *Strangers from a secret land: The voyages of the Brig **Albion** and the founding of the first Welsh settlements in Canada*. Toronto: University of Toronto Press.

Walker, J. St.G. (1976). *The black Loyalists: The search for a promised land in Nova Scotia and Sierra Leone*. New York: Africana Pub. Co.

Wicken, W. C. (1994). Encounters with tall sails and tall tales: Mi'kmaq society, 1500-1760. PhD thesis. Montreal: McGill University.

Williams, R. (March/April 1995). Fooling all of the people. . . . *New Maritimes 13 (4)*, 30-33.

Chapter One

The Vowel Phonemes of Halifax and General Canadian English

A. Murray Kinloch

Editors' Introduction

Visitors to Nova Scotia usually notice the distinct sound of local speech. Asking for directions, they may be told: 'Go out till the light, then go straight on,' and they notice that *out* and *light* sound different from General American, and that *straight* sounds as if it began with 'sh.' Nova Scotians travelling in the US are told that they sound like Canadians. When they come to Ontario or further West, they are told they sound like Maritimers.

Although the study of speech sounds is the special domain of phoneticians, non-professional persons often make accurate observations. An article published in *The Novascotian* (21 Sept. 1985) reported the impressions of Californian writer and performing musician J. B. Grant, who not only noted a peculiarity of Nova Scotian speech, but stated that he found it particularly attractive: it was '[the] manner of expressing agreement by saying "yuh" on the inbreath — a small gasp of being in accord' (p. 6). The indrawn breath, used by speakers to express affirmation was also noted by poet Elizabeth Bishop (Goldensohn 1992, p. 257). Bishop also commented that the indrawn breath is common to all Nova Scotians, young and old alike (p. 258). This is a correct observation, to which it is possible to add that the word *no*, when uttered by itself, is just as frequently accompanied by a sharp inbreath.

Another feature which J. B. Grant found attractive was '[the] way of saying the diphthong "ou" — so that "about" sounds like a cross between "a boat" and "a boot"' In this instance we should add that the words *light* and *right* contain a similarly peculiar diphthong, but one which was perhaps less attractive to the listener.

While such occasional observations help us to identify certain features of Nova Scotian speech, a more detailed examination of the facts is left to phoneticians, who try to provide historical explanations as well as descriptions of present sound-patterns.

While the 'indrawn breath' has not received much notice from phoneticians, the 'diphthong ou' has received widespread attention in linguistic books and numerous articles, both as a 'relic' phenomenon reflecting eighteenth-century speech, British and Colonial alike, and as a peculiar

Canadian sound, termed 'Canadian Raising' from the relatively high position of the tongue required for its production.

This Canadian sound is so noticeable that Canadian actors engaged to play in American movies are coached in pronouncing *out* the American way, but it would be well to remember that, should a movie be set in Colonial times, the Canadian relic pronunciation would be the authentic one, and it would be then appropriate for American actors on the set to learn to pronounce *out* the Canadian way.

Reaching beyond historical and acoustic description of the sound in question, phoneticians also seek to determine the place of this diphthong in the sound system of the language: they find that it is a variant and occurs before voiceless consonants in words like *out* and *mouse*, but not before voiced ones, as in *loud* and *crowd*. The same condition applies to the diphthong in *light* and *right*, as contrasted with *ride* and *hide*. Analysed in this fashion, the peculiar diphthongs are no longer a mere curiosity: they are allophones of the phonemes /aʊ/ and /aɪ/ and are thus an integral part of the system, a phoneme being defined as distinctive sound-unit, capable of conveying difference in meaning. In English /d/ and /t/ are two phonemes because they can serve to distinguish between such words as *tin* and *din*.

A full phonological analysis of Nova Scotian speech would account for all the consonant and vowel phonemes, altogether about forty-three or so — most of them, to be sure, identical with phonemes of general North American English — and for their allophones, that is, for all the alternate realizations of these sounds under special conditions, such as the effect of the sound that comes before them or the sound that follows. The total count of the phonemes might seem high as compared to the familiar letters of the alphabet, but then most of us have always felt that the alphabet was not altogether sufficient as a tool for recording the actual sounds of the language. How do we know how to pronounce *awry*, *bass*, or *dour*?

Since the chapter that follows concentrates on the vowel system, we will comment here on the consonant system. By observing the words discussed in the chapter, with just a few additions, marked * below, and using the American system rather than Kinloch's British system of transcription, one can list the consonants as follows:

/b/ *b*oss, *b*eauty
/p/ ase*p*tic
/d/ *d*oll
/t/ aun*t*
/g/ *g*rease
/k/ hi*cc*up, yo*k*e
/v/ lo*v*e
/f/ wi*f*e
/z/ grea*s*y (one speaker)
/s/ hou*s*e, bo*ss*, *s*tay
/h/ *h*iccup, *h*ouse
/m/ *m*ock, *m*oth
/n/ *n*omi*n*ative
/l/ choco*l*ate, do*ll*
*/r/ sy*r*up, g*r*easy
/ǰ/ fri*dg*e*, *j*am*
/č/ mar*ch*, *ch*air, furni*t*ure
/ð/ *th*e*, *th*at*

/θ/ *th*ree	/ŋ/ dri*n*k, ri*ng*
/ž/ mea*s*ure	/w/ *w*aft
/š/ cu*sh*ion	/y/ *y*olk

The consonants so listed represent an abstraction rather than actual entities. In normal conversation /b/ has a different sound in *boss* than in *beauty*, where it becomes palatalized before the [y] sound that follows it, and /l/ is quite different in *love* than in *doll*; but these differences are ignored in the listing of phonemes because they do not affect the meaning of words: they represent allophones which would be marked in a more precise phonetic transcription e.g., [lʌv]:[dɔɫ]. Among conditioned variants in Maritime speech, the diphthongs have occasioned most comment, but consonants also show certain conditioned variants, such as /s/ being realized as [š] in *strong*, *street*, *string*, *extra*, and *grocery*, /z/ being sounded like [ž] in *misery*, while the /s/ of *reserve* is sounded as [s] contrary to the prevailing tendency to pronounce it as [z].

In commenting on Nova Scotian sounds, we do not attempt to represent the province as speaking in a uniform manner. Not only does speech vary from region to region within Nova Scotia, but even within a community people differ in their speech in accordance with age, occupation, and a number of other factors; moreover, an individual speaks differently in different circumstances: the same person who speaks formally at a board meeting is likely to speak very informally to a young child, e.g., switching from [ɪŋ] endings in *going*, *doing*, etc., to [ɪn] in *darling*. It is therefore more appropriate to consider regional features as points on a continuum between General Canadian and local Standard.

The following chapter was originally a presentation to the Atlantic Provinces Linguistic Association in 1979. Speakers of pure local dialect are hard to find, as A. Murray Kinloch tells us in his discussion of Halifax vowel phonemes. Nevertheless, Kinloch gives a detailed analysis of the vowel system of Halifax speech. He compares a list of phonetically transcribed words which were included in an appendix to American linguist Morton W. Bloomfield's article, 'Canadian English and Its Relation to Eighteenth Century American Speech' (1948), with another list compiled some thirty years later. This approach allows him to make a rare historical study, especially of the trends which seem to have resulted in changes in the vowel system over that period of time.

Bloomfield's article did not deal specifically with phonetics; rather, it offered an overview of Canadian English, stressing its 'relic' features and arguing that Canadian English in general, and Maritime English in particular, is a development of the American speech brought over to Canada by Loyalist settlers in the later part of the eighteenth century, and the early nineteenth. His main contention in the article was that the study of Maritime English can contribute much to an understanding of the early history of American English. Bloomfield's appendix, consisting of four columns of phonetically transcribed words, comparing the pronunciation of speakers from Halifax, Montreal, Ontario, and Saskatchewan, was intended to illustrate 'the General American character' of the phonology of Canadian English.

Kinloch re-interprets Bloomfield's phonetic transcription of Halifax data in phonological terms, and supplements the limited information by astute extrapolation. Unlike Bloomfield, however, he is concerned with Maritime English in its Canadian context, and his discussion leads him to the conclusion that Maritime English, as represented by the Halifax speaker he studied, in comparison with the earlier sample given by Bloomfield, exhibits a trend toward a closer approximation to the speech of Ontario. But not so close, we hope, as to make Nova Scotians quite undistinguishable from others when saying, 'Turn right at the light. . . .' *(LF & MH)*

***

The Vowel Phonemes of Halifax and General Canadian English

by A. Murray Kinloch

At the end of his article, 'Canadian English and Its Relation to Eighteenth Century American Speech,' Morton W. Bloomfield (1948) gives the phonetic transcriptions of forty-three words in a column headed 'Maritime (Halifax)' (pp. 66–67). The transcriptions were not made by Bloomfield himself, and he expresses doubts about the accuracy of some of them — not without justification, it seems, for the transcription of *horror* as [hɑrrər], with its intervocalic [rr], scarcely inspires confidence. Since they use both the symbol [ɪ] and the symbol [ʊ], these transcriptions seem to use the phonetic symbols of the *Linguistic Atlas of the United States and Canada* (see Kurath, 1973, pp. 122–46). Also, since the transcriptions record two forms for the word *greasy*, one with [s] and, surprisingly, one with [z], they appear to record the speech of at least two informants. The transcriptions make no use of minimal pairs, but it is possible to discover something of the vowel phonemes of a Halifax idiolect of the 1940s from them none the less.

The checked vowels of this idiolect are shown by the phonetypes of *grease* [gris], *hiccup* [ˈhɪkəp], *fatality* [fəˈtælɪti], *aseptic* [æˈsɛptik], *aunt* [ænt], *of* [əv] (possibly unstressed), *mock* [mɑk], *boss* [bɔs], *yoke* [jok], *cushion* [ˈkʊʃən], *beauty* [bjuti], *wife* [wʌɪf], and *house* [hʌʊs]. Since this list includes no minimal pairs, the phonemic allocation of these phonetypes must rest on the phonetic dissimilarities among them, but for most of them it is nevertheless fairly certain. The only difficulties are in the phonemic significances of [ɑ] and [ɔ]. It is obvious that the [æ] of *aunt* must represent an allophone of /æ/ and that the [o] of *yoke* must represent an allophone of /o/; the symbols [ɑ] and [ɔ] must therefore represent allophones of two phonemes somewhere between /æ/ and /o/. The symbol [ɑ] is used for the vowel of *mock*, *moth*, *nominative*, *swath*, *waft*, *wasp*, and *what*, although for *swath* and *waft* the transcription gives also forms with [æ]. The symbol [ɔ] is used for *boss*, *chocolate*, and *doll*. The question is: how much rounding is to be given to the sounds that this symbol represents? It is difficult to believe that [ɔ] could have represented a fully rounded phonetic [ɔ]. However, [ɔ] must have represented a vowel with some degree of rounding and hence it has been taken to represent the allophones of a phoneme in the area of /ɒ/. The symbol [ɑ] is thus left to represent a phoneme whose allophones occupy the space from those of /æ/ back to those of the low back rounded phoneme /ɒ/. Since it must thus be a low central vowel, it may be appropriately symbolized by /ɑ/. The checked vowel phonemes in the Halifax idiolect transcribed in Bloomfield's article may hence be represented as /i ɪ e ɛ æ ə ɑ ɒ o ʊ u aɪ aʊ/.

Since Bloomfield gives no words containing vowels in free position, there is no way of telling which of the checked vowel phonemes occurred in free position also.

Bloomfield gives five words which show vowels before /r/; they are *sirup* [ˈsɪrəp], *persist* [ˈpɜ ^{r}sɪst], *march* [mɑrtʃ], *horror* [hɑrrər], and *gourd* [gɔrd]. Obviously, they attest to the occurrence before /r/ of the phonemes /ɪ ə ɑ ɒ/.

The next idiolect described in this chapter is a 'standard' idiolect from the city of Halifax. Although born in Pictou, Nova Scotia, the informant for this idiolect moved to Halifax at the age of seven and had been there continuously until 1968, when his idiolect was recorded, at which time he was twenty-three years old. The informant was a graduate of Saint Mary's University. His father, a native of Halifax, was a BA and an MD, and his mother, a native of Saskatoon, was an RN. (A more purely Haligonian informant speaking a standard dialect proved oddly difficult to find.) The data on which the description of this informant's idiolect is based are taken from a tape-recording made in Halifax on 27th June 1968 over the questionnaire in Davis and Davis (1969).

The responses elicited by this questionnaire provide a number of words which help to identify the vowel phonemes occurring in checked position in this idiolect; these are *beat* [bi^{iˇ}t^{h}], *bit* [bɪt˺], *bet* [bɛt^{h}], *bat* [bæ$^{v> ə\wedge}$t], *butt* [bɐ$^{\wedge>ɐ\vee>}$t], *boat* [bo^{uˇ}t^{h}]; *wail* [we$^{ˇə\wedge}$ɫ], *wool* [wʊ$^{<\wedge ʊ\vee}$ɫ]; *pull* [p^{h}ʊ$^{ˇɔ\wedge}$ɫ], *pool* [p^{h}u$^{\vee ʊˇ}$ɫ]; *hod* [hɑ$^{<\wedge ə}$d], *hide* [ha$^{>ɨ}$d]; *math* [ma$^{\wedge<ə\wedge}$θ], *mouth* [mɐ$^{\wedge>ʊ\wedge}$θ]; *bald* [bɑ·^{ɐ}ɫd], *boiled* [bɔ^{ɨˇ}ɨd]. Obviously, the phonetypes in these words identify respectively the phonemes /i ɪ ɛ æ ə o; e ʊ; ʊ u; ɑ aɪ; æ aʊ; ɑ ɔɪ/. With each phoneme written only once and with all rewritten in a more 'conventional' order, these phonemes are /i ɪ e ɛ æ ə ɑ o ʊ u aɪ aʊ ɔɪ/. It is interesting to note that in pre-voiceless position /aɪ/ and /aʊ/ show the high onsets typical of these phonemes in Canadian speech (Gregg, 1973; Chambers, 1973; Picard, 1977); however, the most important feature of the checked vowel phonemes of this Halifax Standard idiolect is that no allophone of /ɑ/ is rounded.

Some of the free vowel phonemes of this idiolect are shown by the responses *three* [θ^{ɨ}r^{ɪ}i$^{\vee i}$], *stay* [ste$^{\vee ɨˇ}$], *know* [no$^{\vee<ʊ}$], *two* [t^{hʊ}uˇ], *by* [ba$^{>ɨ}$], *cow* [k^{h}a$^{>ʊ\vee<}$]; these phonemes are /i e o u aɪ aʊ/. Although it does not appear in the record, it is difficult to believe that the word *boy* did not exist in this idiolect, and it is difficult to believe that it did not have /ɔɪ/ as its phoneme, even though a tape-recording in the author's possession, made by a native of North Sydney, Nova Scotia, has *boy* as /baɪ/. Emigration to North Sydney from Newfoundland may possibly account for this particular pronunciation. Hence the phoneme /ɔɪ/ will be added to the list of phonemes already given for the free position, but with a cautionary asterisk. The list of free vowel phonemes for the Halifax Standard idiolect should thus be revised to read /i e o u aɪ aʊ *ɔɪ/. Even so, the list may be incomplete; there is nothing in the Davis and Davis (1969) questionnaire to check on the existence of /æ/, /ɑ/, or both in free position.

Before intervocalic /r/, the Halifax Standard idiolect shows *stirrup* [stɪ$^{>}$r̥əp], *Mary* [mɛ$^{\wedge ɨ}$r^{ɨ}i^{v}], *merry* [mɛ̆$^{\vee>}$rɨ], *married* [mæ$^{\wedge>}$rɪd], *sari* [sɑ$^{>}$rɪ$^{\wedge}$], *sorry* [sɔ$^{\vee ə>}$rɪ^{i}]; respectively /ɪ e ɛ æ ɑ ɔ/. However, since there is no minimal pair to distinguish /ɔ/ from /o/ in this position, the totality of vowel phonemes of the Halifax Standard idiolect will be more economically described if the pre-/r/ vowel phonemes are aligned more closely with the checked vowel phonemes and rewritten as /ɪ e ɛ æ ɑ o/. Before preconsonantal /r/, the idiolect shows *beard* [b^{ɪ}i^{ɨ}rd], *sermon* [sɛ$^{>}$rmɪn], *hard* [ha$^{\wedge>}$ṛd], *third* [θɜ·rd], *furniture* [fʌ$^{ˇ<}$rnɪčɜ$^{\wedge}$r], *forty* [fɔˇrṭ̬iˇ], *tired* [t^{h}ɑ$^{\wedge ɨ}$rd]; respectively /i ɛ æ ə (=[ɜ ~ʌ]) o aɪ. In this position, the informant shows a slight difference between *horse* and *hoarse*, the first having [ɔ^{ə}] while the second has [ɔ$^{\wedge ə}$]; in *morning* and *mourning*, however, the informant has [ɔ^{ə}] and [ɔ^{ˇə}] respectively, thus reversing the distribution of the phonetypes [ɔ] and [ɔˇ]. Because of this, it seems that [ɔ] and [ɔˇ] are in free variation before /r/ in this idiolect, and need not be allocated to different phonemes. Before final /r/, the words *ear* [i$^{ˇ>ɪ}$r], *chair* [čɛ$^{\wedge ɨ}$r], *far* [fa$^{\wedge>}$r], *four* [fɔ$^{\wedge ə>}$r], show /ɪ ɛ æ o/ respectively. The diphthongs /aʊ/ and /ɔɪ/ do not appear in any pre-/r/ position in this idiolect; between /aʊ/ and a following /r/, an epenthetic /ə/ appears, while /ɔɪ/ before /r/ is not elicited in the questionnaire.

The vowel phonemes of the two idiolects, so far as it has been possible to discover them, may now be listed and compared with each other; it will also be possible to compare the vowel phonemes of these two idiolects, in some respects, with the phonemes of General Canadian English, the dialect which Avis (1973a) located in and west of Ontario. For the reader's convenience, the vowel phonemes of the Halifax idiolects are tabulated as follows.

Halifax: Bloomfield

Checked	/i	ɪ	e	ɛ	æ	ə	ɑ[1]	ɒ[2]	o	ʊ	u	aɪ	aʊ			/
Free					no evidence											
Before /r	/															
Intervocalic	/															/
Preconsonantal	/	ɪ														/
Final	/					ə	ɑ[1]	ɒ[2]								/

Halifax: Standard

Checked	/i	ɪ	e	ɛ	æ	ə	ɑ[1]	o	ʊ	u	aɪ	aʊ	ɔɪ	/
Free	/i		e					o		u	aɪ	aʊ	*ɔɪ	/
Before /r/														
Intervocalic	/	ɪ	e	ɛ	æ		ɑ[1]	o						/
Preconsonantal	/i			ɛ	æ	ə		o			aɪ			/
Final	/			ɛ	æ			o						/

[1] Rounded
[2] Unrounded

To consider the checked vowel phonemes first, it is noticeable that neither of the Halifax idiolects shows any trace of the phoneme /a/ found in one version of General Canadian English. Of this phoneme, Avis says:

> Although the phoneme /a/ is part of my idiolect, it is by no means common in general Canadian English nowadays. I personally have a contrast between *balm* /bam/ and *bomb* /bɑm/, both of which differ from *bam* /bæm/ and *bum* /bəm/. (1973a, p. 64, fn. 21)

Wherever those speakers of General Canadian English who have the phoneme /a/ got it from, they seem not to have got it from the emigrant sons of Halifax.

In their checked vowel phonemes, the two Halifax idiolects differ also from each other. The rounded vowel /ɒ/ shown by the idiolect transcribed in Bloomfield does not appear in the later Standard idiolect, which shows no checked vowel phoneme at all between unrounded /ɑ/ and rounded /o/. On this point, Avis remarks:

> Most Canadians . . . no longer make a distinction between /ɔ/ and /ɑ/ in such pairs as *caught* and *cot*, *naughty* and *knotty*, which have contrasting vowels in most varieties of American and British English. In General Canadian, in fact, all such words have the phoneme /ɑ/, which may vary environmentally from [a$^{>}$] back to [ɒ], none of which are characterized by rounding. (1973a, p. 64).

Whether or not he actually did distinguish *caught* from *cot*, the informant for the idiolect in Bloomfield certainly had the phonemic ability to do so, although the low and mid back rounded phoneme in his idiolect has been written as /ɒ/ rather than as /ɔ/ for reasons given above. The Halifax Standard informant, on the other hand, made no distinction between *caught* and *cot*; each had [ɑ^{ə}] as its phonetype. Since the informant favoured phonetypes in the area of [ɑ] rather than in that of [ɒ], the symbol /ɑ/ has been used for his phoneme in this area. Despite the difference in symbolization between Avis's /ɑ/ and the /ɑ/ used herein, both represent the same phoneme, and the Halifax Standard idiolect, with its loss of a rounded vowel in the low and mid back area, has moved away from the idiolect recorded in Bloomfield to align itself with General Canadian English.

It is much to be regretted that Bloomfield gave so little information on free vowel phonemes and on the vowel phonemes before /r/. From the meagre information available, it is simply impossible to tell whether or not this idiolect distinguished between /ɔ/ and /o/ before /r/. The very slight difference between *horse* and *hoarse* in the Halifax Standard idiolect may be a reflex of a distinction once common but lost by the late 1960s. However, with its absence of a rounded vowel before /r/ between /ɑ/ and /o/, the Halifax Standard idiolect again aligns itself with General Canadian English, of which Avis, in the continuation of the quotation given above, says:

> Accordingly, [ɔ] occurs only in such words as *door* [dɔr] and *horse* (and *hoarse*) [hɔrs], that is, before /r/. . . .This being the case, [ɔ] . . . may be grouped under the phoneme /o/, so that *door* may be transcribed [dor]. . . . (1973a, p. 64)

Finally, it should be noted that the Halifax Standard idiolect preserves the integrity of /e/, /ɛ/, and /æ/ before /r/. In this regard, this idiolect differs from General Canadian English, of which Avis says:

> Few Canadians of my generation, for example, distinguished *Mary* from *merry*, both having /ɛ/, and in this matter we stand four-square with our children. We did, however, distinguish *merry* from *marry* and *hairy* from *Harry*, having /ɛ/ in the first of each pair and /æ/ in the second. It seems clear that this contrast is breaking down among younger Canadians, for many of whom *Mary*, *merry*, and *marry* all have the same phoneme, namely, /ɛ/. (1973b, p. 113)

In this respect, then, the Halifax Standard idiolect is closer to the older form of General Canadian English.

To sum up, then. The Halifax Standard idiolect differs from General Canadian English in preserving the distinctions among /e/, /ɛ/, and /æ/ before /r/. It resembles General Canadian English, however, in having only an unrounded checked vowel between /æ/ and /o/, and in using [ɔ] only as an allophone of /o/ before /r/. It is at least a possible hypothesis that this idiolect thus shows an attempt to approximate a Maritime speech to that of the more populous, more influential, and wealthier provinces of Ontario and the west.

References

Avis, W. S. (1973a). The English language in Canada. *Current trends in linguistics, 10 (1)*, 40–74.

———. (1973b). Problems in editing a Canadian dictionary: Phonology. In R. I. McDavid, Jr., & A. Duckert, (Eds.), *Lexicography in English*, Annals of the New York Academy of Sciences 211. New York: The New York Academy of Sciences.

Bloomfield, M. W. (1948). Canadian English and its relation to eighteenth century American speech. *Journal of English and Germanic philology, 47*, 59–67.

Chambers, J. K. (1973). Canadian raising. *Canadian journal of linguistics, 18*, 113–35.

Davis, A. L. & Davis, L. M. (1969). Recordings of standard English. *Newsletter of the American dialect society, 1 (3)*, 4–17.

Goldensohn, L. (1992). *Elizabeth Bishop: The biography of a poetry*. New York: Columbia University Press.

Gregg, R. J. (1973). The diphthongs ai and ə in Scottish, Scotch-Irish and Canadian English. *Canadian journal of linguistics*, *18*, 136–45.
Kurath, H. (1973). *Handbook of the linguistic geography of New England.* 2nd ed., rev. A. Duckert & R. I. McDavid, Jr. New York: AMS Press.
Picard, M. (1977). Canadian raising: The case against reordering. *Canadian journal of linguistics*, *22 (2)*, 144–55.
What a Californian sees in Nova Scotia. (1985, Sept. 21). *The Novascotian*, 5–6.

Chapter Two

Some Observations on the South Shore Lexicon

Lewis J. Poteet

Editors' Introduction

Studies in the lexicography of Canadian English have produced impressive reference works in the form of *A Dictionary of Canadianisms on Historical Principles* (*DC*; 1967), and several regional dictionaries, among which the *Dictionary of Newfoundland English* (*DNE*; 1982) and the *Dictionary of Prince Edward Island English* (*DPEI*; 1988) are of paramount importance for the Eastern region. A perusal of these works, with their wealth of information and meticulous scholarship, can give rise to conflicting feelings: pleasure of discovery on the one hand, frustration on the other. Pleasure can come from browsing in these volumes and discovering the meanings of mysterious words like *inconnu* (a fresh-water fish), *terrier* (a variety of beaver), and *deer's tongue* (a kind of plant) — all in the *DC*, while frustration is probably inevitable if we try to look up *northern shark* (a kind of trash fish) in the same dictionary, even though there are twelve other entries with *northern* as the first element.

The lacunae in the *DC* indicate a need for more detailed regional dictionaries. The *DNE* and the *DPEI* meet that need for the provinces whose distinctive lexicon they undertake to describe.

In Nova Scotia no similar project has been undertaken for the province as a whole, but a considerable contribution to regional lexicography has been made by Lewis J. Poteet in his *South Shore Phrase Book* (Rev. ed., 1988).

Poteet had been collecting regional expressions of the South Shore for over fifteen years before he brought out his *Phrase Book* with its over 800 entries. Pleasant to browse through, it is also thorough in its treatment of selected entries whose history and origins are explored in some detail.

In the following chapter, Poteet discusses words under several headings, according to their origins, which he identifies as 'Old English (Anglo-Saxon), German, French, Mi'kmaq, and in a few cases Old Norse' (p.30 following). These origins are not surprising, as even British English is necessarily traceable to earlier stages and shows, in addition to its Anglo-Saxon base, also a vast influx of French lexical items, as a result of the Norman Conquest, and thereafter successive borrowings from all the other languages it ever came in contact with.

The notable part of Poteet's observation, then, is not the presence of such elements as these, but the presence of words which had fallen into disuse in other places, as well as the fact that various words on the South Shore preserved their earlier meanings rather than those which developed elsewhere, in General English. This fact reminds us that the language of colonies has been repeatedly observed to be more conservative than the language of the country of origin, often preserving linguistic relics which disappeared 'back home.' Ian Pringle, in his paper 'The Concept of Dialect and the Study of Canadian English' (1986, p. 226), discusses this phenomenon in detail, stressing especially the fact that once the colonial version becomes established, it will remain stable if no new migrations occur. *Cobbing*, *dinging*, and *spudging* are among the Anglo-Saxon examples of such relics on the South Shore, while *mawger*, *fungee*, and *shimmy* are interesting examples of words borrowed and preserved from French, with *blagarding* as possibly a word of combined English-French origin. Likewise, words of German origin receive attention in Chapter Three, 'The Dialect of Lunenburg.' Here, in the present chapter, Poteet brings to light especially the contribution of folk etymology to meaning.

Finally, Poteet brings in some observations on specifically male and female vocabulary, which complement in some ways the discussion of language and gender which will be offered in Chapter Ten. He ends his discussion with fresh comparisons with the most recent dialect dictionaries, the most important of which is the *Dictionary of American Regional English* (*DARE*, 1985-), whose publication is still in progress. This dictionary, vast in scope and meticulous in execution, will surely inspire lexicographers of Canadian English to produce a comprehensive work, incorporating available knowledge about Canadian regional varieties under one cover — until then, separate regional reference works provide us with words and etymologies to ponder on.
(LF & MH)

***

Some Observations on the South Shore Lexicon
by Lewis J. Poteet

Around 1972, when I began to collect interesting, odd turns of phrase that I overheard along Nova Scotia's South Shore, I did not expect that one day I would be asked to make an attempt to describe the treasure-trove of words in use there. This set of regional words and phrases seemed, and seems to me even now, so diverse and constantly in use — and therefore in some way constantly in change — that to attempt to describe it must be a considerable task.

The linguists from whom I obtained my training and advice, formally in Minnesota and informally in Canada, tended to place most trust in charting the accent, rather than the words, to give a global perspective on the language of any particular place. Harold Allen's *Linguistic Atlas of the Upper Midwest* (1973-76) proposed to do little more with the lexicon than to choose interesting variants to show the lines between different speech fields. Above all, knowing and valuing statistical evidence, these scholars emphasized in their writing the overwhelming uniformity of North American English, while entertaining one another at conventions with odd and curious local usages. I had a sense that their informal, enthusiastic curiosity suggested that their professional view — that the language was mainly the same everywhere on this continent — was incomplete. But I could not yet support my own sense of the variety and diversity I believed existed.

Now accents, the exact slant and colour of sounds, *are* remarkably stable in certain regions, especially among people who have lived in one village all their lives and talked mainly (and a lot) to one another. It is safe to chart the sounds, to draw lines between these language areas, or speech fields. Doing so seems to show that a uniformity based on radio and television announcers' usage is spreading, that old, diverse ways of speaking are dying out. But the lexicon reveals, more clearly than accents, the curious truth that exposure to radio and television with their Radio-Canada French, CBC English, and such American dialects as the Bostonese in which the traffic reports come through to the South Shore, even in the daytime, doesn't wipe out local ways of talking, but merely influences the residents to add on *knowledge* of (if perhaps not use of) another dialect. And rather than joining the linguists in charting accents, I myself have been primarily a student of literature, where the clever or curious (but statistically singular) turn of phrase is prized.

Gradually I have come to perceive that there is common ground between my two passions, for the spoken word of the folk and the elaborate word of the writer. But it took several years of teaching and exploring Victorian literature, the Gothic novel, and adolescent fiction before I discovered that by following one of those grand generalist Victorian professions, that of folklorist, I could document the poetics of folk speech. That is, I could collect South Shore speech items — words and phrases — and meditate fruitfully on their origins, meanings, relationships, contexts, and patterns of use. Beauty and truth came together for me, in the way people talked.

As I studied the group of words I found interesting in South Shore talk, it seemed inevitable to ask where they had come from. So I did research on the origins, backgrounds, and uses of these words elsewhere. I discovered that they could be traced to four or five languages — Old English (Anglo-Saxon), German, French, Mi'kmaq, and in a few cases Old Norse.

First, the selection of words from which people make their choices in this place contains a large number of key words which have changed remarkably little over many years, in some cases centuries. They have passed out of the language in other places, or have been forgotten, or remembered (in the case of proverbial utterances) only in part. From Old English sources, consider: '*Come aboard of* this yard, and you'll get such a *cobbing*, I mean a real *dinging*, that you'll *gimp* away from here.' Or, again, 'When the *glin hove* downshore for a few minutes, you could see the *wrackers spudging* the barrels on deck and getting nothing by *orts and otts* for their trouble.' Or, 'On a *smurry* day, what better to do than take the old gun down and *squib* around for rabbits?'

come aboard of	'enter, intrude upon, walk upon'
cobbing	'beating'
dinging	'beating, with visible damage'
gimp	'cripple,' or as a verb, 'to limp'
glin	'sunny break in the fog'
hove	'stopped'
wrackers	'local people scavenging aboard a wreck under salvage law, or in the belief that it is their right to do so under salvage law'
spudging	'poking'
orts and otts	'odds and ends,' originally 'table scraps'
smurry	'overcast, cloudy'
squib	'fire a gun'

In some cases these words are being used almost exactly as they had been used, especially in the North of England, in the 1300s. In many cases they were in use in the days of Shakespeare (Poteet, 1984). South Shore people are used to knowing more than one way of speaking.

The basic stock on which the vocabulary of this region is drawn is Anglo-Saxon, in some cases preserving even the forms and sounds of the words from before the days when the Norman scribes applied a French ruler to many, sweeping away many old internal vowel changes and adding a simple, uniform set of endings. What is more to the point, it was also before the enormous borrowings of French words into English. In other words, when we say the English language is fairly uniform, we mean the *written* form of it, which acquired its uniformity from the standardizing writing habits of the scribes. Only in regions like Nova Scotia, where a tradition of old *speaking* persists, do we have such old spoken forms kept alive and in use.

But besides these words, new words, too, were borrowed here from French, as early as the late eighteenth century. *Pleasance*, *mawger*, *patti-pans* (from *paté* or *petit pains*), *fungee* (from *fonger* 'to blot up'), *shimmy*, and especially *blagarding*, show that as the people along the Shore met other people, they appropriated and kept using some of their most common vivid terms, particularly among women's words (i.e., words used mostly for activities and the objects associated with them in which women played the largest part, as in cooking, clothing, and gardening).

pleasance	'a small rose garden'
mawger	'thin'
patti-pans	'cupcakes'
fungee	'fruit dumplings'
shimmy	'a shirt'
blagarding	'talking dirty'

Blagarding is a word long known in England (perhaps since 1532, according to the *Oxford English Dictionary*). In the related form *blackguarding*, it has been traced to the 'scurrilous language' of either 'a hypothetical guard of soldiers at Westminster Abbey' (Poteet, 1988b), or of shoe-blacking boys and link-boys (who were hired to carry torches for rich people afoot on London streets) around 1670. This explanation of the origins of the word, obscure as they are, traces it to the Old English word *blæc*. But according to the *DARE* it had, after 1806 in the New World, the particular meaning it has widely on the South Shore, not just 'scurrilous, abusive language,' but specifically 'dirty talk.'

Joseph Ross, author of *History of Cape Negro and Blanche* (1987), has pointed out in conversation with me an alternative or concurrent possible meaning of the word, more strongly suggested by its Nova Scotia form *blagarding*, in the French slang word *blague*, which means 'chaff, humbug, hoax, fib,' according to *Cassell's New French Dictionary* (1951). The case for this etymology of at least the South Shore use of the word is strengthened by our remembering that several other words from the region seem to have come from more than one source. *Cockerwitter*, originally an insulting word for people who live around Cockerwit Passage between Woods Harbour and Shag Harbour in Barrington municipality, has been explained, with nearly equal plausibility, as a word from Old English, French, and Indian sources (Poteet, 1988b). That is, it may derive from *cocker* and *wit*, or 'wits gone all cock-eyed.' Or it may come from the French word *cacaouis*, which may have descended from the Mi'kmaw word *kakawegech*, meaning 'wild duck' (Lewis, 1980). Robie Tufts, an expert on Nova Scotia birds, believed it came from *cock-a-wee*, from the sound made by a local bird (Tufts, 1961). The words *bluenose* 'a resident of Nova Scotia' and *shoe-pack* (for *larrigan* 'a kind of moccasin') are other words which the *DC* suggests were borrowed and used by people who had differing explanations of their origins. In the case of *bluenose*, cold noses, a privateer with a blue cannon on the prow, and a distinctive potato have all been offered as sources.

Folk etymology is worth recording, I find, as it shows how sometimes even a mistaken belief about a word's history may influence its use and meaning. Since language is continually shaped by everyone's use of it, a scientific explanation of a word's origins may be generally disregarded in favour of a mistaken, but seemingly obvious, popular explanation. And so if we want to explain all the ways a language works, we must do more than insist on the 'correct' view: we must also incorporate in our account the widespread misunderstandings which have had effects on the ways words have been used and spread.

The words in use on the South Shore are also in most cases words that came from elsewhere. Many words are not invented in one place by one person, then spread into general use, but rather seem to have come into being in many places at once, echoing greater or less knowledge and experience of several languages and cultures, and exhibiting the human tendency to play with the sounds and meanings of the words we use.

In one example, the word *shimmy* is widely known across North America, but as the name for a dance, not as on the South Shore a form of the word *chemise*, used to denote a shirt. The suggested connection between these two meanings is that the dance was made widely popular after a turn-of-the-century World's Fair in the American Midwest, at which a woman danced in nothing but a shirt. But this event occurred after the word was already in use in Nova Scotia, so it cannot be the source of that local meaning. The *Dictionary of Americanisms* (1951) dates the use of the word (for 'shirt') from 1839, but it was in use in Shelburne County before 1800 (Archibald et al., 1982). It is certainly important to distinguish between this word and words already borrowed from French into English dialect at the time of settlement. There are several such, especially in the world of fashion and clothing. The *Port Roseway Gazetteer and the Shelburne Advertiser* of July 21, 1785, lists, for example, *shalloons*, a word for 'woollen material from Chalons, France,' and in the relatively cosmopolitan boom town of Loyalist Shelburne, it is to be expected that such words will turn up. But *shalloons* disappeared; *shimmy* did not. And it seems to have lasted longer in Barrington than in Shelburne. More in touch with the woods and fishing, older Barrington may well have been the main site of the post-Deportation contact between French and English women which must have occurred to account for the origin and survival of these French words among the local language resources.

My *South Shore Phrase Book* (1988) also gives a sampling of the words borrowed from German in Lunenburg County, such words and expressions as *break together*, *Daks Day*, *fasnak*, *gookemole*, *gut a swilla*, *house-stoy*, *kashittery*, *mother soul alone*, *schimmel*, *schuss*, *schmuck off*, *scluttery*, *smutched*, *wackelass*, and so forth.

break together	'to break apart'; from German *zusammenbrechen*. The parts of the original expression have been carried over separately rather than the whole translated idiomatically.
Daks Day	'Groundhog Day'; *Dachs* is German for 'badger.'
fasnak	'raised doughnuts'; here the food is named for the day on which it was traditionally made and served. *Fastnacht* is the German word for 'Shrove Tuesday night.' The customary English food on this day is of course pancakes.
gookemole	'Look at this!' The German phrase *Gucke einmal* 'look once!' has been a bit slurred as it was carried over into English.
gut a swilla	'God's will be done!' *Gottes Wille!*
house-stoy	'dowry or wedding present'; from the German *Aussteuer*. Curiously, the original German expression does not contain the word *house* (*Haus* is a common word in German), but the English form sounds close enough to suggest it, so there it is!
kashittery	'fuss, mess'; from the German *Geschütterei* 'an outpouring of words.' Again, a sort of coincidence of sounds and meanings brings a new word (here an old Anglo-Saxon four-letter word) that enforces the derogatory connotations.
mother soul alone	'totally alone'; from the German *mutterseelenallein*. An extraordinarily forceful way to say 'alone,' even if *Mutterseele* simply means 'human being.'
schimmel	'blonde, colourless person'; the negative connotations aren't fully clear unless you know that *Schimmel* means 'mould, mildew' in German.
schuss	'a halfwit'; in this case the South Shore word is more derogatory than the original, *Schüssel*, which in German simply means 'a careless, slovenly person.'

schmuck off	'a small bath'; in German *schmucken* means 'to spruce oneself up,' and *Schmutz*, 'filth, smut, dirt.'
scluttery	'fatty'; from German *schlotterig* 'loose, shaky, flabby.'
smutched	'smeared'; see *schmuck off* above.
wackelass	said of a cat that is always underfoot; from *wackeln* 'to reel, totter,' and *Aas* 'carcass.'

From the Cape Sable Island area, I found that at least two seafaring words possibly of Norse origin have lasted: *swale*, for 'a piece of low-lying land below a ridge, often beside a river,' may be related to the Norse *svalr* 'cool.' And *rout*, for 'the noise of the waves on the shoreline, used for determining position in fog,' has a particularly interesting history, appearing in the written reports of the voyages of Henry Hudson by three different sailors, Hudson himself, his first mate, and an ordinary seaman. (These reports appear in a 1625 anthology of travel writings published under the title of *Purchas his Pilgrimes*.) I have found *rout* still in use, as did Helen Creighton (1975), exactly as it has been since it was derived from the Norse *rauta* 'to roar,' and was so used by Chaucer.

The tendency to keep old words in the lexicon is also demonstrated by its offering a plenitude of elaborate, proverbial ways of saying fairly common things. When we compare *happy as a clam*, the generally known simile, with what must surely be the original, which I heard on the South Shore, *happy as a clam at high water*, we see how the local expression has kept what others have lost. Water is *Adam's ale*, a fisherman will *either live in hope, or die in despair*, and to do something self-defeating is not just to *piss in the wind*, but to *piss across a fair wind*. Everybody needs *a pool of still water* 'privacy,' and not just to *wet a line* 'fish.' When I ask you to hang my phrases alongside a while before you heist them aboard, I am in fact *pulling your mouth* 'trying to get you to say something,' but I only do what was done to me, as I listened to people talk.

Much of the proverbial lore is clearly a memorial to the work and words of another age. To notice how smoke rises in the air, to remember *the finer the weather the quicker it goes*, or *the four sides to the weather* have been habits here for a long time. A counting rhyme like *knit one, purl one, 'tis one, 'tain't one, bye and bye* seems out of date, except in a place like this where needlecraft and quilting bees are still primary social and linguistic events, community events where people like to get together and talk and listen. Another kind of expression we find here, terms of 'rough measure,' were mainly used to measure things, like quantities of firewood, in another age (buying and selling *cord*, a *jag*, a *run*). But people still burn wood here, whereas another term of rough measure, *lounder*, originally applied to quantities of rum, is now just as applicable to car windshield cleaning (with *lounders* of snow) — it means 'a good quantity of anything.' Together with Jacqueline Baum, an anthropologist from Brandeis University, I have tried to show the relationship between these terms of rough measure and the habit of metaphorical expression so common on Nova Scotia's South Shore (Poteet & Baum, 1987).

As a record of the relative balance between openness to new words and conservatism of speech tradition, we may well note two related but different sorts of talking. People are quick to make colourful metaphors. If something is about to drive you crazy, it can almost *drive you across the bridge to Dartmouth*; if it frustrates you totally, you're *coopered*. The second is as old as barrels, probably; the first only appeared after the provincial psychiatric facility, the Nova Scotia Hospital, was located across the harbour from the city of Halifax. *Down to the fine shims*, a generally applicable term for the picky parts of any process, includes an old word from the early, crude technology of carpentry and wheels. So words, like people, are either *from around here* or *from away*, but all are available for active adaptation or use, and those adopted bear the marks of their history and that of the people who live here. The local term for the dialect spoken by people from Cape Sable Island's South Side, *Yinkyank*, reminds us that they come from Cape Cod, even though they did so long ago.

The South Shore lexicon also offers a number of words to study the pattern of word-use we might call 'gender-linked' language. Men's words include *getting your skin* 'sexual experience,' *grassing* 'foreplay, petting,' and metaphors adapted from the weather to describe how *growly* the wife is today — *a twenty-nine* is a low, stormy barometer reading. Women's words are drawn heavily from cuisine and clothing (*patti-pans*, *galabashing*, for 'big, crude stitching' in quilting, and *twatching* 'emergency repairs to clothing, darning or mending, not neat or finished work'), but there's at least one, *blagarding*, already discussed as to its origins, which is almost always used by women to describe men's private language. While both men and women know each other's words, they tend to keep their speech communities separate. That is, in a gathering of women, say a quilting circle, while almost any subject may be discussed, the cruder 'men's words' would not be used as they are around the wharf, where only men are present. Where there is any contest, it is the usual power agenda that operates. Aware that 'language writes us,' local people chose to call a new commune *The Cult*, rather than *The Old Schoolhouse Community at Barrington*, as the members would have named themselves (Poteet, 1989). Another example, 'When did you get *home*?' asked of a summer resident, enforces on the visitor the local name of the place, whatever it may be to him or her.

Finally, I should mention that the recent publication of a number of fine regional dictionaries makes possible the comparison of words and phrases that are common to the Maritime speech field or dialect area. First, the *DARE* lists a number of words which are also found in Nova Scotia. Incorporating a number of entries from John Gold's *Maine Lingo* (1975), it gives specific regional distribution in the New England states and beyond for *crocus bag* 'a burlap bag,' *cossit* 'a single lamb specially raised apart from the flock,' *chumming* (a trick of fishing), *buck fever* 'nervousness when first hunting,' *beaslings* 'immunity-bearing substances for a calf in a cow's first milk,' and so forth. In *Maine Lingo* we also find *ash breeze* 'paddling your own canoe,' *big as a barn door*, *down east*, *duff* 'pudding,' *jag*, *jillpoke* (a device used in logging), *make and break* (an early kind of marine engine), and *orts and otts*. T. K. Pratt's *Dictionary of Prince Edward Island English* brings light to the transregional uses of such words as *away*, *flying axehandles* 'diarrhea,' *two axehandles across the ass* 'fat,' *bakeapple*, *black ice*, *Boston States*, *cat spruce*, *ceilidh* 'get-together,' *head* 'to work on the lobster trap,' *jag*, *junk* 'chunk,' *knit* (in lobster trap repair), *line storm*, *make and break* engine, *poor man's fertilizer* 'a late snow,' *Old Christmas*, *one-lunger* (a kind of marine engine), *owly* 'grouchy,' *pinny* (article of clothing), *robin snow*, *scoff* 'steal,' *stog* 'stuff, cram,' *stump fence*, and *weather-breeder*. In some cases the meaning of a word used on Prince Edward Island and the South Shore is slightly different.

The *DPEI* also makes it possible to compare the relative frequency of occurrence of words common to Nova Scotia and the Eastern Townships of Quebec. My phrase book for the Far Eastern Townships *Talking Country* (1992) makes it clear, I think, that Prince Edward Island and the Townships share more words and phrases than Prince Edward Island and the South Shore: the Island and the Townships have in common such items as *skiff* 'a tiny bit of snow,' *popple* 'aspen,' *spreckled*, *cornerways*, *breachy* (said of a cow in heat), *downstreet*, *brookie*, *clart* 'to clean over quickly,' *doty* (*dozy*) 'near rotting,' *fernent* 'opposite,' and *graip*. The large amount of woods work done in these two areas is perhaps the key to this larger common lexicon. The *DPEI* also reveals, from a comparison with the most comprehensive of the Canadian Atlantic region dictionaries, Story, Kirwin, and Widdowson's *Dictionary of Newfoundland English*, that some words occur in Newfoundland and Prince Edward Island, but not in Nova Scotia. *Hangishore* is an example. Additionally, Art Campbell's *Words and Expressions of the Gaspé* (1986) offers interesting comparisons with the lexicons of all these areas: a *chance* there has a similar meaning to the South Shore one — 'a good stand of wood for lumber or firewood' as compared with 'a job on a fishing boat' — both mean money. Words with the same meaning and use in the Gaspé and the South Shore include *buttery* 'pantry,' *big feelin'* 'proud, full of oneself,' and *first going off*; and *mager* (in the Gaspé 'a thin salmon') offers additional evidence of the widespread local borrowing of a few French terms very early in the English settlement of the coasts, probably indicating contact between French and English women. With the publication of the remaining volumes of the *DARE*, it may be possible to trace with more certainty the spread of these words. It would help to have a comparative volume of New Brunswick speech, though there is a lively sketch with examples in A. Murray Kinloch's 'The English Language in New Brunswick 1794-1984' (1985).

In recording, noticing, and comparing the words of these places, we may see a measure of xenophobia, the fear of or rather clear identification of strangers. 'Why don't you talk like us?' is perhaps an unspoken question in the mind, as we may guess only by the familiar comment, 'You're from away, aren't you?' This aspect of the culture may partly reflect the need for precision in an environment in which threat and danger are never very far away. It also signals the place of language in the individual's identification with the community. We are who we are, it says; we are from around here. Talking to or for a stranger fulfills the common local function of entertainment. But language is the key way to pass on information about the environment, for survival and success.

So the words of the South Shore bear the marks of the history and experience of the people, and I believe serve as an index to the culture, with its confidence and stability, its separate and distinct communities, and its openness to language, dialect, and speech field and community contact.

References

Allen, H. (1973-'76). *The linguistic atlas of the Upper Midwest.* 3 vols. Minneapolis: University of Minnesota Press.

Archibald, M., de Molitor, E., & Holmes, C. (1982). *Loyalist dress in Nova Scotia 1775-1800.* Halifax: Shelburne County Museum.

Campbell, A. (1986). *Words and expressions of the Gaspé.* Privately printed.

Creighton, H. (1975). *A life in folklore.* Toronto: University of Toronto Press.

Dictionary of American regional English. (1985-). Cambridge: Harvard University Press.

Gold, J. (1975). *Maine lingo.* Camden ME: Down East.

Kinloch, A. M. (1985). The English language in New Brunswick 1794-1984. In R. Gair (Ed.), *A literary and linguistic history of New Brunswick.* Fredericton: Fiddlehead Books.

Lewis, R. (1980, December). Why did you say that? *Nova Scotia historical quarterly,*

Mathews, M. M. (Ed.). (1951). *A dictionary of Americanisms on historical principles.* 2 vols. Chicago: University of Chicago Press.

Poteet, L. (1992). *Talking Country.* Ayer's Cliff, PQ: Pigwidgeon Press.

———. (1989, March/April). Words and power: the Kingdom Church meets the communities of the South Shore. *New Maritimes,* 10-13.

———. (1988a). Present-day linguistic traces of French-English contact in pre- and post-Deportation Barrington, N.S. Moncton: La société historique acadienne.

———. (1988b). *The South Shore phrase book.* Hantsport NS: Lancelot.

———. (1984). 'Elizabethan English' on Nova Scotia's South Shore. *Nova Scotia historical review, 4 (1)*; rpt in L. Poteet, (1988), *The South Shore phrase book.* Hantsport NS: Lancelot.

Poteet, L., & Baum, J. (1987). Rough measure in Maritime dialect research. *New York folklore, 13,* 5-111.

Pratt, T. K. (1988). *Dictionary of Prince Edward Island English.* Toronto: University of Toronto Press.

Pringle, I. (1986). The concept of dialect and the study of Canadian English. In H. B.

Allen & M. D. Linn (Eds.), *Dialect and language variation*. Orlando: Academic Press.

Ross, J. (1987). *History of Cape Negro and Blanche*. Privately printed.

Story, G. M., Kirwin, W. J., & Widdowson, J. D. A. (1982). *Dictionary of Newfoundland English*. Toronto: University of Toronto Press.

Tufts, R. W. (1961). *The birds of Nova Scotia*. Halifax; Nova Scotia Museum.

Chapter Three

The Dialect of Lunenburg

M. B. Emeneau

Editors' Introduction

The dialect of Lunenburg County has long held a fascination for scholars and the general public alike. With its unique settlement history and a relatively stable population, it seems to offer a Brigadoon-like enclave where old-fashioned speech habits can flourish undisturbed. The more fanciful view would be that everyone in the county speaks a version of Lunenburg Dutch (i.e., German, from *deutsch*) — incomprehensible to all but native speakers, while a more moderate view would be that, given modern trends and living conditions, Lunenburg residents speak very much like other Nova Scotians, and preserve only relics of dialect features in the lexicon, pronunciation, and grammar.

It is, therefore, a happy circumstance that M. B. Emeneau, an outstanding linguist, a Sanskrit scholar of international repute, and a native of Lunenburg, published a description in 1935, which we reprint here. Emeneau's description is detailed and scrupulously accurate, and as such offers a basis for comparison with the speech of today, and possibly an evaluation of the area's conservatism with respect to dialect features.

In lexicon alone, it is evident the Lunenburg dialect preserves many expressions unique to the region. In Lewis J. Poteet's *South Shore Phrase Book* (1988), for instance, some 120 out of the 815 regional expressions are tagged 'Lunenburg,' a substantial number, even allowing for the dozen or so for which Emeneau's article is cited as source.

Among the 'Lunenburg' expressions, many show possible connection with German, as suggested by their sound and meaning, and Emeneau provides the German source of *fasnak* and *apple snits* as well as a number of others. Many of the 'Lunenburg' words in the *South Shore Phrase Book* begin with k, and their initial sound is best explained by Emeneau's remark on the names *Knickle* and *Knock*. Some examples of these words are *kanapp* 'rattle,' *kanutch* 'squeeze,' *kanuttle* 'gather together,' and *knuttled* 'twisted or knotted,' e.g., wool.

In these words, the spelling k-a-n may be a representation of an intrusive schwa [ə] between [k] and [n], resulting in an Anglicized pronunciation of the initial cluster [kn-], which is common in German, but not in Modern English, although it was once found in English too, as in the earlier pronunciation of *knee* and *knight*.

When Emeneau states that Lunenburg '[m]orphology shows little variation from that of standard English' (p. 46 following) except in the use of preterite and participle, he is referring to verbs which have distinct forms in the preterite and past participle, like *came*:*come*, *went*:*gone*, *saw*:*seen*, *grew*:*grown*, and *did*:*done*. Constructions such as *they come here yesterday* and *I should have went* can still be heard, especially among older speakers, but they are not simply the result of confusion; rather they occur in a stable pattern — for instance, the form *he gone there yesterday* is not used. Not only are such constructions still common, but so is also the old-fashioned infinitive with *for to*, especially in the expression of purpose, as in *I went back for to fetch it*. Syntactic constructions such as placing *with* or *you* at the end of an expression, as in *I am coming with*, and *I am coming back, you* can be heard among young speakers no less than among older ones. While *with* in this position appears to echo German, *you* is peculiar to Lunenburg.

In a paper entitled 'Lunenburg Dutch: Fact and Folklore' (1975), R. H. Wilson makes an interesting statement, namely, that knowledge about Lunenburg speech is tinged by certain popular beliefs, so that some incomplete or erroneous observations are often repeated as a matter of common belief, while other features, less easy to identify, remain unnoticed. Thus, Wilson points out, it is often stated that Lunenburgers 'reverse' the sounds [v] and [w], whereas in reality, older speakers use a [ʋ], a sound intermediate between [v] and [w], in words with the sounds [w], [hw], and [v], as in *wail*, *whale*, and *veil*. On the other hand, the tendency towards unvoicing of [b], [d], [g] at the end of words like *lab*, *lad*, *lag* passes unnoticed. According to Wilson, the belief that certain features exist reinforces their use, or at least it reinforces a perception that they are part of the region's dialect.

In the following chapter we have kept Emeneau's original phonetic transcriptions, even though they vary from what might be expected, since they indicate some slight differences in pronunciation between Lunenburg Dutch and the standard dialect. As Emeneau himself noted:

> In transcriptions of words of the dialect I write [ou], [ɑu], [ʌi], [ɑi] advisedly. The second elements of these diphthongs are [u] and [i], not [ʊ] and [ɪ]. For the hypothetical standard dialect [ɑu̯] and [ɑi̯] represent points in the pattern rather than actual pronunciations. In setting forth the treatment of *r* the resultant long vowels are pure, as I have written them, without diphthongal glides. Accents are not written; they are in no way different from those of standard English. (1935, p. 35)

Readers who are interested in the history of Lunenburg will no doubt be critical of Emeneau's rather inaccurate summary at the beginning of the chapter. Emeneau, of course, was writing before the results of more recent historical research were available, and therefore summarized what were the generally accepted views of his own time. As he himself remarks: 'Much work remains to be done on this and other problems of local history' (p. 42 following). Probably the most authoritative work on the subject is Winthrop Pickard Bell's *The 'Foreign Protestants' and the Settlement of Nova Scotia* (1990), originally published in 1961. Bell's work describes in detail the settlement of Lunenburg, listing the settlers by origin and family name, and providing a brief analysis of the political situations the immigrants left behind them, including the complicated status of Montbéliard. It is also clear that while the Palatinate was the source of the largest group of settlers, Switzerland and Montbéliard were at least as significant sources as Württemberg, and the group as a whole was more diverse than Emeneau suggests, including some settlers from the Netherlands. The 'brigade of Braunschweig-Lüneburg troops' (p. 42 following) is also rather dubious, since the Lunenburg militia regiment presumably referred to was drawn from a mixed group of military personnel, several of whom had not previously been in the British service at all (Bell, 1990, pp. 409-17).

In a section entitled 'Languages,' Bell describes the complex mixture of English, German, and French which prevailed in the early settlement, adding some observations and examples of his own to complement Emeneau's analysis. He notes that despite Emeneau's 'short technical study of some phonetic peculiarities' and 'selection of interesting idioms,' and the 'idioms and distinctive phrases' (p. 585) to be found in Helen Creighton's *Folklore of Lunenburg County* (1950), there is still no full-length systematic study of the Lunenburg dialect. While a full-length study is yet to become a reality in the future, Emeneau's essay nevertheless offers a succinct description of the dialect, and an inspiration to those interested in the speech of this region. *(LF & MH)*

***

The Dialect of Lunenburg

by M. B. Emeneau

The town of Lunenburg in the province of Nova Scotia was founded in 1753. Until shortly before that date Acadia, including what later became Nova Scotia, was a French possession with French settlers. To offset the disaffection of these people towards British rule, Lord Halifax originated the plan of offering land to soldiers and other subjects of the House of Hanover and to other settlers who should have no sympathy with the Catholic Acadians. Almost an entire brigade of Braunschweig-Lüneburg troops who had been in the English service in America settled in the province, at Halifax or at Lunenburg which in the earliest church records of the town was known as Lüneburg. They were joined by many shiploads of Germans, some Swiss, and a few French Protestants; a number of English-speaking persons lived in the town from the beginning, as officials, garrison, or settlers. The German settlers were drawn from various sources by a proclamation published in several towns in Germany: German emigrants to North America at this period came predominantly from the Palatinate and Württemberg, and there still survives a tradition that a large proportion of the Lunenburg settlers were 'Palatines.' Incidentally, Montbéliard, the source of most of the French, was a possession of Württemberg at this time (DesBrisay, 1895; Faust, 1927: Vol. 1, *passim*, & esp. pp. 256-8). The German spoken must have been of several dialects. Much work remains to be done on this and other problems of local history; it is, however, recorded that '. . . when the Rev. C. E. Cossmann came to the county, in 1835, he could distinguish by the different dialects the places in Germany to which many of their ancestors belonged' (DesBrisay, 1895, p.41). In 1912 Professor Wilkens of New York University, while visiting the county, heard the German spoken by some of the older inhabitants; he informs me that it was Middle or High German in its more obvious characteristics and probably of the nature of a 'compromise dialect.'

During the early years of the settlement German, French, and English were all spoken both privately and as mediums of religion and teaching. French was the first to die out; there are today no French speakers, and according to oral traditions preserved in some families the language seems to have practically gone out of use four generations ago. German had a longer survival. The county history by DesBrisay records a German sermon, well understood by the older people, delivered by Father Cossmann to his Lutheran congregation in 1888. As was natural, the Lutheran church preserved the language in public use for a much longer time than the other churches. The Church of England seems to have abandoned the use of German at some time between 1775 and 1783. The last German pastor of the Deutsche Reformierte Gemeinde left his charge in 1837 and thereafter Scottish clergymen served the congregation, which is now known as the Presbyterian church and popularly is not thought to have any connection with Germany. So far has this Scottish influence gone that the Born family is now known as Burns and disclaims its German origin. In outlying parts of the county, which was settled almost entirely from the town, the German language was commonly used longer than in the town; in the town itself it was used longest by families engaged in farming and by families of labourers with small social pretensions. At the present time [i.e., 1935] German is no longer spoken within the town; some few persons of the age of seventy or over know the language, which was used in their families when they were young, but they hardly ever speak it.

English, the official language and the common language of most of the rest of Nova Scotia, has displaced both French and German in Lunenburg town and county. The total number of the original settlers was 1453. The town has grown somewhat in size, but settlement of the rest of the county and emigration to the New England states have counterbalanced accretions to the population so that it now numbers only something under 3000. Under the circumstances it is hardly to be expected that German should continue to be spoken as long as it has been in Pennsylvania. The effect, moreover, of the original German on the present English dialect has not been so great as in Pennsylvania. This paper gives an account only of the English spoken in the town of Lunenburg. The other sections of the county show a number of differing dialects, some of them markedly divergent from the dialect here described. All of these dialects, including that of Lunenburg town, approximate more and more as time goes on to the surrounding dialects, which are spoken by descendants of English, Scottish, and United Empire Loyalist settlers. The speech of Halifax, the capital of the province, is perhaps most influential, since it is also the seat of one of the colleges of the province and exerts its influence through the schools and professions. Innumerable ties with Massachusetts probably also have weight in the shaping of the language, and the fact that Lunenburg is a fishing and seafaring port may introduce further influences, though both these factors may prove in the last analysis negligible.

In phonology, the dialect of Lunenburg shares with common Nova Scotian and Canadian the pronunciation of the diphthongal phonemes [ɑu̯] and [ɑi̯] before voiceless consonants as [ou̯] and [ʌi̯]. Examples of the former are [ou̯t], [mou̯s], [krou̯č], [mou̯θ]; of the latter [wʌi̯p], [bʌi̯t], [strʌi̯k], [ʌi̯s],[wʌi̯f], [hʌi̯t] or [hʌi̯θ]. This results in a number of morphological patterns with alternation of [ou̯] and [ɑu̯], [ʌi̯] and [ɑi̯]. The alternation is seen in the following nouns, singular and plural: [mou̯θ]:[mɑu̯ðz]; [hou̯s]:[hɑu̯zəz]; [nʌi̯f]:[nɑi̯vz]; [wʌi̯f]:[wɑi̯vz]; [lʌi̯f]:[lɑi̯vz]; [dɑi̯]:[dʌi̯s] (*die:dice*); (these two are hardly felt as connected, any more than in the other colloquial forms of English). Two nouns with irregular plurals show [ou̯] in the singular, [ʌi̯] in the plural, where the standard speech has [ɑu̯]:[ɑi̯], viz. [mou̯s]:[mʌi̯s]; [lou̯s]:[lʌi̯s]. The alternations [ou̯]:[ɑu̯] and [ʌi̯]:[ɑi̯] are found in the formation of verbs from nouns, [hou̯s]:[hɑu̯z]; [mou̯θ]:[mɑu̯ð]; [ædvɑi̯s]:[ædvʌi̯z], and in the formation of abstract nouns from verbs and adjectives, [flʌi̯t] from [flɑi̯]; [strʌi̯f] from [strɑi̯v]; [hʌi̯t] or [hʌi̯θ] from [hɑi̯]. [hʌi̯θ] is a pronunciation analogical to *length*, *width*, etc. With [soṷθ] one may contrast [saṷwɛst] and [saṷi·st]. Apparently in both cases [oṷ] > [aṷ] before a voiced sound, although the forms may have been borrowed completely made from the nautical vocabulary of the standard dialect.

This dialectal pronunciation results in a few homonyms not found in standard English: [koṷč] for *couch* and *coach*, [goṷt] for *gout* and *goat*, and near homonyms: [oṷt] *out* and [oṷts] *oats*. It should be noted that *mouse* and *moose* are not pronounced alike, as the naive speaker of American English, at least, seems to understand is the case in Canadian speech. On the other hand, we must conclude that phonemically [oṷ], representing /aṷ/, falls together with the standard [oṷ]. The phrase [ʌboṷt ʌ boṷt] *about a boat* not only sounds strange to the speaker of Standard English, but also offers difficulties when an attempt is made to bring it into conformity with standard usage. Both diphthongs may be changed, or the change may be made in the wrong one. It is only by unceasing vigilance that hyper-correction can be avoided by one whose native dialect has this phonological feature and who wishes to correct it.

The treatment of *r* before consonants and final is distinctive and provides a shibboleth for the dialect. The Nova Scotian dialects in general preserve the sound in these positions, either as a weak alveolar fricative, or in some cases as a retroflex fricative. The dialect of Lunenburg town and of some, though not all, of the surrounding country loses the sound. The results are as follows. (1) In stressed syllables. After [ɑ·] it is lost, e.g., [fɑ·m] *farm*, [pɑ·k] *park*, [fɑ·] *far*. After [ɪ·] it is lost, e.g., [hɪ·] *hear* or *here*, [fɪ·s] *fierce*, [gɪ·] *gear*, [gɪ·z] *gears*. After [ɛ·] it is lost, e.g., [ɛ·] *air*, [pɛ·] *pair* or *pear* or *pare*. After [ɔ·] it is lost, e.g., [sɔ·t] *sort* (homonym of *sought*), [kɔ·d] *cord* (homonym of *cawed*), [fɔ·θ] *fourth* or *forth*, [hɔ·n] *horn* (homonym of *Haughn* for the German *Hann*, as this name is spelled in the earliest records), [hɔ·s] *horse* or *hoarse*, [pɔ·z] *pours* or *pores* (homonym of *paws*), [wɔ·p] *warp*, [fɔ·bz] *Forbes*, [wɔ·m] *warm*, [wɔ·f] *wharf*, [ɔ·] *oar* or *or* or *ore* (homonym of *awe*), [wɔ·] *war* or *wore*, [sɔ·] *sore* or *soar* (homonym of *saw*). All other stressed syllables show loss of *r* and the vowel of the syllable is [ʊ·], e.g., [pʊ·pʌs] *purpose*, [kʊ·b] *curb*, [sʊ·f] *surf*, [sʊ·v] *serve*, [wʊ·m] *worm*, [hʊ·t] *hurt*, [hʊ·d] *heard* or *herd*, [fʊ·n] *fern*, [wʊ·θ] *worth*, [sʊ·č] *search*, [ʊ·ǰ] *urge*, [wʊ·k] *work*, [kʊ·s] *curse*, [hʊ·z] *hers*, [fʊ·l] *furl*, [šʊ·] *sure*, [yʊ·] *your*, [wʊ·] *were*, [pʊ·] *poor* or *purr*, [hʊ·] *her*, [fʊ·] *fir* or *fur*. This quality remains when *r* is reintroduced before another vowel, e.g., [fʊ·ri] *furry*, [pʊ·rɪŋ] *purring*, [šʊ·r ʌv] *sure of*, [yʊ·r oun] *your own*. (2) In unstressed syllables. Final *er*, *or*, etc. become [ʌ], e.g., [bʌtʌ] *butter*, [haḭʌ] *higher*. Here belong words of the type *fire*, *hire*, *hour*; i.e., after [aḭ] and [aṷ] *r* appears as [ʌ], e.g., [faḭʌ], [haḭʌ], [aṷʌ]. *Our*, when isolated, is generally [aṷʌ]; in a phrase it is usually [ɑ·] before consonants, [ɑ·r] before vowels. *Ours* is either [ɑ·z] or [aṷʌz]. *Er* followed by a consonant becomes [ʌ], as in *concert*, *pattern* (which is also with metathesis [pætrʌn]), *gathered*, etc.

This treatment of *r* is paralleled in some dialects of English; Nova Scotian dialects generally, however, as was noticed above, preserve *r* in these positions. An independent development of the feature is possible. On the other hand, we might look to the German speech of the original inhabitants for its origin. This suggestion, however, is unsatisfactory, since we cannot ascertain certainly what the character of the German dialect was which we are to allege as a substratum.

It must be noted further that not all the people of the town speak in this way. The sound *r* is heard in the weak alveolar fricative form before consonants (and sometimes, but not so generally, final) in the speech of some people, and is undoubtedly making its way into the speech of most of the younger people. This is brought about by the presence in the town of immigrants from other parts of the province and of people who have left the town for Massachusetts and then returned with an approximation to New England speech, as well as through the influence of the schools. A prediction that the shibboleth of the dialect will disappear in the not too distant future is not unwarranted.

The treatment of German family names provides some points of interest. The spellings of these names are chaotic even in the earliest church records of the town. They show generally an approximation to High German spellings, but the earliest records were written by French clergymen, and after a short interval of educated German clergymen, by English speakers. Under these circumstances chaos was inevitable. At the present time some traditional High German spellings survive, but in many cases spellings follow pronunciation more or less closely. Pronunciations have been changed to accord with English speech-habits. Yet in spite of this a German dialectal basis can sometimes be suspected. Some general phenomena may be tabulated. (1) High German initial [š] before a consonant is represented by [s]; either adaptation to English phonology or retention of dialectal pronunciation may be called upon as an explanation. Examples are [snɛ·] *Schner*, now written *Schnare*; [smʌi̭sʌ] *Schmeisser*; [spɑnʌgl̩] *Spannagel*, now written *Sponagle*; [swɪnɪmʌ] *Schweinheimer*, now written *Swinnimer*; [swɑts] *Schwartz* (in this word we seem to have a hybrid of Low German [swɑt] and High German [šwɑrts]). (2) High German initial [ts] is represented by [s] before vowel or semivowel: [swɪkʌ] *Zwicker*; [sɪŋk] *Zinck*. This accords neither with High German nor Low German speech-habits. It may be a hybridization, or an adaptation of High German sounds to English speech-habits. The English word *zinc* is pronounced in the dialect exactly like the name *Zinck*. (3) High German [z] initial is represented by s: [sɪlɪg] or [sɪlɪk] *Selig*. (4) [χ] is represented by [k]: [hɑi̭nɪk] *Heinich*; [bɑkmn̩] *Bachmann*; [wɑi̭nɪk] *Weinacht*, also pronounced [wɑi̭nɑt] and variously spelled. This is either an adaptation to English speech-habits or a retention of dialectal, specifically Low German, pronunciation. Various more sporadic changes are seen in the following: [nɔ·s] *Naas* or *Nasz*; [ɑi̭znʌ] *Eisenhauer*, also spelled *Eisnor* (is one name or two involved here?); [mʌisnʌ] or [mɑi̭znʌ] *Meisner*; [hʌi̭slʌ] *Heisler*; [bi·nʌ] *Böhner* or *Boehner*;

[mɑi̯rʌ] *Maurer*, now spelled *Myra*. *Jung* has come to be pronounced and spelled as *Young*, *Koch* as *Cook*, *Schmidt* as *Smith*; we have here in part sound changes, in part translation. Two names with initial [kn], *Knickle* and *Knock*, have preserved this non-English combination (with strongly aspirated *k*), and show no sign of losing it. On emigration, however, they are Anglicized as *Nichol(s)* and *Knox*. Even within the county, on the border of an United Empire Loyalist district, the family originally known as *Knock* has now become strongly Scottish and *Knox*, a tendency we have seen already in the case of *Born* > *Burns*.

Morphology shows little variation from that of standard English. Uncultivated speakers tend to confuse preterite and past participle forms, but this need not be recorded here since it is common enough in uncultivated English in general, especially in America.

Syntax and vocabulary show a number of German features. Those most tenacious in the dialect are given first.

In colloquial German in general only one past tense is found. The Lunenburg dialect shows a tendency to use the preterite, in the negative and interrogative forms, rather than the perfect, where standard English would use the latter. *Did you do what I told you? Did you just come? Did you do it yet? He didn't come yet.*

With is used as a final adverb with the verbs *go* and *come*; cf. German *mitgehen. Will you go with? I am going with? Come on with?* So also *off* with verbs of cleaning; cf. *abwaschen. Wash your face off! Clean your feet off!* (= *clean your shoes*). But these idioms are going out of use, the former more slowly than the latter. The adverb *once* is used frequently in the phrase *Come here once!* but this idiom tends to be used only jocularly and will probably soon disappear.

Get awake and *get asleep* are very frequent. These idioms may be based on *wach werden*, but analogical factors may be suspected, viz. *be well:get well* = *be awake:get awake*.

Make in the sense of *prepare* (*a meal*) is frequent: *make breakfast, dinner, supper, tea*. For *make* in the sense 'enjoy, eat,' as in *Did you make your supper?* see the *Oxford English Dictionary* (*OED*) s.v. *make* (v.[1] 60). *Make fish*, in the sense 'cure fish' by drying them in the sun, is said by the *OED* (s.v. *make* v.[1] 39) to be obsolete, but is found in this dialect and in the dialects of other fishing communities, especially in Newfoundland.

Another technical term of the fishing industry is *fish-flake*, a platform on which fish are dried and cured (see *OED* s.v. *flake* sb.[1]). On *yaffle*, to pile up fish at one stage of the drying process, e.g., *you can yaffle fish for me if you want work*, I have been unable to find any light. [Interested readers should check the *Dictionary of Newfoundland English* (*DNE*) for *yaffle* 'to gather an armful (of dried and salted cod, kindling, etc.)' The *DNE* was, of course, not available to Emeneau in 1935.]

All is used for *all gone*; *my money is all.*

Want has the sense of *predict* in such phrases as *The paper wants rain.*

The *was für ein* construction is used, but increasingly rarely, in such locutions as *What for a thing is that? How's that for a jack-knife?* (= *That's a good jack-knife, isn't it?*)

While a translation of *Butterbrot* does not seem to be used, its analogue *lassybread* (i.e., *molassesbread*) is common in children's language.

The language of older people (from about the age of 40 upwards) shows a number of German words, usually with the phonetics of the English dialect; these words are practically unknown to younger people and will undoubtedly be forgotten altogether in another generation. Frequently the words are dialectal in German and sometimes they show interesting semantic developments.

Words connected with food form the largest class. *Sauerkraut* [sɑu̯ʌkrou̯t] is the only exception to the rule that such words are rapidly going out of use. Raised doughnuts have the name [fɑsnɑk]; though this is a general name for the confection in question for those who use the word, it is obviously derived from the custom of making them on Shrove Tuesday, which is called [fɑsnɑkdei̯], from *Fastnacht*. Slices of apple dried for winter use are [æpl̩snɪts]. The singular is [snɪt]. The German word at the base of this is *Schnitte*. The German *läppisch* with pronunciation [lɛpɪš] is used in the sense 'insipid'; *this tastes läppisch*. A cake which has fallen and become heavy or soggy in making is described as [klʌtsi], i.e., *klotzig*. [slʊ·p] or [slʊp] 'drink noisily,' as in *he slurps his soup*, is derived probably from a dialectal *slurpen* rather than from the High German *schlürfen*. [frɛs] from *fressen* means 'eat greedily' or like an animal, and is used when correcting a child's table-manners. *Don't fress!* or in connection with *swill*, as *he fresses and swills like a pig*.

February 2nd is known as [dɑksdei̯], i.e., *Dachs-day*. In local belief, however, the animal that comes out of hibernation on that day is the bear.

Belief in witchcraft is fast disappearing and with it the word [hɛks] 'to bewitch' or 'a witch' or 'a wizard.' A countryman may still say: *My pigs are hext*.

German *grunzen* is used in the form [grʊnts] or [grʌnts] with the meaning 'complain.' The noun [grʊntsʌ] or [grʌntsʌ] denotes a complaining person. English *grunt* also has the meaning 'complain' in the dialect.

Schimmel [šɪml̩] is used in a derogatory sense of a very blond, physically colourless person. The adjective *schimmelig* becomes [šɪml̩li]. Dialectal *Schuss* in the form [šʊs] is used ironically in the sense 'a halfwit'; e.g., *Don't listen to her, she's a Schuss*. Adjectives from it are [šʊsi] and [šʊsl̩li].

A dowry or wedding present is known as [hou̯s-stɑi̯ʌ], formed by popular etymology from *Aussteuer*.

The material here presented shows that the original German speech has left its clear mark in the syntax of the dialect and in its more intimate vocabulary, i.e., in the sphere of 'relational concepts' as defined by Sapir (1949). The less intimate vocabulary, which is in the sphere of 'basic or concrete concepts,' in the first few generations of the transition from German to English contained borrowings; the process of purging the dialect of these elements is now almost completed. In the phonology, the crucial point of any substratum theory, the facts at our disposal in this dialect will allow only the decision 'non liquet' — it is not clear.

References

Bell, W. P. (1990). *The 'Foreign Protestants' and the settlement of Nova Scotia*. 2nd ed. Sackville, NB: Centre for Canadian Studies & Mount Allison University.

Creighton, H. (1950). *Folklore of Lunenburg County*. Bulletin no. 117, Anthropological series no. 29, National Museum of Canada. Ottawa: King's Printer.

DesBrisay, M. B. (1895). *History of the county of Lunenburg*. Toronto: W. Briggs.

Faust, A. B. (1969; 1927). *The German element in the United States*. New York: Arno Press.

Sapir, E. (1949; 1921). *Language: An introduction to the study of speech*. New York: Harcourt, Brace & World.

Wilson, R. H. (1975). Lunenburg Dutch: Fact and folklore. In J. K. Chambers (Ed.), *Canadian English: Origins and structure*. Toronto: Methuen.

Chapter Four

Between Emphasis and Exaggeration: Verbal Emphasis in the English of Cape Breton

Lilian Falk

Editors' Introduction

When discussing a regional dialect, that is, the variety of a language spoken in a particular geographical area, we tend to focus on the ways in which the dialect differs from the standard language. Thus, in Chapter One, we have a phonological study of the vowels of 'Halifax Standard' — a regional variant of General Canadian — which identifies the differences between the speaker's pronunciation and General Canadian or General North American, as well as noting the similarities. In chapters Two and Three, the emphasis is clearly on the differences. Chapter Two discusses some specific words and phrases found in the speech of South Shore Nova Scotians which seem to be peculiar to that region. Such lexical items serve to distinguish South Shore speech from Halifax Standard, thus establishing South Shore English as a regional variety within Nova Scotia. Chapter Three concentrates on the dialect of Lunenburg, a small region within the South Shore, and includes both phonological and lexical discussions. From it we can see that Lunenburg shares many lexical items, especially those derived from German, with the more general South Shore dialect. On the other hand, Lunenburg, which historically is the source of these German-derived words and expressions, possesses many other terms not found generally in South Shore speech. We can also see that the pronunciation of Lunenburg English varies considerably not just from General Canadian, but also from Halifax Standard.

If we were to mark on the map of Nova Scotia the places where certain words and expressions, grammatical constructions, and pronunciations are found, we would then be able to draw lines (called isoglosses) around areas in which the words, constructions, or pronunciations are the same. With these isoglosses we would be able to establish the boundaries of the regional dialects of the province — approximately, of course, since dialects do not end abruptly, but fade into one another. Just with the information contained in the first three chapters of this book, we can distinguish Lunenburg English from general South Shore English, and both from Halifax Standard. However, while we realize from personal observation that there *are* several varieties of English in Nova Scotia, the amount of research which has been done in the province is insufficient for us to be able to identify the boundaries of most of them with any precision.

The next two chapters treat different aspects of the speech of a clearly demarcated geographical area in the province, that is, Cape Breton Island. Since Cape Bretoners themselves feel that their speech differs significantly from that of the mainland (and most mainlanders would agree), we can see these two chapters as the beginning of objective confirmation of this feeling.

While dealing specifically with the speech of Cape Breton, Chapter Four focuses on a feature which has often been neglected in language study: the rhetorical devices used in speech to convey emphasis. These verbal devices rarely have any structural significance in the sentences in which they are employed, and often seem to carry very little lexical meaning. They are frequently dismissed as 'slang' expressions, or as 'imprecise' or 'lazy' speech, and as such are omitted from the written language. Of course, once their function in *speech* as opposed to *writing* is recognized — that they are discourse markers drawing attention to various aspects of the close relationship between speaker and hearer — then their absence from writing, where the relationship between writer and reader is by definition more remote, becomes understandable. All the same, their important function in speech has tended to be neglected until relatively recently, and the possibility of using them as identification marks for regional dialects has largely gone unnoticed.

In the following chapter, Lilian Falk undertakes a description and analysis of discourse markers in the speech of Cape Bretoners. For this purpose she has made use of the body of data available in print in *Cape Breton's Magazine*, which since its foundation has specialized in publishing tape-recorded interviews in which residents share their recollections of life in Cape Breton, with all its richness of experience. While these recordings were not made with the intent of producing a linguistic document, the resulting publication nevertheless provides ample material for a linguistic analysis. Certainly, material of this kind must be treated with some caution, and its limitations vis-à-vis a carefully conducted linguistic survey must be noted, but its advantages, on the other hand, should not be ignored. Firstly, apart from being readily available to the researcher, the interviews are also available to the general public, and readers can therefore read the magazine for themselves, and form their own opinions. Secondly, the interviews published in *Cape Breton's Magazine* were conducted in circumstances that were linguistically as close to the ideal as possible: the people who spoke about their life experiences, or brought up recollections about the past, had no need to feel that their use of certain words and expressions might be subjected to anyone's scrutiny; their speech may be said, therefore, to be free of the spectre of 'Observer's Paradox' which mars so much of professional data-gathering. *(LF & MH)*

***

Between Emphasis and Exaggeration: Verbal Emphasis in the English of Cape Breton

by Lilian Falk

Readers who like to savour a good story, told in the lively and rich speech of Cape Breton Island, can hardly do better than turn to the narratives presented in the Island's long-running publication, *Cape Breton's Magazine*, founded by its editor Ronald Caplan in 1972. Printed from recorded interviews, the many stories of personal recollections are presented to readers very nearly as they were first spoken. Because of this particular feature, they offer a rich source of information about the speech of Cape Bretoners in terms of favoured sentence patterns, frequently occurring grammatical constructions, and the use of special words and expressions.

While it is true that the printed page cannot convey the special quality of the speakers' voices, it can still offer much information not easily obtainable elsewhere. Older grammars busied themselves almost exclusively with constructions acceptable in written edited English, and only more recent research has been directed towards identifying the rules underlying even the most common forms of everyday speech. A recent edition of the widely used textbook *Contemporary Linguistic Analysis* by O'Grady and Dobrovolsky (1996) reflects the new direction by including a discussion of *discourse* and *discourse analysis*. Discourse is understood to mean a segment of speech or writing, and discourse analysis involves a consideration of the conditions under which a conversation took place, or the circumstances under which a written communication was produced and received. Discourse analysis also tries to describe and account for various devices used by speakers to convey their intention in conversation, recognizing that conversations consist of much more than an exchange of thoughts or information. There are, in fact, many expressions which are used solely as signals; for example, that the speaker is about to resume the same topic, to change the topic, to convey a personal view, and the like. Deborah Schiffrin, for instance, in *Discourse Markers* (1987), discusses words which have this special function in conversation, like *oh, well, now, you know*, and *I mean*.

The particular topic which concerns us in this chapter is the variety of means used to convey special emphasis in conversation — a topic which has attracted more attention recently than it once did. There are many ways of expressing emphasis, but these are so deeply entrenched in everyone's speech habits that their special function can easily escape notice, and a special approach, therefore, is needed to identify them.

Our approach in this chapter will be that emphasis and exaggeration are spoken elements which belong primarily to the speaker's performance in the course of a conversation, and which would be omitted in a paraphrase or in recasting into reported speech; e.g., if someone says, '*Geez*, it's *real* cold out,' someone else would paraphrase this as, 'He/she says it is (very) cold out.' An extensive discussion of elements, like *Geez* and *real*, which are characteristic of direct speech as contrasted with indirect speech, can be found in Banfield (1982), where the author analyses many aspects characteristic of direct speech only, such as special word order, repetitions, hesitations, and exclamations.

Of these elements it can be said that, instead of conveying factual information, they convey the speaker's attitude, emotional state, and degree of involvement in what is being said. As we shall see, they also play an important part in establishing the speaker's authority as a reliable source of information.

Syntactic Rearrangement

One important way of conveying emphasis is achieved through altering the sentence structure or creating a special word order, which would be recast in indirect speech. Coleridge's famous line: 'With my cross-bow/I shot the Albatross,' is likely to be rephrased as, 'He shot the Albatross with his cross-bow.' Here, words are not omitted, but the order of elements in the sentences is recast, with a resulting loss of emphasis. Therefore, syntactic rearrangement or inversion of sentence elements in conversation will be regarded as a means of emphasis.

Since instances of syntactic emphasis may come in the same utterance with forms of exaggeration such as high numbers or expressions of intensity, they cannot always be treated separately, as will be seen in some of the following examples, taken from interviews printed in *Cape Breton's Magazine* — the source of all the remaining examples in this chapter.

In creating emphasis by the arrangement of syntactic elements, the speaker achieves the prominence of one component, as in the following:

> And my uncle, he had nothing …

which puts the subject, *my uncle*, into prominence. In the following sequence, a speaker wishes to emphasize the point that his mother played a greater part than his father did in getting him to do responsible work when he was still a young boy:

> Don't forget, our mother had a lot to do with this. *It was her* that got us to do the work.
> … And *it was really her* that got us to do the work.
> … And *it was her* that *really* trained us…. But *it was really her* that got us to do the work.
> … And *it was her* that would get us up in the morning.

In these examples, the emphasis is achieved by a device also common in General English: placing the subject in a main clause, with the significant verb in a subordinate clause. In addition, *really* is also used to stress the significance of the verb, and finally the entire effect is strengthened even more by having the pattern repeated several times in a short, connected sequence in a conversation. The use of the 'objective' pronoun form *her* as emphatic subject is also consistent with the emphatic paradigm: *it is me/you/him/her/us/them*.

An adverb is often put in the initial position for emphasis; e.g., '*Very seldom* would I kill a calf.' The adverb *seldom* is further intensified by *very*, and *would I kill* also shows emphatic order, with the subject pronoun *I* placed between the auxiliary *would* and the main verb *kill*. In the following example:

> I had gone on the ice, and *down* she went …

the position of *down* before, rather than after, the verb creates the emphasis.

Thus it can be seen that stylistic features employed to create emphasis are used not in isolation, but in combination with a variety of such features. Examples of these will be considered further on.

Rhetorical Openings and Closings

If by *rhetorical* openings we mean those discourse markers which serve to signal the fact that the speaker is beginning, resuming, or changing a point of view, or answering a question, then for the most part in Cape Breton English we see signals which are shared with General English, such as *but*, *and*, *of course*, *see*, *as a matter of fact*, *so*, *anyway*, and *so anyway*, and the like, while *yes indeed* is perhaps used more frequently than in General English. In medial positions and in closings we also note common expressions like *you know*, *my God*, *geez* (*jeez*), *oh geez*, and others more specific to the region, such as *holy God almighty*, or *holy jumping God*:

> *Yes indeed* I was in the dory when they [the swordfish] came through.
> *You see* if you died there you had to wait until summertime to be buried.
> *Well, look*, I had that card in my clothes box for I don't know how many years.
> *Well, I'll bet* it's been 45 years since I didn't make that.
> *And* I remember the night he died.

Among examples of closings we note the following:

> Violin places are using it yet *anyways*.
> … Somebody would stick some — there would be fish there *all right*.

And other clinchers can occur:

> *You know*, I think I'm the happiest woman on earth.

These openings and closings serve as links between parts of the discourse, and help to establish the speakers' control of the narrative, as well as their awareness of the control and the attending responsibility. *You see*, in the example above, introduces an explanation to the hearer, not a part of the story as such.

Positive Assertions

But control and responsibility also take other forms. Speakers can testify to their own honesty, accuracy, and frankness, and similar aspects of involvement with the statements they make. Such testifying can take very strong forms, and can easily exceed the measure of whatever the situation vouchsafes objectively, if objective measurement could be applied. The testifying can also take the form of a caution, indicating that the speakers' intent is to be as accurate as possible, but that they fear that their memory or their powers of observation are not fully reliable.

One of the most detailed modern reference Grammars, *A Comprehensive Grammar of the English Language* (Quirk et al., 1985), uses the term *disjunct* to describe expressions of this sort, listing mainly adverbs such as *frankly*, *honestly*, and *simply*. Our Cape Breton texts, on the other hand, show the use of parenthetic clauses and phrases having a function similar to such adverbs rather than the adverbs themselves. Stubbs (1983) speaks of such adverbs as making 'metareferences to the discourse itself' (p.70), and it appears that the clauses and phrases used in this way perform a similar function.

In the following example:

> Snowing? You couldn't see your hand before you. *I'm telling …*

I'm telling carries some of the force of stressing the severity of the snow storm. It can be used only in accounts of first-person observation, creating a link between the fact observed and the person of the speaker.

A link also can be created between the fact observed, the speaker, and the listener:

> Well, people ask, how'd you live? *I'll tell you how we lived.* A hell of a lot better than people live today.

These assertions of the speaker's reliability also heighten the significance of the speech act as an important event in itself, as if the event of the past was receiving a renewed significance through being spoken about:

> *I am safe in saying* I worked there for three years for Robin Jones ... 5 cents an hour.

In addition to clauses, the speaker's assertions can appear as phrases:

> *Not blowing or bragging about it*, I was reared ... the toughest kind of way.
> ... [*B*]*ut as far as my part*, there' not a quarter of the company.

A special way of involving the hearer in the assertion of the speaker's reliability is the use of impersonal *you*. Sufficiently ambiguous as to whether it refers to the speaker or to the hearer, it suggests a reference to both:

> ... [W]e saw that boat coming around Middle Head, *and you'd swear* she was one of those great big slabs of drift ice....

The difference between disjuncts testifying to the speaker's reliability and seemingly objective claims of the truth of a statement may sometimes not be easy to distinguish, as seen in the following:

> That's what's causing cancer today. Because we're not getting the right kind of food — *and that's the whole truth of it.*

Here the form is that of an objective claim, but the claim is in reality a personal opinion. Presenting personal opinions as general truth, or endorsing a general claim by personal testimony are both frequent in personal narratives, further suggesting the extent to which speakers perceive their responsibility, not only in personal, but also in general matters.

Certain assertions may have the force of a denial, as in:

> *Really truly*, I wasn't frightened, but I thought we were going to be drowned.

Here the positive assertion *really truly* is used to confirm the truth of a statement, which is in itself a denial. Negative statements beginning with *Never* and other negations are treated next.

Emphatic Denials

Negative statements are no less subject to emphasis and exaggeration than are assertions. For the speakers, it is as important to establish their trustworthiness in matters of denial as it is in matters of assertion. It is, however, a little more difficult, as the resources are rather limited. Multiple negatives, for instance, are considered nonstandard in Edited English and their use is discouraged. Chaucer's words about the noble Knight, 'He never yet no vileinye ne sayde … to no maner wight,' are fondly recited by scholars, but the construction is infrequent in everyday speech. Still, it is sometimes reflected in Cape Breton speech, as in 'John Simon was from Cape North. Wasn't scared of nothing.' However, most often denials in Cape Breton speech depend on repetitions of certain elements. Below are some examples:

> You *never* were cold, *never*.
> *Never* in my life, *never*.
> You *never* were cold that way, *no way in the world*.… I *never* stopped fishing, *no sir*.
> (Must have been cold.) Yeah, but you'd *never* mind out there. Would*n't* mind *at all*.

The element of exaggeration in the above examples can be appreciated in the context, for in fact the narrative stresses that the weather was very cold, but that it was endured without complaint, and the denial *Never in my life, never* is simply a prelude to a dramatic account of the single occurrence of the incident in question. The speaker was caught on a fishing hook once, and remembers the painful incident vividly.

No way, and the even more emphatic *no way in the world* are used when the denial is one of manner (rather than the denial of an event in actual time):

> And then you couldn't see 50 feet — *no way in the world*.
> You had your winter clothes on you — and once you put your oilclothes on, brother, there is *no way* water can go through them.

The strength of these negations is the more striking, as they are not brought out by any personal provocation, but serve to bolster the speaker's position of trust and authority.

Emphatic Interjections

When we look at emphatic interjections, we see that the words *boy* and *brother* are often used in this function. *My boy* and *my son* also occur, as do *my dear*, *my dear man*, and *my God almighty*. Of these, *my dear* is not gender-specific, and while *boy*, *brother*, and *son* are masculine, their use is not limited to speech directed to male persons. General English also employs these words, but in Cape Breton speech they occur more often. Their function is also different from general use, where *brother* is sometimes used as an exclamation of annoyance, perhaps a polite version of *bother*.

Boy and *brother* are rarely used at the opening of a conversation segment. Rather, they tend to come medially, or as the final element, after some tension has been built up, and the expression helps to achieve the climax:

> The least thing will take them up, but when they come up, *boy*, watch out.
> And, *boy*, the hook got me there.
> (How did you avoid the hooks while hauling?) You got used to it just like everything else, *boy*.
> And that Huey MacKenzie we were talking about, that Huey MacKenzie who had the Gaelic and everything, had a book, *boy*, stories — this knock came one night and the door opened and this hand came on the wall and Huey was sitting somewhere and he had a pillow and he just aimed on the hand — and the hand, *boy*, threw the pillow back in his face. That was going on, *boy*, and she was to priest and she was everywhere — no use.

Brother is similar in use to *boy*; in the example below it seems to intensify the negative *no way*:

> You had your winter clothes on you — and once you put your oilclothes on, *brother*, there is *no way* water can go through them.

My boy, *my son*, and *my dear* act as somewhat weaker emphatic elements than *boy*:

> You'd never stop, *my boy*, — 10 hours.
> Then the last going off, well, there's fish, *my son*, it takes two with a gaff to get in the dory.

Son alone does not function as an interjection.

Dear man occurs along with *man dear*, and *dear*:

> Oh, *dear man*, that roller's as good as two men.
> You had a wonderful sou'wester buttoned underneath your chin, and *man dear*! (You didn't haul barehanded?) You couldn't, *dear*.

Dear man, *man dear*, and even *my dear* resemble, but are not identical with, the use in General English, where *my dear* is more likely to be used to a woman listener as a form of rhetorical address than to a man. In Cape Breton speech it is an emphatic element, which serves to highlight the constituents nearest to it:

> I've seen us out there, *my dear*, in the *Beatrice*, after my father sold the Whitty boat.
> We fished till the drift stopped us — all the young people. But, *my dear*, there's an awful difference.

My God almighty provides a strong element:

> An awful lot of work to them, but they were great boats, *my God almighty*.

Jeez is perhaps a little weaker:

> [The hay] was all stowed and, *jeez*, one man in the hold — it was hard going.

Syntactically, these expressions come not only between such separate elements as clauses and phrases, but also in the middle of a syntactic construction; e.g., between subject and verb, as in, 'and the hand, *boy*, threw the pillow back in his face.'

Intensifiers

In drawing a distinction between emphasizers and intensifiers, Quirk et al. (1985) reserve the term *intensifier* for those elements which add force to gradable constituents. Thus *very* in *very good* is seen as an intensifier.

In our examples, we see certain intensifiers with adjectives of size and quality, including adjectives which are themselves a part of an adverbial phrase. We also see that adjectives can be intensified by repetition of the adjective itself, or by the use of a synonym. The following example shows repetition of *big*:

> [They] even went onto the Grand Banks swordfishing. They took *big, big* fish.

Below are several examples of *big* being intensified by *great*:

> We knew they [the fish] were going to leave, because of the *great big* fish we got.
> … And you'd swear she [the boat] was one of those *great big* slabs of drift ice….
> *Great big* pair of rubber boots on us and our oilclothes — walked over 8 miles.
> But hauling gear, you had to haul with a *great big* pair of woollen mitts on.

The following example shows the use of *great big*, as well as *big* standing alone, in the same sentence:

> And there was a *great big* square-rigger going into Englishtown. And there was a *big* sea on, a *big* roll, you know.

As in general use, *big* can be intensified by *very*:

> And there's *very big* sores on the side of them — and that's the sign of the last school of fish.

The last example shows *very* as intensifier, before a constituent which differs somewhat from the ones mentioned earlier. The constituents which were modified with *big big*, or *great big* can usually be seen to be concrete and, in a sense, stable in size, like a fish, a square-rigger, a pair of rubber boots, and even a slab of ice, whereas a *big sea*, and *big sores* are not stable in size. *Tremendous* sea and *quite a* sea show other expressions used to underscore the size and force of a gale. An abstract term, like *difference*, is modified with *great* only:

> … *great* difference [= awful difference].

Although there is also a distinction between *big* and *great* in General English, with *big* being favoured as a qualifier of concrete nouns and *great* of abstract (e.g., *big house*, *great improvement*), the distinction is not strict, and *big difference* is possible. What we see here in our texts is the absence of *great big* as modifier for an abstract noun.

The form of a superlative adjective can have the function of an intensifier, as follows:

> … the *healthiest* life *on earth* …

where *on earth* forms a part of the intensifier;

> … the *toughest* kind of a way …
> … in the *hardest* kind of a way …

where the entire expression functions adverbially; and

> The *very best* stuff …

where *very* functions as intensifier to *best*, in itself an expression of highest quality.

As much as a superlative can be established by being the best/worst or greatest anywhere, so it can be established as the best/worst or greatest ever, at least in the speaker's experience:

> That was about the *worst* experience that ever I had on the water.

In Cape Breton, as in General English, the comparative sometimes requires a strong reinforcement, as in:

> ... *a hell of a lot* better than....

Of course, the expression *about ... worst* is not a pure intensifier, as it is also modified by an approximator, *about*. Such seeming inconsistency will be considered next.

Much as we tend to think of intensifiers as words which help to suggest that something was unusually large, strong, or powerful, we know that some words serve to express hesitation or uncertainty on this very point. In their discussion of intensifiers, Quirk et al. (1985) also discuss a subclass of *downtoners*. While downtoners may seem too far removed from intensifiers to be included in this part of the discussion, it is possible to see them as points on a continuum. All the same, how can an approximator or even diminisher (e.g., *partly*) function in conveying emphasis? The answer lies again in the connection between emphasis and the need of the speakers to establish themselves as reliable narrators. Thus hesitations, concessions, expressions of approximation, and even inexactitude give an aura of a genuine effort to be as accurate as possible. Some forms of approximation also involve the hearer — when the hearer is called upon, as it were, to participate in evaluating the degree of accuracy. The parenthetic *like*, *kind of*, and *about* occur in Cape Breton as they do also in General English. Both *kind of* and *like* can occur in one sequence:

> And on the roll of the sea, *like*, if you are rowing you've got to *kind of* back water — don't let your dory go ahead too fast.
> ... [M]y father would haul *like* three or four lines to give the other fellow a chance to warm up, *you know*.

Here *like* expresses the approximation, and *you know* involves the hearer, as does also the following statement of concession:

> [S]ometimes when it was cold — *what you call* cold....

An approximator may also be used with a very strong intensifier:

> That was *about* the *worst* experience that ever I had on the water ...

or with an estimator of measure:

> *About* three foot six or something like that.

When *about* is used with *worst*, the expression of approximation strengthens the intensifier contained in the superlative by showing that speakers are aware of their own hesitation, but go on to express the superlative in spite of it. *As high as* is used when numbers are approximate, but at the same time the expression conveys the notion that the number is relatively high, thus:

> In the evening we'd have *as high as* 16 to supper.
> And there'd be *as high as* 70 men working there.

Giving the exact time, size, or location pertaining to an event is also a part of stressing the function of the speaker. This often comes in the form of *right* before a prepositional phrase, as in:

> Yes, indeed, I was in the dory when they [the swordfish] came through the dory *right* to their eyes ...

or:

> And the boats came down from everywhere. *Right* from Digby, *right around* down Nova Scotia and all down the shore ...
> It will rot *right* in no time....

Expressions like *went right down*, *went right back*, and *went right through* are very common.

There is also another use of *right* as an intensifier of adjectives — as in *right good* or *right hot*, both widely used in Nova Scotia — which is similar in function to *very* in General English, yet differs from it in several ways: *very* can be repeated for added emphasis, as in *very very good*, but *right* is not repeated in this manner.

Right as an intensifier of adjectives differs also from *quite*, in that *right* with adjectives refers more often to actions, processes, and events rather than static conditions, where *quite* is more common.

Exaggerations

Exaggerating numbers and amounts is a common feature of everyday conversation. 'Thousands of ants,' and 'millions of mosquitoes' will liberally embellish an account of a less than perfect picnic. And yet even this feature of conversation, so common that it can usually pass unnoticed, has an important function. It is much more likely to occur in first-person narratives than in secondhand narratives (e.g., 'We didn't stay long, because of those millions of mosquitoes' versus 'They didn't stay long, because the mosquitoes bothered them'). In other words, the amounts and quantities have a share in establishing the narrator's fortitude or endurance, or some other outstanding quality. They also, by the same token, establish the narrator's trustworthiness, for participants in events acquire a special right to exaggerate.

In Cape Breton, quantities can be overstated:

> (Did you ever have it happen? [i.e., the painful experience of getting

> squid 'ink' in the eyes.]) Yes, *thousands* of times.
> Used to go to the Bird Islands. Used to go up these to get bait, to bait our trawl gear. We'd stay there in the night. (What kind of bait?) Squid. *Thousands and thousands* of them.
> You had your vegetables, everything. Lots of meat, *piles* of meat, *piles* of potatoes, turnips — all kinds of stuff to eat.

Here *piles* means, evidently, 'large quantities,' while in General English it is normally used literally for items that can be stacked or piled or, metaphorically, for money. *Scads* is used similarly to *piles*.

When we look at the various ways in which speakers introduce emphasis into their discourse, or intensify certain elements in a given region or speech community, we see a mirror of what obtains in General English. The desire to establish one's position as a trustworthy and reliable reporter of events, and perhaps the pleasure of occupying such a position, is universal. The choice of words and expressions used to this effect may, on the other hand, be different in different regions. The speakers of Cape Breton English have, in addition to the shared resources of linguistic emphasis, a number of expressions which are regional. This chapter has looked at a sampling of such expressions, confirming, perhaps, what speakers and hearers of Cape Breton speech have observed before.

References

Banfield, A. (1982). *Unspeakable sentences: Narration and representation in the language of fiction*. Boston: Routledge and Kegan Paul.

Caplan, R. (Ed.). (1984a). *Cape Breton's magazine, 35*.

———. (1984b). *Cape Breton's magazine, 36*.

———. (1973). *Down north: A collector's edition of Cape Breton's magazine*. Toronto: Doubleday.

O'Grady, W., & Dobrovolsky, M. (Eds.). (1996). *Contemporary linguistic analysis: An introduction*. 3rd ed. Mississauga, ON: Copp Clark.

Quirk, R., Greenbaum, S., Leech, G., & Svartvik, J. (1985). *A comprehensive grammar of the English language*. London: Longman.

Schiffrin, D. (1987). *Discourse markers*. Studies in interactional sociolinguistics, 5. Cambridge: Cambridge University Press.

Stubbs, M. (1983). *Discourse analysis: The sociolinguistic analysis of natural language*. Oxford: Blackwell.

Chapter Five

The Use of Nicknames in Cape Breton

William Davey & Richard MacKinnon

Editors' Introduction

Our personal and family names are an essential part of our identity, establishing our uniqueness on the one hand and our link to a larger group, such as family, clan, Band, ethnic or religious group, and even nationality on the other. Names also link us to the past and the future, making it possible to seek our connection to previous generations, and to leave behind us a record of our lives for the generations to come.

Given the importance of names, it is not surprising that nicknames receive less attention from scholars and students of language than do names. But nicknames, though more elusive and seemingly less significant, are a fascinating part of how we refer to ourselves and others, and in Cape Breton we find an especially well established custom of nickname use. In Cape Breton whole families are known by a joint nickname, a tradition that spans generations, having been possibly brought to the island from an old custom of the Highland Scots. While nicknames often derive from an event or trait associated with a person's past, they do not merely 'add' descriptive details. They become an important part of referring to individuals, and serve to distinguish between individuals and between families who bear identical names and surnames, as the *Goats* and the *Bears*, where both families have the same last name of MacDonald, and many members of the family share the same first name.

Nicknames, then, not only divide, but unify: they help to distinguish members of different groups, but at the same time, confirm that each of these groups (e.g., the *Bears*) is really a branch of a larger group (i.e., the MacDonalds). Nicknames also tie generations together, and can give individuals a strong sense of belonging.

In the present study, based on extensive surveys. William Davey and Richard MacKinnon offer a detailed discussion and analysis of Cape Breton nicknames.

Starting with the distinction between internal methods of creating nicknames (where the name is based on some features of the language, such as alliteration or rhyming), and external methods (where external circumstances give rise to a nickname), the authors proceed to discuss examples of nickname creation in both methods: phonetic features, alliteration, contraction and substitution, phonetic derivatives, and semantic association in the first method, and a variety of external events and circumstances, such as physical or personality traits, habitual actions or expressions, important events, occupations, geographic association, and even humour in the second. The authors then evaluate the significance of the nicknames as an aspect of the way society functions, quite apart from the need to identify individuals who bear identical names.

The following chapter gives insights into the practice prevalent in Cape Breton; it will also evoke readers' memories of nicknames they may have encountered in their own experience, funny or embarrassing as these may have been. *(LF & MH)*

***

The Use of Nicknames in Cape Breton

by William Davey & Richard MacKinnon

Nicknames are a pervasive feature of English and probably of language in general. The *MLA Bibliography* (1981-1995) contains articles discussing nicknames in over thirty languages including Russian, Portuguese, Greek, German, French, Gaelic, Spanish, Dutch, Czech, Serbo-Croatian, Scottish Gaelic, Italian, Peruvian, Hindu, Mandarin, and Old Norse. The practice of nicknaming spans continents and the ages. In England, political leaders have always been given nicknames, at times complimentary, like Alfred *the Great*, and at times derisive, like those given to some of the Viking rulers who led invading armies into England; Ivar *the Boneless*, Eric *Bloodaxe*, and Harold *Bluetooth*. Even monarchs who have long been dead have new names attached to their memory: combining history and modern technology, a London woman recently described Henry VIII as the *Wife Dispatcher*. The British press continues to delight in using nicknames for political leaders. When Prime Minister Thatcher first came to power, she was called the *Grocer's Daughter* (because she succeeded Edward Heath, who had business interests in the food industry); one of her later names is the *Iron Lady*. The list might go on to include two other groups that are notorious for generating nicknames — professional athletes and teachers — but this chapter considers nicknames of ordinary people in Cape Breton from three perspectives: the naming practices, classification of the nicknames, and the social importance of these names.

Before considering the names themselves, however, two qualifications and a definition are needed. Firstly, while some of the names are unique to the area (such as *Biscuit Foot* McKinnon), other names, like the *Red* MacDonalds and Joe *Priest*, are as easily found in Cape Breton as they are in any place where red-headed MacDonalds live, or where a priest has a caretaker named Joe. Secondly, because of the oral nature of nicknames, one cannot claim that nicknames are more numerous in Cape Breton than in other areas or cultures. At the same time, however, evidence indicates that the practice of nicknaming is a lively and important oral tradition in Cape Breton that reflects the cultural values and local history of the various communities.

In order to better understand the term *nickname*, it might be useful to consider the origin of the word and its etymology. As Jan Jönsjö notes in his study of Middle English nicknames: 'Etymologically OE *ekenama* (OE *ecan* + OE *nama*) is synonymous with ME *surname* (OF *sur* + OE *nama*) and both terms mean "additional name," i.e. a name added to the name (the Christian name) that a person was already known by' (1979, p.11). Historically, then, the *surname* was an additional name, but through the centuries it has lost the sense of being something added to the person's name. It is now an oddity for a person to use only one name, an aspect that some entertainers like Cher have exploited. In a similar way, many nicknames in Cape Breton are perceived as the person's actual name rather than an additional name. As one male informant explained, his wife once tried to call him at work, but failed to reach him until she used his nickname rather than his given name. David Crystal gives a working definition of the term:

> The word *nickname* is first recorded in the 15th century; 'an eke-name'(Old English *eke*, 'also') was an extra or additional name used to express such attitudes as familiarity, affection, and ridicule. Nicknames are usually applied to people, but places and things can have them too. (1995, p.152)

This broad definition accounts for additional nicknames, like Allan *Big Hughie*, but substitution is also used for some nicknames, such as the *Cow Hooks* for the surname of a family in Glace Bay. Nicknames are also applied to places and things, but these will not be considered in this chapter (cf. Davey, 1990).

There are several conventions or naming practices followed in the formation of Cape Breton nicknames. An obvious but nonetheless important feature is that nicknames survive in an oral tradition. Occasionally, nicknames appear in print, but more usually they are kept alive by word of mouth in the local community. There are at least two consequences of this oral circulation. First, these nicknames are subject to the strengths and weaknesses of the human memory. As occupations change and generations die, names are lost, and it becomes impossible to answer statistical questions about the prevalence of nicknames one hundred years ago, or to define the exact origin or meaning of certain names. An associated characteristic of oral circulation is that several versions of even a current nickname may exist. For instance, a family from Glace Bay is known there as the *Big Pay* MacDonalds, but are remembered as the *Pay Cheque* MacDonalds by an informant from Sydney. A further consequence of their oral nature is that the survival of certain nicknames depends on phonetic qualities, but more detailed consideration of this factor is found in the following classification.

A second naming practice is that many are traditional and familial. Although some nicknames are, of course, short lived, other nicknames may last a lifetime, or may be passed to the second, and occasionally to the third generation. As several informants commented, these names have a habit of 'sticking' to the person being named. One woman was born during a storm and has been called *Stormy* ever since. In Ingonish, Allan, the son of *Big* Hughie, is called Allan *Big Hughie*; both father and son were known and respected for their strength. Such compound names are common all over Cape Breton Island: John Joe *Red Angus*, Allan *Paulie*, Willie *Duncan* and his brother Jimmy *Duncan*. A family of MacDonalds is known as the *Piper* MacDonalds because a grandfather was known for playing the bagpipes.

As well as being traditional and familial, nicknames are mainly patrilineal (Dunn, 1953; Frank, 1988). For example, three generations ago the community of Black Point called Angus MacKinnon *Big* Angus; his son Derrick later became Derrick *Big Angus*; in the third generation Derrick's two sons are known as Philip *Big Angus* and Johnny *Big Angus*, taking their grandfather's name rather than their father's. Similarly, when a woman marries, she is often known by a compound name consisting of her own Christian name and her husband's Christian name or his nickname, thereby creating an oxymoron such as Aggie *Tom* to identify the Agnes who married Tom. Jessie *Big John* is the wife of *Big* John, and their daughter is called Katie *Big John*. In the same way, Maggie *the Sailor* does not sail, but is the daughter of Alex *the Sailor*. About 32% of the women's names collected in this study follow this pattern. While the nicknames are usually patrilineal, occasionally the woman's name is attached to her son's Christian name. The son of Lizzy MacKinnon is called Simon *Lizzy*, and Tommy *Peggy* MacDonald refers to Thomas, the son of Peggy MacDonald. Alec *the Plug* is the son of a short woman called Peggy *Plug*, and Angus *the Widow* has a mother who is known as the *Widow*. However, only about 1.5% of the names follow this pattern. In general, the first name of the compound identifies the individual, and the second reveals the family relationship — similar to the way that last names are, or used to be, passed from one generation to the next.

Because of the traditional nature of these names, the nickname often outlives or fails to describe the social reality that generated it. In Dominion, a family is widely known as the *Bore Hole* Macdonalds because two generations ago, the grandfather bored holes in the coal mines. The name persists although none of the present generation bores holes. Similarly, because Joe Doucette has a lame leg, he is called Joey *Peg*, and his family — all of whom have healthy legs — have inherited the nickname *Peg*: for instance, his wife is Mary *Peg*. As Alexander Laidlaw, a native of Port Hood, points out, the names can be misleading; *Young* Donald is always called *Young*, even if he dies at 95, 'Or maybe *Little* Sandy goes through life with a name which does not very well describe his giant stature at six foot two' (Creighton, 1962, p.72).

Although most people receive one nickname that remains with them for life and that may survive into succeeding generations, a small group have multiple nicknames. Morgan, O'Neill, and Harré (1979, p.42) found multiple nicknames among schoolchildren in England, and Apte (1985, p.54) states that occupational nicknames often differ from those known in the community. For example, a big man from Sydney Mines is known to his friends as *Moose* because of his size, but for a short while he was called *Jesus* because he had a beard and long hair, and he is also known by his family name, the *Dukes*.

With these naming practices in mind, it is now possible to classify nicknames according to the factor or factors that generated them. In their study of school-age children in England, Morgan, O'Neill, and Harré conclude:

> A fundamental distinction in all naming systems is between internal methods of formation where a name is generated by some feature of

> the language, such as alliteration or rhyming, and external methods of formation where matters of history, appearance, family relationships, local culture, and so on are involved in the genesis of the name. (1979, p.37)

The fundamental distinction between names generated by internal methods, or some phonetic feature, and those generated by external methods, or social factors, provides a useful starting point for analysis. Within these two general classes of nicknames, Morgan et al. (1979, pp.35- 45) discuss several features that are also found in nicknames common in Cape Breton.

Since nicknames exist primarily in an oral tradition, one would expect to find that phonetic elements foster the survival of many of these names. The most frequent phonetic feature of Cape Breton nicknames is the suffix tense [i] or slack [ɪ]. Instead of Big *Dan* or *Tom* Cod, the two names are Big *Danny* and *Tommy* Cod (the smallest kind of cod). This suffix is found on many Christian names. Examples abound: *Johnny* Mink, *Mickey* Hay Cove, *Tommy Peggy*, Big *Hughie*, Big *Johnny*, and *Charlie* Beaver. Similarly, the substituted names frequently end with this suffix: *Birdy*, *Scratchy*, *Sharky*, *Sporty* Peter, and *Mossy* Face. Approximately 31% of the names collected in this research have this suffix. Although Morgan et al. (1979, p.41) found suffixes like *-bo*, *-kin*, and *-bug* popular among school-age children, this study found only one such suffix, for a man called Johnni*kin*, who apparently received the name as a child, since as an adult he is known for his toughness.

Alliteration is another common feature of these names. Examples are the *Court Crier* (who habitually visited the lawcourt), *Bully* Brown, *Beer Bottle* (who was short), and Billy *the Brat*. Other nicknames combine alliteration with some physical characteristic, such as *Freckly* Flora, *Red* Randy, *Spotty* Steward (who had a growth or spot on his eye), and *Monkey* Malcolm (who reminded people of a monkey). Other names combine phonetic derivatives and alliteration. For instance, Ronald *the Rooster* at first suggests some physical affinity to the bird family, but, in fact, the name is a phonetic derivative from Gabarus, the man's place of origin. According to one informant, Gabarus is referred to as the *Roost*, and people from that area as *Roosters*.

Other nicknames are generated from contractions of or substitutions for longer names. Accordingly, names like MacDonald and Buchanan become the clipped forms *Mack* and *Buck*. In the Italian community in industrial Cape Breton, a man named Calisthanius is called *Cal*, and Cassamiro is reduced to *Miro*. In the previous generation, many long European names were replaced by substituted nicknames: a Mr. Calavisortis was called Nick *the Greek*, and a man named Szerwonka was called *Bubble Gum*, partly because he chewed bubble gum instead of tobacco in the coal pit, but partly because his name may have been hard to pronounce by speakers of English.

Phonetic derivatives are responsible for some nicknames as well. One man is known as *E-Boy* because as he heaved and pulled in his nets, he would say, 'Heave, Boy.' Because a man named Dougall habitually stutters his name as 'Dou- Dou- Dougall,' he is known as *Dougall* Dougall. Other nicknames resulting from phonetic derivatives are generated by mispronunciations of words. *Mossy* Angus received his name because he habitually mispronounces 'Mercy me' as 'Mossy, mossy me.' Jim *the Jampion* pronounces *champion* with the initial sound of *jump*, and his pronunciation is recalled in his name. Other nicknames originate from childhood mispronunciations. For instance, one man, widely known as *Bucko* or *Buck*, received this name because as a child he mispronounced the name of his father's fishing boat, the *Buckaroo*. Similarly, a family from the northeast are known as the *Bootchers* because the father mispronounced the word *butcher* as a child. The nickname was reinforced because the child looked like a butcher who visited the community. As an adult he is called *Bootcher*, and his wife is Mary *Bootcher*. Other phonetic derivatives depend upon rhyme and partial rhyme. For instance, Carl *Snarl* and Jake *the Snake* rhyme, but these names belong to boys aged seven and twelve, in contrast to the other names in this study, which belong to adults. Far more usual for adults is partial rhyme: *Cute* Hughie, *Pan* Dandy, Sam *the Wake Man* (who used to go from one wake to another) *Hucky* Tuck Finn (who smoked a pipe like Huck Finn), and *Hobby Gobby* (who was associated with hobgoblins because he worked as a watchman on Hallowe'en night).

A small but interesting group of names are formed by semantic association. As Morgan et al. (1979, p.41) point out, a name like *Gardener* is altered to *Weed* by the association between gardens and weeds. During the 1930s, the president of the Orange Lodge was called — not surprisingly — *Orange* Dan, but by association the treasurer became known as *Yellow* Jack (McCawley, 1936, p.4). The nickname of a brother, or of one's friends is often the source for semantic association. The brother of John *the Bear* became Allan *the Buffalo* as one big animal apparently suggested the other. The brother of Joey *One Time* became Tony *Half Time* because of a semantic slip made by a friend's mother. Again, semantic association seems to be responsible for the nickname of a man called *Birdie* in Glace Bay: he lived beside a man with the surname of *Sparrow*. Similarly, a group of boys who grew up together in Sydney Mines all have names associated with the animal kingdom: *Duck*, *Goat*, *Toad*, and *Moose*. Within this group, some names combine both phonetic and semantic changes. A man from Sydney Mines reflects this pattern. Originally called *Moose* because of his size, his name was shortened to *Moo*, which by semantic association became *Moo Cow*. Following the same principle, Ray MacDonald was given the name *Doug* (for reasons unknown to the informant); then *Doug* became *Rug* as a phonetic derivative, and finally the name became the alliterating Ray *Rug*.

Finally, when nicknames are considered in a family grouping, the result is often more lyrical, and the phonetic similarity is more evident than when the names are considered individually. In a sense, when considered together, some of these names have the quality of oral formulaic. For example, there is little to suggest phonetic similarity in the nickname Joey *Peg*, when it stands by itself, but there is when he and his family members are described as Joey *Peg*, Mary *Peg*, Eddy *Peg*, Teddy *Peg*, and Granny *Peg*. Using formal names, we might say that Marcella MacLellan is married to Archie MacKinnon. Locally, it would be stated more lyrically as *Micey* is married to Archie *Gookin*. Phonetic similarity is also seen in the nicknames of children in a Glace Bay family: *Googie* and *Boogie*, a sister named *Booboo*, and a cousin called *Butchy*. In part, at least, phonetic similarity and near rhyme seem to generate these names.

Although we might expect phonetic or internal features to play a more prominent role in these nicknames, especially given their oral transmission, a partial explanation is suggested by Morgan, O'Neill, and Harré's study (1979, pp.40-41) of students in junior and senior high school. Citing a study by Peevers and Secord (1974) and their own research, they conclude that as students grow older, they depend more on physical or social aspects to provide nicknames, rather than the free wordplay that is characteristic of younger children. This tendency to rely more on sense than on sound is also true of nicknames in Cape Breton, as roughly 70% of the nicknames collected in this study depend on external or social features. They are generated by various factors: physical characteristics, habitual actions and expressions, events of local importance, character traits, occupations, and references to places. Closely related to these are the descriptive nicknames or aptonyms that are given as a result of humour and popular culture. At times, more than one cause may generate one nickname, and consequently some nicknames could be placed in more than one class. For example, the nickname *Livers* originated because of an event and habitual behaviour: this man was once caught stealing cod livers, but the name was reinforced because he was an habitual thief.

Within this broad class of nicknames, the largest group is that which refers to physical qualities of a person. Since physical size and strength are valued in rural and industrial Cape Breton, adjectives like *big*, *little*, and *long* appear frequently in nicknames. In addition to these common names for size, *Hunk* and *Ox* indicate large people, in contrast to those called *Stump*, *Bump*, *Splinter*, and *Pancake*. Adjectives referring to size also distinguish two or more people with similar names. A generation ago, *Big* and *Little* identified the two Carlos who worked at the same coal mine in Dominion. Where a surname such as MacDonald is common, nicknames like the *Red* MacDonalds distinguish that family from the *Blue* MacDonalds and from the *Ditty* MacDonalds. In a small town, three men in their thirties have the name Kenny, and two of them have the same last name; the three are known as Kenny *Turk* (because of his dark complexion), Kenny *Mugs* (because of his ears), and Kenny *Auger* (because of his neck). A fourth Kenny, who lives just outside of the town, is *Lame* Kenny *from the Creek*. The two Lisas in the area are *Black* Lisa and *White* Lisa, because one is brunette and the other is blonde. Thus, physical appearance is an important means of generating nicknames, but even slight differences may be used in nicknames to distinguish people with identical or like names.

Others receive their nicknames because of habitual actions. A miner from Dominion who habitually carried sugar cookies in his lunch is called *Sugar Cookie* Smith. Dan *the Dancer* was known for his habit of dancing for money during the Depression. And a man who repeatedly sat on a pickle barrel in the Company Store was dubbed *Pickle Arse* MacLean, and his family members are known as the *Pickle Arse* MacLeans. *Spider* and Sammy *the Flea* are nicknames of two men known to move quickly on the ice floes, and *Dynamite* Dan earned his name by breaking dynamite boxes with his bare hands as a sign of his strength. Occasionally, the nicknames given in childhood because of habitual actions last longer than the habit itself. A man from New Aberdeen is still called *Scratchy*, even though he has outgrown his childhood scratching. A young boy who used to hide in a wood box is still called Billy *Wood Box* now that he is an adult, and Charlie *Beaver* bears his name because, as a child, he liked to chew sticks. *Little Hell*, a man with teenage children, received his name when misbehaving as a child.

In addition to repeated actions, habitual expressions can also be a source for nicknames. Oft-repeated expressions and expletives, and even the manner in which a person speaks may be commemorated in a nickname. A couple who owned a store in Sydney habitually responded to comments with 'Is it?' They became Mr. *Is It* and Mrs. *Is It*. In like manner, two other men are known as Johnny *What Is It* and Joe *Me Fix*. A pair of identical twins, Malcolm and Norman, received their name because of their mother's habitual greeting to the boys when they were small. Apparently, the mother found it difficult to distinguish one from the other, and so she would greet the unidentifiable boy with 'Malcolm, is that you, Norman?' As the boys grew older, the expression stuck to them, and they are now called *Malcolm Is That You Norman* as adults. Others receive their names from characteristic expletives. One man who habitually said, 'Jingers, Cripes of war,' was christened *Jingers*; through family association, his son became *Little Jingers*. By the same process others are called *Gee Hosifer* Dan, *By Cracky* Tom, and *The Bloody Awk* (for a Cockney living in Sydney who used this term to criticize others). One's manner of speech might also generate a nickname. When John Eliot laughed, he sounded as though he were crying; he is accordingly called John Eliot *the Crier*. A man with a high-pitched voice was christened John *the Piper*, presumably because his voice sounded like bagpipes. *Swearing* Dan and *Swearing* Peter use profane language, and a man from the southern part of the Island who used to strike his breast while speaking is called *Through My Fault*.

Other nicknames are formed because of some event that is historically important or unusual. For example, when a group of strikers raided the Company Store in 1925, a man named McKinnon was injured when a box of biscuits fell from a top shelf and crushed his foot (Mellor, 1983, p.306). Thereafter, he was called *Biscuit Foot* McKinnon. Another well-known nickname also comes from the practices of the Company Store. Before the miners received their pay, the Company Store deducted money from the workers' wages to cover the bills owed to the store. When Johnny MacDonald collected the small pay left after the deductions (two cents, according to one informant), he sarcastically boasted about his big pay. He is known as *Big Pay* Johnny, and his family as the *Big Pay* MacDonalds. Other nicknames are created from unusual events rather than those of interest to local historians. One man is called *Turkey* because he once stole a turkey from his mother-in-law. An Italian man from the industrial area received his nickname Tony *Vin* from his habit of selling his home-made wine on Sunday afternoons, but his lasting fame was assured by an incident well known locally. Having been served a new batch of wine made from unknown berries, his customers were stricken with diarrhea. With only one toilet on the premises, the afflicted drinkers retreated to the trees and bushes in the yard to seek relief. The informant explained that this story is often retold, and just as often embellished in the retelling.

Character traits or quirks of personality also foster nicknames. One man is called the *Silver Fox* partly because of his white hair and partly because of his characteristic of reporting infractions by fellow workers to his brother, who worked for the administration of a local company. Billy *the Brat*, an engineer, received his name because of his characteristic arrogance, and a *Leo* (Italian for 'lion') received this nickname because of his noisy, aggressive behaviour. A man called *Two Dans* received his name because of his 'two-faced' character.

In industrial Cape Breton, nicknames associated with occupations are also common, especially those connected with the coal mines and the steel plant (Frank, 1988). One family is known as *Twelve-to-Eight* because the husband regularly worked this shift. Two MacDonald families in Glace Bay are identified as the *Bore Holes* and the *Beveller* MacDonalds because of their respective occupations in an earlier generation. The family known as the *Gobs* probably received this name because of a father or grandfather who worked in the gob, the place in the mine where the coal has been removed. *Jack Hammer* refers to Joe MacKenzie, who used a jack hammer, and John *Clinker* MacMillan pulled the clinkers (pieces of fused coal) from the furnace used to generate steam power. Two of the Joe MacNeils from Dominion are called Joe *Priest* (a caretaker for a local church) and *Radio* Joe (a steel worker who repaired radios). Jimmy *the Barber* is better known in Glace Bay by his nickname (according to one informant) than by his official name, Jim MacDonald.

Geographic nicknames indicate either a place of origin or a place visited by the bearer of the name. Danny *Plaster* designates the Dan who comes from northern Cape Breton where gypsum was mined for plaster. *Smokey* Joe refers to the man who lives at the base of Cape Smokey.The *Light House Brothers*, Donald *Bridge End*, Hughie *Alders*, and the *Goose in the Bog* are nicknames which depict where these people live. *Yankee* Dan, one of the few general nicknames, is used in Port Hastings, industrial Cape Breton, and in the Ingonish area for men who came from or visited the United States (except that in Port Hastings the son is known as Danny *Yankee Dan*). Some people received their names as a result of a prolonged or important visit to a place. *Montana* Dan worked in Montana as a shepherd for several years before returning to Cape Breton, the *Klondike* MacKinnons lived in the Klondike during the Gold Rush, and *Ottawa* Angus visited the capital only once, but repeatedly referred to the trip in conversations.

Other nicknames are generated because of various kinds of humour. Occasionally, the humour depends on irony. *Hairy* Johnny describes a balding man, *Tiny* Power describes a man who is six feet tall, and two town drunks were called the *Senator* and *Doctor* Angus. Three Sydney men better known for their drinking than for their boxing ability used to fight in the preliminary matches behind the Harness Shop. Because of their comic attempts at pugilism, they were ironically called *Knock Out* Kelly, the *Belgium Panther*, and *Slippery* Tom. Other humorous nicknames seize upon a physical or personality trait to ridicule. Cassie *Skillet* is a thin woman, and the *Blob* is a man with the opposite characteristic. *Bump*, Leo *Pancake*, and the *Pancake* family are all short. In the days before artificial limbs were as sophisticated as they are tody, those who had lost a limb might be called *Wooden* Allan or *Stiff* Angus. Yet even in the face of these grim injuries, humour was used against the dangers faced every day by miners and soldiers. As D. MacDonald (1980, p.14) notes: 'A Cape Breton miner with one arm shorter than the other was dubbed Alex the Clock.' Another Alex, who lost a leg in the First World War, had to swing his wooden leg as he walked. Because of his need for a wide path, he was called *Broadway* Alex. Other humorous names emphasize disreputable characters: *Sharky* (described as a 'wheeler dealer'), Eco *Bis* (*biscia* is Italian for 'snake'), *Slick* Jim, *Turkey* George, and *Livers*. A sly bootlegger from the Coxheath Mountains avoided being caught and earned his name, the *Fox*. A man from Port Hastings who talks excessively is called the *August Gale*. Other names depend on vulgar language for their humour; *Piss Pot* Mary, *Flat Assed* (the smallest of a short family), *Pickle Arse*, and probably many more that informants were too well mannered to mention. Other humorous nicknames depend on incongruous sound for humour, such as Alec *the Boo*, *Bozo*, and the group of children called *Boogie*, *Googie*, and *Booboo*. A few humorous nicknames are connected with stories that probably have some truth, but have become apocryphal in the retelling. One such story explains the nickname given to a derelict from a small town on the west side of the Island. One night, the man was lying drunk on the road when an old lady ran over him. Surprised by the bump, the woman supposedly backed up to discover the problem, and ran over the man a second time. According to the story, the man survived the accident, continued to drink, and was christened with the whimsical nickname *Speed Bump*.

One small group of nicknames have their genesis in what might be called popular culture, as these names are borrowed from a well known person, a character on a television program, or a famous event. Names like *Gandhi*, *Tokyo Rose*, *Squiggy* (after Squigman on the television series *Laverne and Shirley*), *Smurf* (for a short cleaner who wears a blue uniform), and *Sputnik* (a girl born in the year the first Russian spacecraft was launched) all attest to this cultural influence. Other names recall notorious characters: *Jack the Ripper* and *Captain Kidd* (for a man who sailed on a ship that smuggled rum during Prohibition in the United States). One of the local characters who habitually moves his head from side to side is called *Wimbledon*.

Clearly, then, these two broad categories — internal and external methods for forming nicknames — provide a diverse array of nicknames. In part, the social function of these names within the community is implicit in this classification. The most obvious of these social functions is identification. The frequent occurrence of certain surnames among the Highland Scottish immigrants, and the custom of naming a child after a relative are two factors which encourage the use of additional and substitute names to distinguish one person or family from another with a similar name (Creighton, 1962, p.71). Of the nicknames in this study with known surnames, 75% are Scottish in origin, with MacDonald and MacKinnon being most frequent. In conversation, Prof. A. Murray Kinloch mentioned that the practice of giving the same name to members of a large family occurs in some areas of Scotland. Studies (e.g., Smith, 1968) also indicate a parallel situation among the Amish, where both first and second names recur frequently, and nicknames are needed to identify individuals and families. Even within a single family, there may be a need to use nicknames to identify two children, because occasionally members in the same immediate family have the same Christian name. Reporting on the nicknames used in the Port Hood area during the 1960s, Alexander Laidlaw states:

> Many of the Cape Bretoners have large families, very often eight or ten children, and sometimes the same name was used twice, perhaps for lack of imagination, or respect to some relative. Thus we have such names as Big Sandy and Little Sandy, Old Donald and Young Donald, or Brown Jack and Black Jack after the colour of their eyes. (Creighton, 1962, p.72)

Three informants reported a similar pattern in their areas, and one of them mentioned the high infant mortality rate as a reason for giving the same name to two children in one family. Because of this similarity in first names and surnames, clearer identification is needed at home, in the community, and in the workplace. Thus, *Black* Allan is distinguished from his younger brother *Red* Allan, and the two Dan MacDonalds from East Bay are easily identified as *Business* Dan and *Sydney* Dan. As one informant from Glace

Bay noted, nicknames were essential in the coal mines, as workers were paid according to the daily tonnage that they produced. Those recording this information each day had to have a more specific name to identify each worker accurately.

Another important function of nicknames is social control. Many of the derisive nicknames stigmatize the bearers of the names for some behaviour of which the community disapproves. Derogatory names such as *Livers*, *Slick* Jim, Jimmy *Skunk*, *Sharky*, *Bully* Brown, and the *Silver Fox* clearly criticize those engaged in either criminal or antisocial behaviour. While useful in identifying the antisocial or deviant members of the community, these pejorative names also have a negative side. Those with a physical defect or a conspicuous physical feature have a more difficult life if they have to bear a name like *Lumpy* (because of the bumps on his head), the *Hook* and the *Nostril* (because of their noses), or *Popeye* (because of a bulging eye). At the same time, however, it is difficult to generalize about what names are derisive, as people react differently to their nicknames. In the previous generation, Allan *Big Hughie* did not mind being called *Ox*, but another family called the *Oxes* resented the name. While *Boozer* is usually seen as insulting, it is not for one family, because the name was given as a joke when the person was a child. As mentioned above, the nickname *Spider* is valued by one man, as it refers to his speed on the ice, but the same name is derisive to another person, as it refers to his appearance when wearing glasses. As with most names, the context in which the nickname is used determines its meaning and the reaction to it.

One final importance of these names is to preserve the local values, culture, and history of a community. As indicated above, strength is admired and consequently reflected in the many epithets like *Big*, *Tall*, *Long*, *Hunk*, and *Ox*. Names such as Tommy *Cod* and Paul *Fish*, and others like the *Gobs* and the *Bore Holes* attest to two of Cape Breton's major industries. *Big Pay* MacDonald, *Biscuit Foot* MacKinnon, and *Pickle Arse* MacLean all record the importance of the Company Store in industrial Cape Breton, and to some extent the animosity between managers and workers. Tony *Vin* and the *Fox* — for those who know the origin of the names — recall the custom of selling alcohol illegally. Nicknames like *Gandhi* and *Sputnik* indicate an interest in people and events of international importance.

In conclusion, the naming practices, the diverse classification, and the social functions of these names indicate that nicknames are a lively and important tradition in Cape Breton. Although adjectives like *big*, *little*, *long*, *black*, and *red* recur frequently in the nicknames gathered, these five adjectives account for only 11.3% of the nicknames in this study. With a few exceptions, most of the nicknames do not recur and show remarkable creativity and imagination. Instead of using a nickname like *Speedy* to describe a man known for his speed in hauling logs out of the woods, he was given the imaginative and memorable name of *Split the Wind* Billy. While a thin person might be called *Skinny*, there are also interesting variations like *Hair Pin* Angus (McCawley, 1936), *Splinter*, and the *Spavin* (a disease contracted by horses that makes the bones become more pronounced). This imaginative use of language is also inspired by humour, as illustrated by the examples given above, and by many other names such as *Ten to Six*, used to christen one man who had the habit of tilting his head to one side. The examples given in this chapter illustrate a sensitive ear and an intelligent interest in words.

While this study provides some insight into the use of Cape Breton nicknames, there is more research to be done. Although trying to cover representative areas, the study does not analyse any one area exhaustively, nor does it cover every location in Cape Breton. Of the fourteen informants used as a source for this study, most come from industrial Cape Breton, with one or two informants from the northeast, the west, and the south of the Island. The most important written sources report on Port Hood (Creighton, 1962) and the industrial area (McCawley, 1936; Frank, 1988). More thorough research is needed on the nicknames in each of the Island's regions, on occupational nicknames, and on a few specific groups, such as the Mi'kmaq, Acadians, and Gaelic speakers.

We are grateful to the following people who generously volunteered their time to be informants for this study: Terry Campbell, Mary Margaret Chiasson, Peyton Chisholm, Kate Currie, Redmond Curtis, George Hussey (who provided nicknames from Meat Cove to Cape Smokey), Dan Alex MacLeod, Brenda MacKinnon, Mr. and Mrs. L. MacSween, Robert Morgan, Percy Peters, Lino Polegato, Lois Ross, and Mr. and Mrs. Arthur Severance.

References

Acadiennes de Chéticamp, St. Joseph du Moine et Magré. (1977). Généalogie des familles. Unpublished paper. Sydney, CB: Beaton Institute.

Allen, I. L. (1983). *The language of ethnic conflict: Social organization and lexical cultures*. New York: Columbia University Press.

Apte, M. (1985). *Humor and laughter: An anthropological approach*. Ithaca: Cornell University Press.

Beaton, E. (1974). Nicknames. Unpublished paper. Sydney, CB: Beaton Institute.

Creighton, H. (1962). Cape Breton nicknames. In H. Beck, (Ed.), *Folklore in action*. Philadelphia: American Folklore Society.

Crystal, D. (1995). *The Cambridge encyclopedia of the English language*. Cambridge: Cambridge University Press.

Cumming, P., MacLeod, H., & Strachan, L. (1984). *The story of Framboise*. Framboise, CB: St. Andrew's Presbyterian Church.

Davey, W. (1990). Informal names for the places in Cape Breton: Nicknames, local usage, and a brief comparison with personal nicknames. *Onomastica Canadiana, 72*, 69-81.

Dunn, C. W. (1953). *Highland settlers: A portrait of the Scottish Gael in Nova Scotia*. Toronto: University of Toronto Press.

Frank, D. (1988). A note on Cape Breton nicknames. *Journal of the Atlantic provinces linguistic association, 10*, 54-63.

Jönsjö, J. (1979). *Studies on Middle English nicknames*. Lund: Gleerup.

MacDonald, D. (1980, Oct.). Nova Scotia's wacky nicknames. *Readers' digest*, pp.13-14.

MacKenzie, C. (1926, June). Creating a New Scotland in Canada. *Travel, 47*, pp.16-19, 42, 44.

MacPhee, R. (n.d.). Sydney Mines, Cape Breton nicknames. Unpublished poem. Sydney, CB: Beaton Institute.

McCawley, S. (1936, Oct. 13). Cape Breton tales. *Sydney post-record*, pp.4, 7.

McCrum, R., Cran, W., & MacNeil, R. (1986). *The story of English*. New York: Viking.

Mellor, J. (1983). *The company store: James Bryson McLachlan and the Cape Breton coal miners 1900-1925*. Toronto: Doubleday. Rpt. Halifax: Goodread Biographies.

Monteiro, G. (1962). *Alcunhas* among the Portuguese in southern New England. *Western folklore, 20*, 103-7.

Morgan, J., O'Neill, C., & Harré, R. (1979). *Nicknames: The origins and social consequences*. London: Routledge & Kegan Paul.

Noble, V. (1976). *Nicknames past and present*. Foreword by Eric Partridge. London: Hamilton.

Peevers, B. H., & Secord, P. F. (1974). The development and attribution of person concepts. In T. Mischel (Ed.), *Understanding other persons*. Oxford: Blackwell.

Rees, N., & Noble, V. (1985). *A who's who of nicknames*. London: Allen & Unwin.

Seary, E. F., with Lynch, S. M. P. (1977). *Family names of the island of Newfoundland*. St. John's: Robinson-Blackmore.

Smith, E. L. (1968). Amish names. *Names, 16*, 105-10.

Urdang, L. (1979). *Twentieth century American nicknames*. Comp. by W. Kidney & G. Kohn. Foreword by L. A. Dunkling. New York: Wilson.

Chapter Six

The Place Names of Nova Scotia

Margaret Harry

Editors' Introduction

Just as children must be named in order to be integrated in society, so places, especially places of human habitation, must be named for administrative, economic, and political reasons. The giving of names is a seemingly pleasant task: here is a chance to put a stamp of one's own on a hitherto unnamed piece of landscape; here is a chance to exercise one's poetic and creative instincts, not to mention a flair for originality. But, just as the naming of children is subject to tradition on one hand, and fashion on the other, so place-naming is more traditional and ruled by fashion than innovative.

The present chapter examines place names of Nova Scotia, and finds that they fall into categories which are common also in other parts of the globe: namely, commemorative names like Amherst, Kentville, Halifax; descriptive names like Salt Springs, Black Brook, Flat Lake; possessives like Peggy's Cove, Sullivan's Pond; and shift names, that is, names given by extension from one community to one or more adjoining ones, like Pubnico and West Pubnico.

Tradition and fashion are intertwined in such names as Kentville, where the first part honours the Duke of Kent, and the second part introduces the suffix *-ville*, which became popular in the nineteenth century, So, although it would seem that place-naming is an invitation to linguistic extravagance, in reality there are many constraints on this activity.

These constraints are both linguistic and cultural, at least in the sense that people tend to create new names from existing linguistic elements in their own language, or in a language they know, and they do it within the norms dictated by their culture. Thus it goes without saying that places honour heroes, not villains, and if military battles are remembered, it is the victorious ones, not the ones that brought no glory. Of course, with the passage of time, perceptions of heroism and glory may change, and then names sometimes need to be changed too. A combination of linguistic and cultural constraints can be seen in the avoidance of ordinary taboos and of names which resemble taboo words.

An important linguistic constraint is that place names must be pronounceable in conformity with the phonetic patterns of a given language. The concern that it must be possible to record them in writing is relatively late, for in pre-literate societies all names were known in their spoken forms only.

Even a consideration of minimal constraints shows that place naming cannot be totally arbitrary. Furthermore, it becomes evident that even if there is a measure of freedom in the naming of a place itself, all derived forms usually conform to existing grammatical patterns. For instance, the Mi'kmaw name Malagash (N.S. Dept. of Tourism, 1973, p.86) combines into Malagash Station and Malagash Point according to accepted English word order. Earltown, reportedly named by Gaelic speakers (p.87) is a compound of two nouns, as English as *bookcase*.

Of particular interest is the name of the province itself: Nova Scotia. Nominally Latin (meaning 'New Scotland'), it is formed on the pattern of adjective plus noun, both in the feminine declension, in accordance with Latin grammatical structure. Like Earltown, it was formed in a language foreign to the name-giver King James the Sixth of Scotland and First of England, who probably thought little of the necessary permutations of this name if it was ever to be used by an English-speaking population.

Eventually the name has become much more English in character than Latin; it is pronounced in accordance with English, not Latin, phonetic rules. It also functions grammatically like an English phrase. We say *Nova Scotia's prosperity*, for instance, with *'s* used once as a mark of the possessive, whereas the Latin would have *Novae Scotiae prosperitas*, with both the adjective and the noun showing the possessive ending of the feminine declension. In English the province is not grammatically feminine — it takes the neuter pronoun *it*, whereas in Latin *I love Nova Scotia* would be *Novam Scotiam amo* — with both parts of the name showing the feminine accusative ending.

Also, in Latin, noun-phrases do not function as adjectives, as in *Nova Scotia schools*, nor would Latin derive an adjectival form like *Nova Scotian schools*. Many other derivations, as those created from the first or second element of the name, would not be possible in Latin, let alone the nominal and adjectival use of the initials *NS* which are fully English in function and pronunciation [ɛn ɛs]. Unlike *PEI* and *BC* the abbreviation *NS* is not used by itself in conversation, so we must say 'I took the ferry from PEI to Nova Scotia,' but it is pronounced in the beginning of longer acronyms, such as *NSTU* (Nova Scotia Teachers' Union) and even more bravely in *NSCUFA* [ənskufə] (Nova Scotia Confederation of University Faculty Associations) — a combination of initial sounds not normally heard in English.

From the distant days of King James to the present, Nova Scotians have been naming their communities, using, beside English, place-name elements from a variety of other sources; among English speakers, these elements have eventually, though not without exceptions, conformed to the linguistic patterns of English. The chapter which follows examines these developments both from a historical and a linguistic point of view. *(LF & MH)*

***

The Place Names of Nova Scotia

by Margaret Harry

When they move to a new locality, all settlers have to decide on names by which their settlement and all its surrounding natural features, both on land and along the coast, will be identified. This was a problem facing the settlers of Nova Scotia, from the Native peoples on, and they employed many familiar and not so familiar methods of arriving at suitable appellations. The study of place names, or toponymy, can often reveal a great deal about the history and culture of a particular area. However, as far as Nova Scotia is concerned, relatively little work has been done in this field, and the few studies which exist tend to concentrate on curiosities, rather than attempting to provide any kind of systematic survey, whether linguistic or otherwise. Gazetteers, and lists of names, including the extensive *Place-Names and Places of Nova Scotia* (*PN*) originally published by the Public Archives of Nova Scotia in 1967, while they explain the origins of individual names, do not identify patterns of nomenclature or link together related names. There is also a tendency to concentrate on the names of settlements alone, and to ignore various natural features, especially lakes and seamarks, as well as the names of artificial features, such as municipal subdivisions and streets. In addition, there is a fairly widespread assumption, arising from the pervasive linguistic influence of Loyalist settlers, that the dominating influence on the English place names of Nova Scotia has been taken from the naming patterns of New England.

While the Loyalists obviously made some impact on the place names of the province, it is clear from a glance at a map that it has not been a very large one, and in many cases it can be argued that what we see are the effects of much more general nineteenth-century naming fashions than the particular influence of this specific group of settlers.

Many place names in the province cannot by any stretch of the imagination be associated with the Loyalists, since they date from an earlier period. The first settlers to give identifying names to the area were the successive groups of Native peoples who inhabited the Maritimes before the arrival of any European visitors. Most of these very early names have not survived, and what generally remains are Gallicized or Anglicized forms of Mi'kmaw names, whose meanings can sometimes still be deciphered, but not always. The earliest visitors of European origin known to have given names to the region were Norse explorers from the Greenland settlements, who travelled in the general area from the tenth to the thirteenth centuries, but unfortunately the precise locations referred to by recorded Norse names cannot be identified with any certainty, and have been variously assigned to Newfoundland, Maine, and other New England states, as well as to Nova Scotia. The Norse settlement itself is still commemorated in Markland in Yarmouth County and in occasional business names using the elements *Mark- /Merkland* and *Vinland.* In the late nineteenth century a temporary settlement of Icelandic immigrants at Mooseland Heights in Halifax County was also called Markland (Kristjanson, 1965), but the name is no longer used there, and so must be regarded merely as an ephemeral and sentimental usage.

Later arrivals in the province included fishermen, who were seasonal settlers, from the fifteenth century on, principally of Irish, English, French, Basque, and Portuguese origin, and permanent settlers of French origin from the seventeenth century, of British (including Irish and Scottish Gaelic speakers) and to a lesser extent of German and U.S. (Loyalists and others) origin from the eighteenth century, and of many different European backgrounds from the nineteenth century on. While the naming of subdivisions, streets, and so on, continues into the present, the naming of most other Nova Scotian places, including towns and villages and natural features of the landscape and seascape, seems to have been largely completed by the end of the nineteenth century, so that more recent immigrants, and especially those of non-European origin, have had virtually no influence on the naming process. What we would expect, therefore, would be a system of place names which follows English (including Loyalist), French, Gaelic, or German patterns, and to some extent this is what we find. But it is interesting to note that, although the majority of Nova Scotian place names are evidently European in origin, many of them do not conform completely to the linguistic place-name patterns found in the previous homelands of the settlers.

Given that Nova Scotian names date mainly from the nineteenth century, and that European names may date from classical times or earlier, with very few indeed dating from later than the Middle Ages, it is possible to argue that what we find is not a departure from original patterns but rather the effect, entirely to be expected, of general eighteenth and nineteenth-century naming fashions — current in Europe as well as in Canada, the United States, and other outposts of European empires. In the few examples of nineteenth-century European place names we certainly find those fashionable elements more usually expected in North American names. For example, Bournville in England (founded by the Cadbury company in 1889) uses the element *-ville*, recently imported from French into English in general, rather than from French into the United States exclusively. It is not surprising, therefore, to find in Nova Scotia such places as Waterville and Kentville, which are superficially rather peculiar mixtures of English and French place-name elements, usually associated with U.S. (and therefore Loyalist?) naming practices. The early adoption (1826) of Kentville as a place name may certainly be seen as an example of American influence. Yet nineteenth-century fashions, whether American or more general, do not altogether explain Nova Scotian place names.

George R. Stewart, in *Names on the Globe* (1975), an examination of toponymic practices throughout the world, divides place names into ten different categories, to which he adds several possible combinations of categories. The main categories are, briefly, commemorative names, descriptive names, possessive names, shift names, associative names, incident names, commendatory names, manufactured names, mistake names, and folk etymology. All of these categories with some of their sub-groups and possible combinations are represented in Nova Scotia, but most of the place names of the province fall into the first six categories, with only a few examples of the last four.

The majority of names in Europe appear originally to have been descriptive or possessive or associative, even if the descriptive and possessive elements in particular have become fossilized and may no longer be generally understood by the local inhabitants. Mi'kmaw naming practices were largely descriptive. Indeed, descriptive names seem to form the basic pattern of place names throughout the world, without regard to cultural origins; they serve the primary function of providing a specifically recognizable identification for a place, even if what is in question is only the demarcation of property.

By the nineteenth century — the most prolific naming period in Nova Scotia — the basic criterion was bound to have become somewhat blurred in the minds of many settlers. First, many European place names had been established by long-vanished races or cultural groups, in languages no longer spoken, and had merely been taken over by later settlers, for whom they were arbitrary rather than descriptive, and therefore no longer fully meaningful identifications. The survival of Roman, Celtic, Scandinavian, and often French place names in England provides a good example of this practice, e.g., Chester, Penrith, Grimsby, Beaulieu, and so on. Second, even when the local inhabitants still spoke the 'original' language, a large number of European place names no longer had anything other than arbitrary meaning for their users, for languages change while, as mentioned above, place-name elements become fossilized. The two elements in an English name like Canterbury, for example, are not obviously explained by the ordinary non-etymological dictionary definitions of *canter* and *bury*. Third, even when descriptive names remained superficially meaningful, as for example in cases of foundation, ownership, or tenure, the particular attribution had often been lost. Who, for example, would know which king had founded Kingston, or even if any king had had so direct a connection with the place? This kind of experience would not suggest that place names must necessarily be descriptive, or even meaningful to anyone apart from the original namers.

Along with these factors, there was also the need even in Europe (a need which explains the development of new fashions) to find new names for places. There was an ongoing population explosion, which led to the rapid expansion of existing settlements (as well as in part to emigration to Nova Scotia and other locations), and also considerable industrial development, which led to the establishment of new settlements, including new towns (such as Bournville mentioned above). Thus the settlers in Nova Scotia did not necessarily come to the selection of place names as to an altogether unfamiliar problem.

In Nova Scotia, as elsewhere, most names were established either formally or informally by group or community agreement, and confirmed by usage. In a few cases, a single individual can be identified as having chosen a particular place name, but in general local consensus and usage are more significant. The identification of a place is, after all, a community rather than an individual need. However, it should be noted that municipal subdivision and street names have increasingly since the early nineteenth century been selected by a very small group of individuals (chiefly those involved in municipal government), and may often be considered an imposition on the general culture rather than growing naturally out of it.

Classes of Place Names in Nova Scotia

(a) Commemoratives

One of the largest classes of place names in Nova Scotia is that of commemorative names, i.e., names which are mainly honorific or sentimental, forming an arbitrary means of identification, dependant on cultural connotations alone. In Nova Scotia, this complex category has several sub-classes, of which the two most obvious are places named after places in Europe and elsewhere (usually, but not always, the original homes of the settlers) and places named after well known (at the time, at least) people who had no direct connection, in the sense of foundation, ownership, or tenancy, with the particular location. Most of the names in both these sub-divisions are British in origin, reflecting the dominant culture of the province, although they are not necessarily English.

Places named after places include such oddities as small settlements named after whole countries, provinces, states, and so on. For example, Ireland, Devon, Laconia, Oregon, and Russia are all to be found in Nova Scotia. But far more usual is a settlement named after a town, village, or other relatively small area in the country of origin. The place names of England are, for example, represented by such settlements as Liverpool, Mersey, Oldham, Preston, Truro, and Watford. From Scotland come such names as Aberdeen, Arisaig, Balmoral, Coldstream, Glengarry, Loch Lomond, Renfrew, Scotsburn, and Ulva. From Portugal comes Mira (after Mire, near Oporto). From France come Cannes, the Basque Cape Breton (after Cap Breton), Fauxbourg and Lourdes — but the two latter may have been named for religious, rather than nationalistic reasons. And this qualification itself serves as a bit of a warning about such arbitrary names, that the cultural connotations may be something other than the most obvious ones. For example, Lunenburg, which many assume was named after Lüneburg in Germany, seems rather to commemorate a family title of the House of Hanover, Duke of Braunschweig-Lüneburg, and parallels New Brunswick in the way it honours the royal family (Bell, 1990, p.407). Wittenburg in Colchester County was certainly named after Wittenburg in Germany, but its settlers did not include any Germans. According to *Place-Names and Places of Nova Scotia*: 'About 1885 the name Wittenburg was suggested by Reverend E. T. Miller because the church resembled that on which Martin Luther nailed his thesis' (1974, p.741). And the Assyrian name Nineveh, found in both Lunenburg and Victoria counties, is equally religious in origin, deriving from the Bible, rather than from any romantically minded Middle Eastern settlers.

This leads to a further caution, which is that a name chosen for its sentimental connection with an original homeland may not represent the homeland it superficially appears to. A fairly large number of settlements in Nova Scotia were established in the late eighteenth century by Loyalists, both white and Black, and for most of these settlers 'home' was New England. Many nineteenth-century settlers also arrived from the United States. These settlers gave their new homes the names of the old, and such names include not only such obvious commemorations as Oregon in Victoria County, but also Bangor, named after Bangor, Maine; Cambridge, Hants County, named after Cambridge, Massachusetts (whereas Cambridge, Kings County, seems to have been named after Cambridge in England); Denver, after Denver, Colorado; Londonderry, after Londonderry, New Hampshire; Plympton, from Plympton, Massachusetts; and Westchester, from Westchester County, New York. On the other hand, Ohio, in Yarmouth County, was not named by settlers from the United States, but celebrates the 'Ohio Fever' of 1826 (*PN*, 1974, p.507).

Frequently, in order to distinguish the new home from the old, settlers used the adjective *New* in combination with the old name — a common practice with migrating peoples from the earliest times. Thus we find New Britain, New France and New Germany, and on a smaller scale, New Annan, after Annandale in Scotland, New Boston, after Boston, Massachusetts, New Cornwall, New Edinburgh, New Gairloch, New Glasgow, New Harris, New Waterford, and New Yarmouth. Yet even here appearances can be a bit deceiving. While New Canaan is fairly obviously a Biblical reference, the slightly mysterious New Dominion is only to be explained by a fairly relative local newness: it is named after Dominion in Cape Breton County. Equally local is New Chester, which is probably named after Chester in Lunenburg County.

The second large sub-division of commemorative names consists of places named after well known people whose connection with the locality was not necessarily very close. Some of these are still obvious, such as Victoria County, named after Queen Victoria, along with all the *Victoria* roads and streets found throughout the province, and accompanied by Queens County and its attendant *Queen* streets. Equally, Prince Albert and even Albert Bridge, along with the various *Albert* streets, are easily identifiable, although *Prince* by itself does not necessarily refer to Prince Albert. For example, Prince's Lodge in Halifax refers to the Duke of Kent who was Queen Victoria's father. Indeed, such appellations indicate the ephemeral nature of fame. What purports to be the name of one prince proves somewhat of a mystery in the city of Halifax, where in the mid-eighteenth century a sequence of downtown streets was named Prince, George, Duke, and Buckingham. In 1882, George W. Hill observed that Prince Street 'no doubt was so named in honor of the Royal family; but I am puzzled to know which of them' (Rpt. 1911, p.6). If the sequence was named by Governor Cornwallis after the death of Frederick Louis, Prince of Wales, in 1751, then the reference could be to his son George. However, this particular Prince George was never Duke of Buckingham — a title which had become extinct and which was not 'revived again until George IV's time' (Hill, rpt. 1911, p.7). Nowadays, the absolute forgettability of this particular scion of royalty is underscored first by the reduction of Buckingham Street to a tiny fragment of its former self as a result of the 1960s construction of Scotia Square, and later, ironically, by its final disappearance in the Historic Properties development. And here the ephemeral nature of fame may be of some consolation to citizens concerned about the recently developed practice of naming streets after incumbent members of municipal governments. In a case where a local politician was subsequently found guilty of a crime, the municipality was embarrassed by the already well established identification of a street by his name, and the suggestion was made that streets should be named only after dead people. This would be a considerable departure from the traditions of the province, where almost all place names containing personal names commemorate people who were alive when the name was given.

Of course, commemorative names of this kind can often be useful in dating a locality or settlement, since the identification of the individual provides at least an earliest possible date for the establishment of the name. The various *Jubilee* roads in the province, while only indirectly referring to a person, nevertheless reveal their dates. An early example is Jubilee Road in Halifax, which celebrates George III's Jubilee of 1810. Several others celebrate Queen Victoria's Diamond Jubilee in 1897. Various members of the British Government and military forces, otherwise forgotten, date settlements all over the province. Stormont celebrates the Lord Stormont who was Secretary of State from 1779 to 1782, Halliburton is named after Sir Brenton Halliburton, Chief Justice of Nova Scotia, 1833-1860, and Strathlorne remembers a Marquis of Lorne who was Governor-General, 1878-1883. Many other examples can be found: Abercrombie for General James Abercrombie, Addington Forks for Henry Addington, Viscount Sidmouth, Digby for Admiral Robert Digby, Hammonds Plains for Sir Andrew Snape Hammond (and his wife in Lady Hammond Road in Halifax), and so on. Sometimes, the identification can be a bit more elusive: Guysborough town and county, for example, rather unusually employ the first, not the last, name of Sir Guy Carleton, while Earltown is hardly an immediately recognizable reference to the Earl of Dalhousie who was Lieutenant-Governor, 1816-1820, and who is more clearly remembered in the name of Dalhousie University.

In many cases, what appears to be a place name commemorating another place actually commemorates a person. Halifax, the capital of the province, was named not after the town in England but after George Montagu Dunk, 2nd Earl of Halifax, who was President of the Board of Trade from 1748 to 1761, the period of Halifax's foundation, and who was known as the 'Father of the Colonies' (*PN*, 1974, p.273). It is doubtful whether many Haligonians nowadays care about this eighteenth-century politician, and certainly the primary association in people's minds seems to be with the English town. (However, it is rather amusing to reflect that the city could well have been called Dunktown.) Other places which commemorate not places but people include Amherst (Lord Jeffrey Amherst), and Kentville (Duke of Kent). On the other hand, Dartmouth, which is often thought to have been named after William Legge, Earl of Dartmouth, actually seems to commemorate the English port (*PN*, 1974, p.155). In addition, some place names which appear to be commemoratives may turn out to be altogether different. For example, Sheffield Mills in Kings County is not a commemorative at all, but a possessive, named for a family of early settlers including Mason and Frank A. Sheffield (*PN*, 1974, p.618). On the other hand, Chaswood, which looks like a first-name possessive, actually commemorates Charles Wood, the first Nova Scotian to be killed in the Boer War (p.121). And the rather odd looking Glen Tosh turns out to commemorate the Rev. Abraham McIntosh, who was a Presbyterian minister in the district from 1856 to 1889 (p.245), while Giant Lake, in itself a fairly small lake, celebrates Duncan McDonald, the 'giant' (p.231).

A relatively minor division of commemorative names, consisting of abstractions, is also fairly well represented in Nova Scotia. The name Harmony occurs several times, both alone and in combination, reflecting both the hopes (if not the actual dispositions) of the settlers and their feelings about the land. On the other hand, Economy tells us nothing about its inhabitants, since it is an example of folk etymology, rather than a true abstraction. The name seems originally to come from a Mi'kmaw word *kenome*, meaning 'a long point jutting far out into the sea' (*PN*, 1974, p.191), with an intermediate Acadian version, Vil Conomie, later given a reasonable sounding English interpretation. In contrast, Sober Island does seem to represent the aspirations of its inhabitants, while Diligent River at least reflects the view of an outsider, Governor Parr, who was 'impressed with the diligence and industriousness of Lieutenant Taylor in his efforts to make a home' (p.170). The Folly, settled by James Flemming in 1762, and giving the shift names Folly Lake, Folly Mountain, and until 1909, Folly Village, is one of the few negative abstractions, taking its name 'from the old saying that it was folly for Mr. Flemming to settle in so poor a place' (Miller, 1873, p.131).

In this category also belong a few literary and other references: among others we find Arcadia (for the Classical region of rural peace and contentment), Hawthorne (named in honour of American novelist Nathaniel Hawthorne), Mantua (celebrating the birthplace of the Roman poet Vergil), and Nerissa (named after a character in *The Merchant of Venice*).

Miscellaneous commemoratives also occur, the most common being places named after commercial companies. Among these are Imperoyal, actually a manufactured commemorative, celebrating the Imperial Oil Company. Dominion takes its name not merely from the Dominion of Canada, but more specifically from coal mining — the Dominion No. 1 shaft gave its name to the Town of Dominion No. 1, which was changed to Dominion alone by Provincial Statute in 1906. Eureka, which sounds like an exclamatory incident name, was actually named after the Eureka Milling Company, and Greenwood in Pictou County seems to have been named after the Greenwood Coal Company.

(b) Descriptives

Descriptive names, unlike commemoratives, have some connection with the landscape or general geography of a place, in that they relate, if only in the vaguest way, to some specific detail of the place itself, and require no cultural explanation for their basic meaning to be understood. Examples of almost all of Stewart's sub-headings of descriptive names occur in Nova Scotia.

Sensory descriptives include a few examples of sound (Loud Lake) and taste (Salt Springs), and the very much larger group of sight, with examples of size (Big Pond, Little Harbour), colour (Black Brook, Blue Mountain, Greenwood in Kings County, Red Islands, White Point), configuration (Flat Lake, Round Island), and material (Mud Lake, Granite Village, Sandy Point). The division of size is by far the biggest, despite the relatively small number of specifics: *big*, *little*, *great*, *grand*, and *long*.

Relative descriptives occur very frequently, and in almost all cases the relationship is purely a local one. The specifics in use include compass direction (*east*, *eastern*, *north*, *northeast*, *northwest*, *south*, *southwest*, *west*, *western*), and other relative locations (*back*, *central*, *centre*, *first*, *halfway*, *lower*, *middle*, *rear*, *second*, *upper*). These specifics sometimes appear in combination, producing lengthy compound names (Lower Middle River, Upper West Pubnico), which can be meaningful only to someone with an intimate knowledge of the locale. Yet such names are very characteristic of the province as a whole.

Stewart's remaining categories of descriptives certainly occur in the province, but generally there are very few examples. Intellectual descriptives, which require some technical knowledge on the part of the namer, are virtually non-existent, with the exception of the geological Syenite Point, and the manufactured descriptive Ferrona (from *ferrum*). Some metaphorical descriptives can be found, such as Chimney Corner (for the shape of a nearby rock), Roaring Bull Point and Hell Rackets (both presumably for the sound made by the water), Saddle Island (shaped like a saddle), Pudding Pan Island, Frying Pan Island, and probably Whale Lake, which does vaguely resemble the shape of a whale. Cape Negro probably belongs to this group, since it seems to have been named by Champlain, who thought a nearby rock resembled the head of an African. There are a few subjective descriptives, such as Lonesome Lake, but virtually no negative, ironic, or hortatory descriptives, and only a few, mainly seamarks, such as Squally Point, that can be reasonably identified as repetitive descriptives, that is, places named after events or actions that habitually recur there. However, the unusual Gunning Cove, Sporting Lake, and Sporting Mountain record the use of these areas for hunting and fishing as sports, often involving expensive vacations for Americans and other visitors. The scarcity of names in these groups does not mean, of course, that the settlers lacked imagination, but rather that their imaginations were directed towards different methods of creating place names.

(c) Possessives

Possessive names are usually fairly clear in their meaning, although whether they denote ownership, or merely habitation, or even some other relationship with a place may not be so obvious. In Nova Scotia they form a large category, usually recording actual ownership of land, or a close association between a person or a group and the natural feature being identified. Where there are good records of settlement, ownership names are easily recognized, even if the particular families have since vanished from the neighbourhood. These names generally appear in the form of compounds—specific name of individual or family + generic (natural or artificial feature). So we have Aldersville, Barronsfield, Cook Brook, Roachvale, and many others. In the majority of cases, such ownership is recorded by surname, but fairly often first names, and even nicknames, are found: Barney's River (for Barnabas McGee); Jimtown (for James McDonald); Peggy's Cove (for Peggy Rodgers); and Kingross (for 'King' Angus Ross). While most names of this kind are male, as would be expected from the history of property ownership, there are also a fair number of female names, and it seems likely that there is often an overlap between ownership and association (by habitation, or other relationship). Names such as Ellen Brown Lake and Colin Chisholm Brook are more likely to fall into the second category of possessives, and even Peggy Rodgers, of Peggy's Cove, is identified as the wife of settler William Rodgers at a time when married women could not really own property. Isaac's Harbour, one of the very few places known to have been named after Black settlers, records Isaac Webb's living in the district, but not his proprietorship (as is also the case with Brass Hill, named after a very early Black settler, remembered only as Brass, living there in the 1760s). And where a designation, rather than a name, is used, it seems even more likely that what is being recorded is not ownership, but association. What matters is where the doctor lives, so we have Doctors Brook (for Dr. Alexander MacDonald), and Doctors Cove (for Dr. Andrew Collins). So also Glen Bard (for the Gaelic poet John Maclean), Piper Glen (for Neil Jamison), Pipers Cove (for Norman McNeil), and probably also Clarks Harbour (for Michael Swim, a clerk). Captain Island was owned by Captain T. W. Hierlihy, but he probably only lived at Captain Pond. Glendyer refers to Donald McLean MacDonald, who erected a dyeing mill in the locality.

Occasionally, personal names are used alone to indicate possession; that is, they are not combined with a generic. Usually such names are in the possessive form, with *-'s* or just *-s* (the spelling conventions vary), but this is not always the case: alongside the grammatical possessives Goff's, McAulays, Meiseners, and Pemberton's are to be found Burton, Gibbon, Probert, Quinan, and Watson. Reynolds (for Thomas Reynolds), Rogers (for the Rogers family), and Stevens (for Robert Stevens) are all understandable forms, for *-'s*, even if it had been used originally, would quickly have been lost from such names.

Associations with groups also occur, are mainly ethnic or national in form, and provide an interesting kind of record of the history of the province. In most cases, these names refer to habitations, both permanent and seasonal. The original inhabitants are usually merely given the designation *Indian* — Indian Harbour, Indian Point (in both Halifax County and Lunenburg County), and Indian Rear, near Whycocomagh — although Micmac does occur in Hants County, and Lake Micmac is a suburb of Dartmouth. Indian Brook probably refers to the habitation of a specific individual whose name has not been recorded. Lingan, which seems to be an attempted pronunciation of the French *L'Indienne* (*PN*, 1974, p.355), presumably also refers to an individual, since the feminine form would hardly have been used for a group reference.

The fishing industry is remembered in such names as Basque Islands and possibly Portuguese Cove, which may have been a Portuguese fishing station, but may also have been the location of a Portuguese wreck, and therefore an incident name. Jerseyman Island, in Richmond County, is probably either a possessive or an incident name, but almost certainly has some reference to the involvement of Jersey fishermen in the industry.

Other settlers are remembered in such names as French River in Pictou County, French Village, Frenchville, Dutch Brook, Dutch Settlement, Dutch Village (all for German settlers, from the German *deutsch*), Englishtown, Irish Cove, Irishvale, Scotch Hill in Pictou County, Scotchtown, Scotsville, Welshtown, the former Halifax district of Africville, Maroon Hill (after deportees from Jamaica, many of whom later emigrated to Sierra Leone), Yankee Harbour, and Yankeetown. As usual, these names can sometimes be deceptive. Danesville was probably called after an early settler, but there is no certainty. Italy Cross is a shift name, given because of its proximity to an old settlement called New Italy. Scots Bay should probably be considered an incident name, referring to the wreck of a ship full of Scottish immigrants (*PN*, 1974, p.610). The survivors remained only temporarily in the district.

Later settlers have not been remembered for their ethnic backgrounds, mainly because they came to settlements that had already been named. However, it is interesting to note that municipal division and street namers have on the whole preferred to stick to the naming patterns already established in the nineteenth century, and that when they venture away from these it is very rarely that they recognize the diverse ethnic backgrounds and cultures of twentieth-century Nova Scotians.

A few other groups are remembered: for example, Waldeck Line is in the area where some of the Waldeck troops, who fought in the American Revolution, settled after the end of the war. Pirate Harbour, traditionally a refuge for pirates, including Captain Kidd and Paul Jones (*PN*, 1974, p.528), recalls what now seems like a romantic aspect of provincial history. And Goshen in Guysborough County recalls not so much the Biblical place itself as the Goshen Society, which 'was formed for the purpose of sending one of its members to Halifax twice a year to bring back supplies much as did the sons of Jacob who went to Egypt to buy corn' (p.249).

(d) Shift Names

Shift names, which occur frequently in Nova Scotia, are names in which different generics and/or specifics are added to already existing names. Even though these names often overlap with relative descriptives, they rarely pose any problem of meaning, since the geographical relationship between the various places is usually fairly clear. For example, a glance at the map of Guysborough County shows the connection between Country Harbour itself and Country Harbour River, Country Harbour Head, Middle Country Harbour (a relative descriptive), Country Harbour Mines, Country Harbour Gold District, Cross Roads Country Harbour, and Country Harbour Lake. Such names appear, in many different combinations, in every part of the province. Occasionally, as mentioned in reference to Italy Cross above, one or other of the shift names takes prominence, with the original name losing importance, or even vanishing altogether.

(e) Associative and Incident Names

Two lesser but still large categories of names in Nova Scotia are associative names and incident names. Associative names, in which a place-generic is combined with a specific associated with the place, are very common, with the specifics including many different features. The maritime heritage of the province is recorded in names such as Fishing Cove, Ketch Harbour (for the good 'catch' to be obtained there, rather than a meeting place for ketches), Lighthouse Point, and Ship Harbour, with many more numerous examples, such as Clam Harbour, Duck Island, Eel Cove, Gannet Point, Goose Island, Gull Rock, Mackerel Point, Oyster Point, Seal Rock Cove, Shad Bay, Shag Rock, Shag Roost, and Trout Cove, referring to the different species of fish and birds found along the sea coast.

Moving inland, we find the industrial history of the land in names referring to nineteenth-century mills, generally sawmills and gristmills: Millbrook (occurring several times), Mill Creek, Millstream, and Mill Village, but Factorydale refers to a carding mill. Two examples of Mill Town have both been shortened to Milton. Mining and quarrying also produced many names, including Coalburn, Copper Lake, Goldboro, Goldenville, Ironville, Limerock, Mineral Rock, Mineville, Plaster Cove, Quarry Point, and Steam Mill Village.

Many associative ideas of this kind appear without a generic, especially (although not always) when the inclusion of a generic would have produced a lengthy combination name, so that a number of these names appear as possessives or as sensory descriptives. Thus we have such locations as Balmoral Mills, Blue Mills (for Dugald Blue), Cochran Hill Mine, Conquerall Mills, Gardiner Mines, Gypsum Mines, Iron Mines, Kavanaugh Mills, Lochaber Mines, Mabou Mines, Montague Gold Mines, Moose River Gold Mines, Newton Mills, Plaster, Plaister Mines, Quarry St. Anns, Rawdon Gold Mines, Reserve Mines, Sheffield Mills, Silver Mine, Soapstone Mine, Sydney Mines, Victoria Mines, and White Rock Mills.

When it comes to natural features of the landscape, the examples are numerous, with flora (mainly trees) and fauna forming the largest source groups. Thus we find Alder Point, Apple River, Ashfield, Birch Grove, Blueberry Pond, Cherryfield, Cloverdale, Cranberry Lake, Forest Glade, Framboise, Maplewood, New Elm, Oak Island, Poplar Grove, and Bass River, Beaver Brook, Deerfield, Loon Lake, Mooseland, Otter Brook, several examples of Salmon River, Trout Brook, and so on. It is clear that these examples represent the flora and fauna of the area, and in general it can be accepted that the location is associated with an abundance of the plant or animal specified. In some cases, however, as Stewart suggests (1975, p.100), the names may be incident rather than associative names, particularly with 'animals which are neither sedentary nor given to leaving permanent and conspicuous traces.' Without research into local records and traditions, supposing they exist, it may be impossible to tell whether, for example, Turtle Lake is a known habitat of turtles, is a place where some incident involving a turtle occurred, or merely is vaguely shaped like a turtle. Given the infrequent appearance of snakes in the province, Snake Lake sounds like an incident name. It also seems unlikely that a whole family of giant geese inhabit Giant Goose Lake, and while domesticated animals do gather at watering places, so that Cow Pond could reasonably be treated as an associative name, the generally remote locations of such examples again make the category of incident names more likely. It seems probable that Heifer Lake, Horse Lake, Hog Lake, and so on, commemorate something other than the proliferation of these animals in the neighbourhood.

Nearby physical or geological features provide another source of associative names, and as usual with such names there often seems to be nothing particularly remarkable about the specific feature identified. Thus we find examples of Brookdale, Brookfield, Hillside, Hillsvale, Lakeside, Lakevale, Riverside, and Riverville. Most of these names are self-evident, and hardly distinguishing, although the usual caution needs to be given: Hilltown, in Digby County, for example, is not an associative but a possessive name, celebrating an early settler called John Adam Hill (*PN*, 1974, p.296).

Places named after single events or occurrences fall into the category of incident names. In Nova Scotia this category provides a number of interesting examples, since such names often have stories attached to them, although, unfortunately, where the story is not a matter of general knowledge it may be difficult to establish for certain that a given name actually is an incident name. However, most incident names in the province belong to only two of Stewart's sub-groups, that is, places named after incidents involving animals or after incidents, especially accidents, involving human beings, with a scattering of names which seem to include exclamations.

The absence of names recording 'Acts of God' is not really surprising, since the province is not usually subject to severe occurrences of earthquakes, hurricanes, flash floods, and so on. Storms at sea are relatively commonplace, and are remembered mainly in 'wreck' names, which belong to the group of accidents involving human beings. Given the early French settlement of the province, and the known French liking for calendar names, that is, names given because a settler happened to be in a location on a particular day, we would expect a few such names. But most of the places named for saints seem to commemorate a church or parish around which the settlement has developed rather than its first discovery or foundation. *Noel*, although the French word for Christmas, is also a fairly common personal name, and Noel Bay in Hants County, with its accompanying Noel, Noel Road, and Noel Shore, are all possessives, named for Noel Pinet, an early settler. This personal name was often given by the French to Mi'kmaw converts, and still appears as a Mi'kmaw family name, along with the English Christmas, the name bestowed on Anglicized Noels. So Christmas Island is also a possessive, rather than a calendar name, remembering a chief called 'Noel' (*PN*, 1974, p.129). Saturday Lake and Sunday Lake, both in Lunenburg County, are probably calendar names.

On the other hand, incident names involving animals occur fairly frequently, and often tradition still records the original incident. The most famous of these examples is probably Port Mouton 'Sheep-port,' apparently named by French explorer De Monts after a sheep jumped overboard and was drowned during his 1604 voyage (*PN*, 1974, p.554). Other examples include Bear Cove, whose name 'was probably prompted by some experience with a bear' (p.45), Caribou, named for a sighting of a herd of caribou (but unlike Caribou Gold Mines and Caribou Marsh, not particularly associated with the animal), and Moose Brook, which records an incident involving a moose, 'wounded and pursued by two hunters, who succeeded in escaping by concealing his trail in this brook' (p.449). It seems likely that many other names, whose traditions are not so well known, also involve incidents with animals: for example, Beaverskin Lake, Beavertail Lake, Snake Cat Lake, and possibly even Moosehorn Lake. The frequent occurrence of the name Hog Island, and the association of various other unlikely animals with offshore islands also suggests that the kind of incident recorded in the name of Port Mouton may have happened fairly often.

Incidents, especially accidents, involving people provide a few more examples of incident names. As suggested above, the most common of these, especially along the coast, are 'wreck' names. Scots Bay has already been mentioned, and to it we can add such names as Litchfield Shoal (for the wreck of the *Litchfield*), Malignant Cove (for the wreck of the *Malignant*), Saladin Point (for the wreck of the *Saladin*), Tribune Head (for the wreck of the *Tribune*), and Wreck Cove itself. The Hawk is interesting, traditionally named after a ship grounded there which 'lay on the beach for many years during the early settlement' (*PN*, 1974, p.670).

Spanish Ship Bay may be an incident name, recording the wreck of a Spanish ship (*PN*, 1974, p.637), or it may be a metaphorical descriptive, comparing a nearby headland with the shape of a Spanish galleon. Frenchmans Barn is a curiosity, since it involves a metaphorical descriptive, a rock shaped like a barn, near which a French ship was wrecked (p.223).

Brûlé 'burned' is an interesting incident name, since it 'allegedly originated with an incident involving the Quebec Indians who burnt the woods on the point when they came to fight with the Micmacs' (*PN*, 1974, p.92), and therefore had nothing to do with the subsequent European settlers in the area. On the other hand, one of the traditional explanations for Burntcoat does involve European settlers, recording a marsh-burning incident in 1795 in which Thomas and Robert Faulkner 'lost a coat by hanging it on bushes too near the fire' (p.95), although the other possibility, involving a member of a Privateer's crew who got too near a fire while spending the night ashore, again is not directly related to settlers. Names such as Bobsled Lake, Buckshot Lake, Handsled Lake, and the sinister Murder Lake suggest incidents, but any stories associated with them are not well known. River Philip, if it is not a possessive but rather, as one tradition suggests, is named after 'an Indian called Philip Pedoristack [who] is said to have killed five hundred moose there in one season' (*PN*, 1974, p.578), is yet another incident name, and it seems likely that there are others of this kind, particularly among the many inland lakes and streams named after individuals, but without records they cannot be identified.

Conquerall, with shift names Conquerall Banks and Conquerall Mills, could be regarded as an exclamation incident name: according to *Place-Names and Places of Nova Scotia*, it was the 'Conquerall of the river bank' (1974, p.144), but it is not recorded who actually said this or why.

(f) Minor Classes of Place Names

Stewart's remaining categories account for a relatively small number of Nova Scotian place names. There are a few commendatory names, mainly employing the adjective *pleasant*: among others for example, Pleasant Bay, Pleasant Hills, Pleasant Point in both Halifax and Shelburne counties, Point Pleasant in Halifax itself, and Pleasant Valley in Antigonish, Colchester, Halifax, Pictou, and Yarmouth counties. Goodwood also occurs. Devils Island, the habitat of ghosts, should probably be regarded as a possessive rather than an anti-commendatory name. Great Village, built on marshes which, according to tradition, two explorers agreed 'would be ideal as the site for a great village, and reported that they had seen the Great Village' (*PN*, 1974, p.258) could be regarded as a commendatory name, although the story in itself is rather dubious, since an early Acadian settlement, Vil Le Cadets, already existed on the site, and an alternative English name, Port of Londonderry, was also in use for some years.

Manufactured names, that is, names created out of non-traditional place-name elements which may have been specially invented for the purpose, are very rare indeed. Imperoyal and Ferrona have already been mentioned. Waldegrave, according to *Place-Names and Places of Nova Scotia*, was created from the German *Wald* 'forest' and *Gräf* (a title) (1974, p.705). If this explanation is correct, then the name does not approximate any kind of German place name, but apparently follows the pattern of English names such as Mulgrave in Guysborough County. However, it seems at least as likely that the settlement was named after General Waldegrave.

A few mistake names, generally involving erroneous spelling, occur: Rights River was actually named for a settler called Wright; Weatherley seems to be an attempt, after the original meaning had been forgotten, to make the name look more like an English place name (following the pattern of names such as Beverley), if indeed the origin was actually that it was 'sheltered from Atlantic storms somewhat by the topography of the country' (*PN*, 1974, p.714) — that is, a 'weather lee'; and River John probably results from an attempt to give a sensible English spelling to an Anglicized pronunciation of the original French Rivière Jaune 'yellow river.'

River John, in which the misunderstood second element has been replaced by an English name that makes some sort of sense, leads into the related category of folk etymology. The example of Economy has already been discussed, and it is probable that names such as Hoppenderry, explained as a commemorative (Derry) where the settlers were *hopin'* 'to make sizeable settlement' (*PN*, 1974, p.297), and Joggins in Digby County, apparently a 'jog-in' from the sea (p.317), should be included in this category. An earlier version of Hoppenderry, Obiderry, certainly casts doubt on the suggested etymology. Also interesting are Tennycape, supposedly a locality with ten high points, and Donny Brook, most probably a possessive or straightforward commemorative, but explained as having been given the name Donnybrook for its pejorative connotations of fighting and rowdyism after a number of Irish settlers moved in. Jordan, however, from the Portuguese Ribera des Jardins 'river of gardens' is a straightforward example of folk etymology in the style of River John.

Discussion

Just these few examples of folk etymology show that some of the determining factors in the development of Nova Scotian place names have to do with the forms of the language itself. In some cases, the elements composing the place name may well be English in origin, but in the course of time their meanings have become opaque, so that people no longer recognise their original significance, and substitute meaningful, or more-or-less meaningful elements in their stead. Without good records of earlier versions of the name, it may be impossible to work out what it was intended to mean in the first place. In other cases, the modern version of a name may be a result of language contact. Whether or not European newcomers to Nova Scotia decided to adopt earlier place names or invent their own seems to have been largely a matter of chance. If the European settlers were aware of earlier names, whether in their own language or not, they were often perfectly happy to take them over. Otherwise, they would make up new names. And in a number of cases, settlers decided, for varying reasons, to change earlier names, including those in their own language.

The decision to maintain existing names from other languages is not as surprising as it seems. As mentioned above, Europe is full of place names whose origins are so far in the past, and often in foreign or forgotten languages, that they no longer have any lexical significance to most of the inhabitants, and remain as purely formal identifications of places. (This does not, of course, prevent them from attracting all kinds of emotional connotations.) Thus, there would have been no intrinsic difficulty for most settlers in the idea of taking over an already existing name, even if the name itself were in Mi'kmaq, Acadian French, Portuguese, or Gaelic. There is a strong motivation on the part of most individuals or family groups to devise their own names for their own houses or farms, their own territory, but this feeling usually weakens as the location involved becomes less directly linked to the individual or group. What would matter, therefore, was not necessarily the intelligibility of a given name, but whether it was pronounceable in English (or in French), whether it could be written down in some English (or French) form, and whether it sounded reasonably as if it might be a name. The last factor was not very limiting, since English speakers were long used to all kinds of different names originating in different languages.

Mi'kmaq is an Eastern Algonquian language which is still spoken by many Native people in the Maritime provinces, Maine, and the Gaspé region of Quebec. At the time of European settlement in Nova Scotia, the Mi'kmaw people belonged to the Wapenaki Confederacy, which extended along the northeast coast of North America. The traditional lands of the Mi'kmaq, *Mìgêmewèl Maĝamigal*, are extensive, and do not coincide with twentieth-century political divisions. Of the seven lands of the Mi'kmaq, four, *Gespogwitg*, *Sugapungègati*, *Esgègewàgi*, and *Ùnêmàgi*, are entirely contained within Nova Scotia, *Epegwitg aĝ Pigtug* is partly in Nova Scotia and partly in Prince Edward Island, *Sigunigtewàgi* is partly in Nova Scotia and partly in New Brunswick, and *Gespèg* is partly in New Brunswick and partly in Quebec. Until restrictions were placed on them by the white governments, the Mi'kmaq were a nomadic people, following established seasonal movement patterns related to hunting, trapping, and fishing. However, there were well established villages within the seven lands, even though some of these villages may have been occupied only during certain seasons. For example, there were summer villages '*nipgewèl utann*,' which were regarded as permanent settlements, and the names of several of them, along with other Mi'kmaw names, were taken over by the later European settlers.

The Mi'kmaw language belongs to the class of languages known as polysynthetic; that is, its words tend to consist of a base or stem and one or more affixes. This means that from the point of view of languages such as French or English it appears to have an extremely complex grammatical system, in which the individual words often do not correspond to individual words in the European systems. A further complication for European settlers is the existence of different Mi'kmaw dialects, with subtle variations between them. In addition, many of the sounds of Mi'kmaq are found neither in French nor in English, and the reverse is also true.

The result of these differences is that direct translation from Mi'kmaq to French or English is often difficult, and very few, if any, French or English place names can be considered translations of Mi'kmaw names. For example, Barachois in Colchester County (from *barre-à-cheoir*, referring to 'small ponds near the sea separated only by a sand-bar or neck of land' (*PN*, 1974, p.33)) is not connected linguistically in any way with Tatamagouche (from *Taĝamigujg* 'barred across the entrance with sand'), despite the geographical proximity of the two places. The geographical features of the two locations are in themselves sufficient to produce the similarity in the meanings of the names. Further, in the absence of a written form of the Native language before Dr. Silas Rand's pioneering *Dictionary of the Language of the Micmac Indians* (1888), the actual forms of Mi'kmaw place names could often only be roughly approximated by their European hearers. Thus we find that in cases where the original names have survived, the modern Anglicized forms of identical elements may vary from place to place. For example, modern Pictou represents the element *pugtug*, but so also does the Halifax County district of Chebucto (Mi'kmaq *Jipugtug* 'big *pugtug*').

The suppression of much of the culture of the Mi'kmaq by the white settlers, their general exclusion from many areas where traditionally they had lived, the replacement of many of the original place names with unrelated European names, and the Gallicization and/or Anglicization of the pronunciation of the names which did survive, has led to some obscurity in regard to the basic meanings of some Mi'kmaw place names. For example, *pugtug* is a relatively common place-name element, occurring not merely in Pugtug itself, and Jipugtug, but also in such names, among others, as *Elsipugtug* (now known as Big Cove). The word itself seems to mean 'explosion' or 'fart,' but the significance of this meaning in relation to the specific places so identified has been lost. On the other hand, it is clear from numerous examples that Mi'kmaw place names were chiefly descriptive, with some incident names.

The district of *Sugapunègati* (Anglicized as Shubenacadie) means either 'ground-nut land' or, more probably, 'land of wild potatoes,' and *Esgisoĝonig* (Anglicized as Eskasoni) means 'green boughs.' *Waljìg*, near Pictou Harbour, a name which has not been Anglicized, means 'little snowballs,' which sounds very much like an incident name. Even where the meaning of a name is now obscure, as in *Whycocomagh*, which is thought to mean 'head of the waters' or 'end of the bay,' but which according to Rand meant 'beside the sea' (*PN*, 1974, p.734), the basic descriptive pattern is still evident. In examples where the English 'translation' seems surprisingly lengthy, such as *Gespogwitg* (not Anglicized), which is explained as 'an island that partially disappears with the rising tide' (Delisle and Metallic, 1976, p.516) and *Pubnico* 'land from which the trees have been removed to fit it for cultivation' (*PN*, 1974, p.564), we should probably regard the English explanations as definitions of Mi'kmaw words which have no corresponding term in English. The names themselves are still descriptive.

The chance survival of some Mi'kmaw place names in English forms while others have been replaced with European names poses problems for the Native people which should not be ignored by English-speaking Nova Scotians. At the very least, there is the possibility of a divergence between the name actually used in a locality and the 'official' name (although, of course, this kind of divergence is not limited to English-Mi'kmaq contact situations). For example, in the report of Mi'kmaw guide Henry Peters:

> The biggest trout we ever caught was in the Shelburne River at a place on the map called Sand Beach Lake. That's not the right name for it. All the Bear River guides knew it as Koofang. (Parker, 1990, p.100)

Where the place is larger and better known, the problem may be more significant. For example, in their description of Sugapunègati, Delisle and Metallic write:

> Ula tet nigè sàĝ nèw tèsêgêpênn nipgewèl utann. Nigè gisgug pasêg tapùgul tàn èwasêgêl, Sugapunègati aĝ Gopegwitg. (1976, p.516)

But in their translation they give the English names, not translations of the Mi'kmaw place names, which is also how they deal elsewhere with Mi'kmaw names:

> Now here, a long time ago, there were four summer villages. Now, today, there are only two which are used, Shubenacadie and Truro. (p.516)

The point here is that it would be extremely difficult for the Native people to resist the overwhelming usage of a name such as Truro. Ironically, there is ample evidence that they use not merely the Anglicized forms of such names as Shubenacadie and Kejimkujik, but actually adopt English abbreviations for them, as in the following statements:

> … Terry and me went over to Shubie and we found Wilson Brown working on an old Ford…. and him and Terry and me and two other fellas from Shubie piled in … (Guillemin, 1975, p.166)

and

> My grandfather Freeman Peters and Johnnie Peters came from Peters Point in what is now Kedgie Park…. The biggest Indian settlement was at Kedgie. (Parker, 1990, p.95)

Yet while such abbreviations and even a clearly English name such as Truro may seem a relatively neutral examples of cultural imposition, the replacement of original names by names commemorating such white Governors as Lord Jeffrey Amherst and Lord Edward Cornwallis, whose atrocities against the Mi'kmaq have been clearly demonstrated by Daniel Paul (1993) and others, is a continuing insult to the Native peoples. A further irony lies also in the fact that when renaming does occur, as in the recent decision to rename Cornwallis Place in Halifax Summit Place, the action is not the result of any recognition of the offensiveness of the original name, but rather of the wish to commemorate another external imposition (in this case the 1995 G-7 Summit Meeting).

Folk etymology has already been mentioned, and while not especially frequent in the formation of Nova Scotia place names, it does provide some examples, usually resulting from the Gallicization and/or Anglicization of earlier names. At least one original Mi'kmaw name is interesting in this context: Main-à-Dieu 'God's Hand' in Cape Breton County is actually a Gallicization of the Mi'kmaq *mên'tu* 'devil.' The Basque name Petit-de-Grat (probably 'little fishing-station') also seems to have achieved a certain reversal of meaning in popular usage. As Archibald MacMechan commented:

> On the eastern coast of Cape Breton lie two small islands called Isle Madame and Petit de Grat, familiar to all sea-captains as 'Peter the Great.' (1928, p.125)

However, folk etymology often seems to be an aspect of a more general factor in the development of Nova Scotia place names, and that is the shifting of pronunciation at first toward French, and more recently toward English, or a combination of English and French patterns, as in Sable Island and Sable River, pronounced [sebl]. In the case of Port Mouton, a series of alternative names given by more recent explorers and settlers than De Monts (St. Luke's

Bay, Gambier Harbour, Lebanon) and an Anglicization (Port Mutton) have failed to disturb the original French name, which remains Port Mouton, but the pronunciation has changed considerably to something approximating [pot mʌtun].

Complicating this kind of development is Acadian pronunciation, which differs from Standard French, and in which certain sixteenth and seventeenth-century pronunciations are maintained. Thus L'Ardoise is pronounced not as a French speaker would expect, but more like [lɔdwez], leading R. MacG. Dawson to point out in a note:

> Fr. F. Black, C. S. B.... informs me that the pronunciation of this ... name is regularly /lordways/.... The inhabitants of the village are aware of the meaning of the word *ardoise* ['slate'], but he feels, 'derive a certain small satisfaction out of the religious overtones of /Lordways/.' (1960, p.6)

And keeping the same archaic French pronunciation of *oi* as [e], Port Razoir has moved by folk etymology to the name Roseway, now surviving chiefly as a river-name in Shelburne County.

Occasionally, pronunciation similarities between French and English words of different meaning can lead to confusion, and although the result is usually an English rather than a French name, this does not always happen. River John, from the French Rivière Jaune, and Bear River, in Digby County, from earlier Hebert River (Rivière Hébert, or possibly Rivière Imbert, commemorating a settler) are not altogether surprising. However, Port Hebert in Shelburne County shows the process in reverse. In this case, the earliest French form of the name seems to have been Port-à-l'Ours or Port-aux-Ours, 'because bears were common in the area' (*PN*, 1974, p.548). These were apparently usually translated as Bear Harbour, and less frequently as Port Bear. Later, presumably because bears became less common, or less remarkable, the original meaning of the name was forgotten, although the French origin was not, and it was assumed that the settlement had been named after a settler, although a continuing variation between Port Hebert and Port L'Hebert indicates some uncertainty.

Despite J. B. Rudnyćkyj's assertion that 'the most obvious and common way of adapting the original toponym in the colonial or immigrant languages in Canada was the simple translation' (1972, p.294), it seems that the French and English settlers of Nova Scotia did not on the whole adapt Mi'kmaw names in this way, nor has the dominant English-speaking culture used the method in dealing with names in the languages of other European settlers. Once a name has been established in the opinion of the dominant culture, it does not seem to matter whether its origins are Mi'kmaq, French, Gaelic, German, Portuguese, or any other language. Commonly, an Anglicized pronunciation has developed, but that is all. Where terms, particularly generic terms, are similar in each language, the English form may take over, resulting in hybridizations, such as the replacing of French *rivière* by English *river* in such names as River Bourgeois, River Denys, and River Hébert, and the substitution of the English pronunciation of *port* for the French in such names as Port La Tour and Port Royal (in Annapolis County, where the whole name is pronounced as if it were English). In other cases, especially with the Gaelic generic terms *brae*, *glen*, and *loch*, the terms are treated, as in England and in other former British colonies, as if they were English words, and thus used to form 'English' names. So it is not at all surprising to find such hybrids as Glen Haven and Glen Margaret in areas far from the main Scottish settlements, and the very English Lockside (for *loch*-side) on the banks of Loch Lomond. This does not mean that all settlers understood these terms. As Dawson suggests, the settlement-name of Lochaber was evidently treated as a single morpheme, not composed of two elements, *Loch* and *Aber* 'Lake Aber,' so that 'although Lochaber is indeed on the water, Lochaber Lake is a pleonasm' (1960, p.10).

However, with the cultural dominance of the English language, the formation of hybrid names became very common indeed, giving such examples as Ben Noah 'mount Noah,' Cape Sable 'sandy cape,' Glace Bay 'ice bay,' Port Ban 'white port,' and Shinimicas Bridge 'shining river bridge.' Almost all shift names based on non-English roots are hybrids of this kind, and are also generally given an Anglicized pronunciation, so that we hear, for example, [kep sebl] rather than [kep sabl].

It is possible that this kind of hybridization, as much as the influence of Loyalist settlers, affected the adoption of the element *-ville* mentioned earlier. In addition to the American fashion for this term, English-speaking settlers would have found it in use, following ordinary French naming patterns, in the Acadian areas of the province. Familiarity with such names as Comeauville and Saulnierville may well have reinforced the use of this term in Nova Scotia. There is also the likelihood that English speakers of British descent were in any case more familiar with French place-name elements as opposed to those derived from other languages, as a result of the historical influence of Norman French on English names as well as on the language in general. On the other hand, an overview of place names in Nova Scotia, southern New Brunswick, and the New England states suggests that the place-name elements form a continuum moving southwest through the Maritimes into New England rather than west into the rest of Canada. Such a continuum agrees with patterns of settlement and association, and also allows for the kind of local influence described above.

What is clear from such an overview is that certain elements are common throughout the area. These are mainly English in origin and refer to very ordinary geographical features, e.g., *bay*, *beach*, *boro*(*ugh*), *brook*, *dale*, *fall*(*s*), *field*, *glen*, *hill*, *island*(*s*), *lake*, *land*(*s*), *mo*(*u*)*nt*, *mountain*, *point*(*e*), *pond*, *river*, *spring*(*s*), *to*(*w*)*n*, and *-ville*. Slightly less common, but widely distributed throughout the area are *bluff(s)*, *bridge*, *cap(e)*, *cove*, *ford*, *harbo(u)r*, *haven*, *head*, *isle* (*île*), *junction*, *meadow(s)*, *mill(s)*, *neck*, *port*, *ridge*, *rock(s)*, *station*, *stream*, *valley*, *view*, and *village*. *Glen*, of Celtic origin, was well established as an English term by the eighteenth century, and while some of these terms, including *cape*, *isle*, *point*, *port*, and *-ville*, are certainly supported by French usage, they can also be regarded as established English elements. Notably, almost entirely absent from Nova Scotia is the German element *-burg*, which becomes increasingly common throughout the New England states. However, it is not possible always to appeal to the relative Englishness of a particular element to account for its presence or absence. English elements found in New England but absent from Nova Scotia include *-bury*, *common* (with the exception of the Central Commons in Halifax), *farm(s)*, *gap*, *-ham*, *notch*, *peak*, and *pool*. The equally English *arm*, *creek* (in the sense of a tidal inlet), *glade*, *knoll*, *siding*, and *square* are all found in Nova Scotia but are generally absent from New England.

Reflecting settlement patterns in the area, the most obvious Gaelic terms, such as *ben*, *brae*, *craig*, and *loch*, are peculiar to Nova Scotia. French terms, such as *anse*, *barachois*, *désert*, *étang*, and *portage*, are found in Nova Scotia, New Brunswick, and Maine, where they slowly peter out, sometimes being replaced by translations, as in the Maine term *carry* for *portage*. On the other hand, the common element *station* is gradually replaced in New England by the French *depot*, and *reservoir*, of French origin, appears there alongside *dam*, although neither is found as a place-name element in Nova Scotia.

In the context of translation, the use of *carry* for *portage* is unusual, but it seems reasonable that some of the English terms adopted in Nova Scotia are attempts at translation from French and other languages, rather than traditional English usages. Big Pond, for example, would be a most unexpected name in England itself, where neither element is used in place names, but it seems reasonable as a translation of the French Grand Etang, also found as a place name in the province. In traditional English usage, the most common opposite for *little* is *great*, but by the eighteenth century *great* had acquired other stronger connotations in common use, and the ordinary opposite of *little* was *big*. Given the existence of the easily Anglicized French word *grand*, its use as an alternative for *big*, in names such as Grand Lake, Grand Narrows, and Grand River, is also reasonable.

Pond poses a slightly different problem, since the English element *pool* was available for use, as attested by some place names in New England. However, the French distinction between *lac* and *étang* was one that was not familiar to English speakers, the very few lakes in England having been identified by the archaic English element *-mere*. Again, translation may account for usage in the province, with the French pair *lac/étang* being replaced by the English *lake/pond*, although a glance at the map shows that if the distinction was one of size, it was certainly not applied consistently.

Translation equivalents of this kind may also account for the kind of phrase-name which seems to be unique to Nova Scotia. The group of place names Garden of Eden, Head of Amherst, Head of Jeddore, Head of Loch Lomond, Head of St Margaret's Bay, Head of Wallace, South Bar of Sydney River, South Side of Baddeck River, South Side of Boularderie, and West Side of Middle River have no equivalent in England, although following French practice, some English place names do include prepositional phrases, e.g., Barrow-in-Furness, Newcastle-under-Lyme, and Shoreham-by-Sea. However, the Scottish Gatehouse-of-Fleet probably provides a better clue to the Nova Scotia names, since it is an Anglicized equivalent of a Gaelic naming pattern. In fact, the Scottish Kinlochleven (= *Kin* 'head' [of] Loch Leven) gives the precise pattern of Head of Loch Lomond, with the English *of* inserted to show the grammatical relationship which in Gaelic is indicated by the word order.

In certain other place names in the province, it also seems clear that a Gaelic word order is being followed, without even the insertion of the necessary English preposition. Possessives such as Glen Campbell and Glen Margaret, with a Gaelic word order and no *-'s*, stand alongside Barra Glen and Pipers Glen. With further reinforcement from French word order, in which the adjective generally follows rather than precedes the noun, it is not at all surprising that Nova Scotia is rich in such pairings as Lake Pleasant and Rocky Lake, Point Michaud and Smith Point, Port Malcolm and Ingramport, and River Ryan and Larry's River.

Finally, very characteristic of Nova Scotia is a pattern of complex relative descriptive names which indicate distance, direction, age, size, and so on, in the context of an earlier, but not necessarily central, settlement. In some cases, especially those involving direction, the elements involved come from the English tradition, but a few are relatively new. Both *back* and *rear* are used to indicate a settlement further inland than the original one (Back Settlement, Rear Black River) and *centre* and *central* are used alongside *middle* (Central New Annan, Centre East Pubnico, Middle Musquodoboit). The main elements used are *back*, *big*, *central*, *centre*, *east*, *grand*, *halfway*, *little*, *lower*, *main*, *middle*, *north*, *northeast*, *northwest*, *over*, *rear*, *south*, *southwest*, *upper*, and *west*. The word order is not fixed, so that Iona Rear occurs as well as Rear Forks, and Feltzen South as well as South Brookfield.

As can be imagined, the existence of such compounding elements can lead to the development of complex systems of place names, often including shift names as well, in which a number of places are linked together. The district of Pubnico in Yarmouth County provides an excellent example, with settlements around Pubnico Harbour named Lower West Pubnico, Middle West Pubnico, West Pubnico, Upper West Pubnico, Pubnico, East Pubnico, Middle (or Centre) East Pubnico, Lower East Pubnico, and off to the northeast, Great Pubnico Lake. The meaning of such names is usually self-evident, but they can occasionally be cryptic, as in First South in Lunenburg County. The explanation that this is the first settlement south of the town of Lunenburg is all right if one accepts a local definition of the term *south*, and also helps with two other Lunenburg place names, First Peninsula and Second Peninsula. Ultimately, with such names, we need to know the local priorities, the direction to start from.

This sense of locality, of the centrality of the community itself, is of course what gives many otherwise prosaic Nova Scotia place names their charm, and also the subjection of pedantic rules of English grammar to the feelings of the namers themselves. If a compound works in Gaelic or French, then it can work in English, and produce such attractive names as Sunset Cape North or Quarry St. Anns. If we know where we are, then we should have no trouble gathering at West Branch North River or even at North Side East Bay.

References

Bell, W. P. (1990). *The 'Foreign Protestants' and the settlement of Nova Scotia.* 2nd ed. Sackville, NB: Centre for Canadian Studies & Mount Allison University.

Dawson, R. MacG. (1960). *Place names in Nova Scotia.* Onomastica series: 19. Winnipeg: Ukrainian Free Academy of Sciences.

Delisle, G., & Metallic, E. (1976). *Micmac teaching grammar (preliminary version).* Ecowi, PQ: Manitou College.

Guillemin, J. (1975). *Urban renegades: The cultural strategy of American Indians.* New York: Columbia University Press.

Hill, George W. (1882, rpt. 1911). Nomenclature of the streets of Halifax. *Collections of the Nova Scotia Historical Society 15,* 1-22.

Kristjanson, W. (1965). *The Icelandic people in Manitoba: A Manitoba saga.* Winnipeg: Wallingford Press.

MacMechan, A. (1928). *Old province tales.* 2nd ed. Toronto: McClelland & Stewart.

Miller, T. (1873; 1972). *Historical and genealogical record of the first settlers in Colchester County down to the present time.* Halifax: A. & W. MacKinley; Rpt. Belleville, ON: Mika.

Nova Scotia. Department of Tourism. (1973). *Nova Scotia tour book: An official guide to the highways of Nova Scotia.* Halifax.

Parker, M. (1990). *Guides of the North Woods: Hunting and fishing tales from Nova Scotia 1860-1960.* Halifax: Nimbus.

Place-names and places of Nova Scotia. (1974). Belleville, ON: Mika.

Rand, S. (1888). *Dictionary of the language of the Micmac Indians who reside in Nova Scotia, New Brunswick, Prince Edward Island, Cape Breton and Newfoundland.* Halifax: Nova Scotia Printing Company.

Rudnyćkyj, J. (1972). Names in contact: Canadian pattern. In H. Dorion (Ed.), *Les noms de lieux et le contact des langues: Place names and language contact.* Quebec: Les presses de l'université Laval.

Stewart, G. (1975). *Names on the globe.* New York: Oxford University Press.

Chapter Seven

Reactions to Three Types of Speech Sample from Rural Black and White Children

John Edwards

Editors' Introduction

The traditional study of linguistics has largely concerned itself with an examination of language, both written and spoken, from a fairly objective point of view; that is, linguists are concerned with identifying systematic variations in language and working out what these patterns mean. For example, certain grammatical features, along with specific items of vocabulary, and pronunciations may be used to identify a regional dialect. Lexical items alone, and especially the use of otherwise ordinary words in very specialized meanings may be helpful in identifying an occupational jargon. At a very detailed level, noting which individual sounds carry meaning, and which are merely variations caused by the surrounding sounds, allows a systematic distinction to be made between the phonemes and allophones of a language or dialect.

Using a somewhat different approach, sociologists have long recognized that language is essentially a social act, and that systematic language variations, and especially speech variations, are identifying features of particular socioeconomic groups. The study of language in a social context, as opposed to a purely linguistic one, comprises the special discipline known as sociolinguistics. But in fact, it is not merely sociologists and linguists who recognize the social significance of language use. Almost all of us are able to tell from the speech of strangers whether they speak our own regional dialect or another, even if we do not have the knowledge to tell what the other dialect is. And in so far as we recognize a 'standard' dialect of English, we can tell whether strangers conform to that standard or not. Further, we generally recognize from experience whether an occasion is formal or not, and so vary our register appropriately; that is, we can tell from the circumstances whether we should be careful about our choice of words, or whether it is okay to use slang.

In the past, the attitude taken by linguists towards these variations has been a relatively neutral one. Linguists are not concerned about so-called 'correct' English, since from a linguistic point of view any one dialect is just as correct as any other: the patterns of Lunenburg English may not be the same as the patterns of Halifax Standard, but linguistically neither of the dialects is superior or inferior to the other. Equally, sociologists are not concerned with correctness, seeing the speech patterns as identifying features of a group, or of an occasion, and correct or incorrect only in so far as they are appropriate to the group or the occasion.

Both linguists and sociologists are aware, however, that dialects and registers of English are not viewed by most speakers in this neutral way, but are assigned certain social values. The dialect generally recognized as standard, usually the dialect of the educated, urban, professional classes (that is, a specific socioeconomic dialect), is widely thought of as being superior to other dialects, and people who do not use the standard dialect are therefore considered in some way inferior to those who do. Since institutionalized education has insisted for a long time that students should use the standard English dialect rather than a local variation, we have become used to nonstandard speech being described in such terms as 'rough' or 'uneducated.'

There is no point in denying the general usefulness of a standard dialect for any communication outside a small local area, but it is debatable how far a nonstandard dialect interferes in any serious way with such communication. Recently, attitudes of educators and others have softened towards many nonstandard usages, and some variations are even regarded as attractive, adding (ironically, as the following chapter may suggest) to the charm or friendliness of a particular speaker. However, most educational institutions still insist on fluency in the standard dialect as an essential feature of successful 'education.'

Given this insistence, it is easy enough to understand that a Grade 1 student whose family speaks a nonstandard dialect is not in any sense less 'educated' than a student from a family speaking standard English, but that the latter student begins formal education with a definite advantage. If the former student has not merely to learn the standard dialect, but also suffers from a variety of prejudices directed against nonstandard speakers, then the burden of acquiring the standard language, and the formal education associated with it, may well become intolerable.

Most educators nowadays are aware of such problems, and would not deliberately put down a child just because he or she is Black, or comes from an Acadian family. In fact, they may think that they go out of their way to encourage such 'disadvantaged' children, without ever realizing the extent or the effect of their own cultural prejudices.

We are all used to the phenomenon of disliking another person, and may even say we dislike the way the person speaks, quite sincerely regarding the particular mode of speech as an aspect of the individual's personality. Indeed, if what we refer to is the use of sarcasm, or the deliberate use of distant and unfriendly terms, then we are arguably correct in our judgment. However, if what we dislike is a 'nasal twang,' or a 'drawl,' then we may well be using a prejudice against a regional variation in language to put down the speaker, and if such a linguistic feature is the chief basis of our dislike, we may be altogether unjustified in our feelings. The point is that we make judgments about other people based on our contacts with them, and our own linguistic prejudices enter quite largely into these judgments.

In the following chapter, John Edwards describes and analyses a sociolinguistic research project carried out a few years ago with a group of student teachers in Antigonish, Nova Scotia. These student teachers listened to a number of tapes of individual children performing various linguistic exercises, and made judgments about each child's intelligence, attractiveness, potential for success, and so on, based on what they heard. The student teachers were not familiar with the children in the way their class teachers would have been, so the question of personally liking or disliking individual children, or even of identifying them, did not arise, and since audio tapes were used, the possibility of prejudice against *visible* minorities was eliminated. The results of the study are complex, showing that the judgments we make based on an individual's speech alone include such apparently extra-linguistic factors as the speaker's sex. On the positive side, they do not reveal the existence of gross prejudices among the student teachers, many of whom presumably work in the provincial school system now. However, they do not establish the absence of prejudice either.

Sociolinguistic studies like the following one may give us a lot of information about how our language works in a social context. The 'how,' of course, is often intrinsically interesting in itself. But what is also interesting, and perhaps of greater significance to us, is the revelation of the complexity of our use of language in our social relationships, and the close connections between our linguistic and our social attitudes. *(LF & MH)*

***

Reactions to Three Types of Speech Sample from Rural Black and White Children

by John Edwards

Central to any study of language in society is the question of *attitude*. Different varieties of language may evoke different perceptions of their speakers and, indeed, most readers will know themselves that virtually everyone has linguistic preferences or prejudices, that we often categorize people at least partly on the basis of their speech, and that differences in social status are often associated with language variations. The contribution of language to stereotyping in this way is a very long-standing one — in fact, we might well suppose that wherever language varieties have differed, someone has thought to attach social significance to this difference.

In 1605, Richard Carew, an English poet and antiquary, observed that Italian was 'pleasant, but without sinews,' French 'delicate,' and Spanish 'majestical but fulsome.' This would seem to accord roughly with the views of Charles V, Holy Roman Emperor (1500-1558), who allegedly said that he spoke Spanish to God, Italian to women, and French to men. German, incidentally, was for his horse. Later, when Voltaire visited the court in Berlin, he found French language and culture emphasized, while '*l'allemand est pour les soldats et pour les chevaux*' (Waterman, 1966, p.138). These are all preferences at the level of *language* itself, but varieties *within* languages (including dialects, accents, and styles) have also attracted attention throughout history. About 50 B.C., Publilius Syrus noted in his *Sententiae* that 'speech is a mirror of the soul,' a sentiment echoed seventeen centuries later by Ben Jonson: 'Language most shows a man: speak, that I may see thee.' More contemporary still is George Bernard Shaw's observation that '[i]t is impossible for an Englishman to open his mouth, without making some other Englishman despise him'; or Thomas Hardy's statement about the 'use of dialect words — those terrible marks of the beast to the truly genteel.' Finally, here, the common phenomenon of linguistic manipulation or incongruity — as, for example, having a stage duchess speak with a Cockney accent, or as found in innumerable jokes and comic routines — indicates the rich evaluative dimension in language. The extent to which we, as members of a given speech community, can appreciate and give meaning to this is surely evidence of both the power of language attitudes and their deeply ingrained nature.

It is not surprising, then, that within the disciplines of linguistics, sociology, and psychology there exist subdisciplines — sociolinguistics, the sociology of language, and the social psychology of language — primarily concerned with what we could generally term the 'social life of language.' We want to know how attitudes and perceptions arise, how different groups come to possess different varieties of language, and what the consequences may be. Again, at an anecdotal level, we can all appreciate that not only does linguistic variation give rise to incongruity and humour, but that it may also reflect, or create, more serious matters. The fact, for example, that we would notice and be disturbed by a doctor or lawyer who said something like, 'Just take a seat, would ya? I ain't gonna be too much longer with this guy on the phone,' reveals how powerful are our expectations of the relationships between speech and status. And, of course, the subject of this chapter has to do with linguistic issues in the important educational context. However, before turning to specifics, let us briefly consider some important general issues.

First, how is it that different speech styles evoke differing reactions? How do negative reactions to some lower-class speech patterns develop, and positive ones towards the speech styles of the upper middle class? Three possibilities suggest themselves. Firstly, perhaps different speech varieties differ in terms of linguistic effectiveness, logic, or succinctness. That is, perhaps there exists a purely linguistic dimension along which varieties range and according to which they are judged, thus acquiring over time particular connotations. Secondly, perhaps different varieties have different degrees of attractiveness. Perhaps the language used by an educated CBC news reader is inherently more pleasant than that of, say, an outport fisherman, and perhaps it is this *aesthetic* quality which elicits positive attitudes. Thirdly, different reactions to varieties of speech might be due to the differing social and political status of their speakers. This implies that, regardless of alleged linguistic or aesthetic qualities, the speech styles of the powerful would come to have the most favourable connotations.

In fact, evidence suggests that only the third of these possibilities is at all likely. Linguistic and anthropological evidence has shown that, at the level of *language*, no reasonable claim can be made for one form being 'better' or 'worse' than another; it is thus not possible to say that French is better, or more logical, or more expressive than English. And this evidently applies across the board, whether one restricts oneself to standardized and written languages, or whether one includes *all* languages. Gleitman and Gleitman (1970) have been quite explicit on this point, and state that no one has been able to find a 'primitive' language. Lenneberg (1967) made much the same observation. The notion, he states, of the primitive language has been 'thoroughly discredited by virtually all students of language' (p.364). Many years ago, Sapir noted that 'when it comes to linguistic form, Plato walks with the Macedonian swineherd, Confucius with the head-hunting savage of Assam' (Guy, 1988, p.64); although we might not put things quite like that today, Sapir's thesis has proved convincing to anthropologists and linguists. The extension of this point to varieties within a language, however, has been a more recent phenomenon, although it is clearly a logical extension. Trudgill (1975) points out that 'just as there is no linguistic reason for arguing that Gaelic is superior to Chinese, so no English dialect can be claimed to be linguistically superior or inferior to any other' (p.26). In short, the linguistic 'logic' attaching to different varieties is simply equivalent to the relevant grammar — which itself is clearly a product of long-term convention and usage. It must be noted, though, that, even within the academic community, the linguistic 'goodness' of all dialects has not remained unchallenged (see Honey, 1983; Edwards, 1983).

The second possibility, that some forms are inherently more aesthetically appealing, or pleasant, is impossible to test within the speech community in which connotations are deeply ingrained. If it could be found, however, that listeners unaware of the social conventions relating to certain speech styles still judged some to be more 'pleasant' than others, then there would clearly be something to the aesthetic hypothesis. Two studies by Giles and his colleagues are relevant here. Giles, Bourhis, Trudgill, and Lewis (1974) asked British undergraduates ignorant of Greek to evaluate the aesthetic quality of Athenian and Cretan varieties. The former is, within the Greek community, the prestige form, while the second is perceived as a low-status variant. Yet, these British judges were able to make no significant distinctions between the two in terms of pleasantness or prestige. In fact, there was a slight tendency for the Cretan variety to be evaluated more positively. In the second study, Giles, Bourhis, and Davies (1975) had Welsh students rate European French, educated Canadian French, and working-class Canadian French voice samples. Although within Quebec there existed clear preferences, on aesthetic grounds, for the European variety, these judges were unable to single out any one of the varieties as being more pleasant than the others. Things have changed in Quebec, of course, since the Giles studies; one might suggest that the full impact of the 'Quiet Revolution' and the resurgence of Quebec nationalism, with its renewal of group self-esteem, will have altered language perceptions. This makes a good argument, incidentally, for using language studies as windows into social dynamics. Generally, it seems reasonable to suggest that, when preferences are expressed for a certain speech style on aesthetic grounds, these are the products of a great deal of social learning. Aesthetic qualities do not appear to inhere in the varieties themselves.

This leaves us with the third explanation for differential dialect evaluation. It is that such evaluation rests upon social stereotypes which reflect differing perceived status of the speakers. Thus, we would expect that in stratified societies the speech styles of those in power would be the ones evoking the most favourable judgments. Although not possessing any inherent linguistic or aesthetic superiority, these varieties float to the top, as it were, along with their speakers. The so-called Standard English *is* standard because of the formidable influence of its speakers. Standards, where they exist, are the dialects of those who dominate. It follows, then, that all other varieties can be logically termed *nonstandard*, but this must be understood as a completely non-pejorative description (and certainly not equivalent to the inadmissible *substandard*).

I have simplified things somewhat here. Although it is the case that national or regional standards are generally evaluated most favourably in terms of prestige, they may not evoke such reactions along other dimensions. Lambert (1967) categorized dimensions along which speech is usually evaluated into three broad groups. Some reflect speaker *competence* (e.g., dimensions like intelligence, industriousness, etc.), some *personal integrity* (helpfulness, trustworthiness, etc.), and some *social attractiveness* (friendliness, sense of humour, etc.). Thus, Giles (1971, 1973) found that the British 'Received Pronunciation' (RP: roughly, 'BBC English' or 'Queen's English') evoked most positive ratings in terms of competence; regional varieties of English were seen more favourably in terms of integrity and attractiveness (see also Edwards, 1989). It is clear, in other words, that evaluations of speech varieties need not be unidimensional; local varieties may evoke sentiments of 'solidarity' which will be reflected in more positive ratings of the warmth and friendliness of the speaker. There also exist differences among nonstandard variants. Trudgill (1975) suggests, for example, that in Britain urban speech patterns are often seen as more unpleasant than are rural varieties. A speaker of Devon English might therefore fare better than a Liverpool speaker. And, as well, there is also the factor of the dialect possessed by the evaluator. To summarize here: standard varieties usually evoke greater prestige or competence ratings, although some regional varieties may elicit positive evaluations of speaker integrity or attractiveness, at least when the judges are themselves regional speakers (and possibly when they are not, too; see Edwards, 1989).

A recent study by Edwards and Jacobsen (1987) revealed some further complications. In a Nova Scotia context in which speakers and judges were university students, four varieties of English were assessed — Cape Breton, Newfoundland, mainland Nova Scotia, and Massachusetts. While the mainland variety clearly operated as a standard here, inasmuch as it evoked high ratings of speaker competence, success, and status, it *also* fared well in terms of integrity and attractiveness. The suggestion is that this variety figured as a 'regional standard' and thus possessed *both* the status/competence attributes of standards *and* the solidarity dimension of a local and (in the larger context) nonstandard form.

It is probable that the competence dimension on which standard varieties are seen most favourably is the single most important one in contexts of *contact* between nonstandard and standard speech. The salient feature here is that this contact usually involves groups of unequal power or status; consequently, it is not difficult to guess which group's language is downgraded, nor to understand how speech *differences* become translated into substantive social *deficits*.

Here, the educational context in particular may prove problematic: the school is the single most important point of contact between standard and nonstandard speakers, for several reasons. First, the school is a powerful and visible standard-speaking institution; second, school usually represents a child's first sustained 'break' from the home environment and local dialect community; third, the school receives and works with the child at a young and impressionable age; fourth, the influence of the school extends over at least a decade for most children. We might expect, then, that certain children may find the way they speak disadvantageous. In particular, members of low socioeconomic status groups and minorities are most important here. Of course, membership in these two groups is often held jointly. Visible minorities in America, immigrants to the New World, 'guest workers' in Europe — all these are minority groups which are also poor in material terms and subordinate in sociopolitical status.

Many studies have demonstrated that the speech styles of children from such groups are negatively characterized by teachers and others, and some examples will be discussed here. Before doing so, however, it is salutary to recall exactly what it is that negative evaluations imply. Proceeding not from any inherent linguistic or aesthetic basis, but related instead to the low status of the speakers, these evaluations may unfairly hinder children's school progress. Two decades ago, Rist (1970) sketched out the well-known 'self-fulfilling prophecy' here. Teachers, on the basis of children's speech and other attributes, may feel some to be less capable than others and may communicate this in subtle (and not-so-subtle) ways to the children. Sensitive to this, the children may respond at the level expected, do less well than others, and in time confirm the initial expectations. The important aspect of extrapolating from speech and using preferences and prejudices as bases for educational assessment is that teachers' evaluations of children contribute to this circular process in an unnecessary, unfair, and damaging way.

Two studies by Edwards (1977, 1979a) investigated reactions to lower-class and middle-class speech in Dublin, Ireland. In the first study, it was found that the lower-class children's speech was rated less favourably than that of their middle-class counterparts, by adult middle-class judges, on the dimensions of fluency, intelligence, vocabulary, pronunciation/intonation, and communicative ability. In the second study, teachers-in-training evaluated lower-class children less favourably on *every one* of 17 dimensions (e.g., fluency, intelligence, enthusiasm, likely school achievement, social status, etc.). It was suggested that these reactions proceeded from an overall stereotype of disadvantaged children (and a rather unidimensional one, at that).

Another study is that of Seligman, Tucker, and Lambert (1972), conducted in Montreal. Evaluators were presented with eight 'hypothetical' children who had been constructed out of all possible combinations of pre-judged 'good' and 'poor' voices, photographs, and drawings/compositions. While all types of information affected the evaluations made, the authors noted that speech was always a cue of importance. Even in the presence of other information (which, here, could be manipulated as desired) speech remained a salient and potentially stereotype-provoking variable.

While an increasing degree of linguistic tolerance nowadays has been documented (Edwards, 1989), a recent investigation by Edwards and McKinnon (1987) showed negative reactions of Nova Scotia teachers to certain groups of children; these were linked, by the teachers themselves, to speech characteristics. Black and Acadian-heritage children in English schools in the northeastern part of the province were particularly referred to by the 96 teachers surveyed as incapable of properly articulating their thoughts, as placing little value on receptive and expressive language skills generally, and (in the case of the Black students) as having a 'slang' language all their own — and being unwilling to use 'proper' English.

Given the larger social treatment of lower-class and minority populations, it is perhaps not very surprising that children from these groups should fare poorly in speech-evaluation studies. Nevertheless, the matter remains one of concern, especially within the school context. While we realize that teachers are people first, and thus not at all immune to social conventions in linguistic matters, it is still disappointing to see them conforming to larger and inaccurate social stereotypes. Teachers, after all, are rather special here. We can recall the work of Rist on the self-fulfilling prophecy, and how teachers' expectations may lead to performance differences among children. This indicated how important the bases for these expectations are. For, while expectancies are perfectly normal things for teachers (and others) to possess, it is disturbing to realize their potentially harmful effects if based upon inaccurate or stereotype judgments (useful discussion of teacher expectancies is found in Dusek & Joseph, 1983; see also the classic, if much-criticized, studies of Rosenthal & Jacobsen, 1968).

So, the crux of the matter is this: we know that certain social groups are viewed less favourably than others, that their speech patterns are a factor in this, and that children may be unfairly or inaccurately perceived at school. This is a phenomenon of some generality; indeed, we may expect it wherever there exist both social stratification and a standard dialect — in other words, very widely indeed.

It should be noted here that speech studies do not all use the same *type* of sample when eliciting judges' evaluations. Edwards (1979a) and Seligman, Tucker, and Lambert (1972) employed reading passages; Edwards (1977) used a story-retelling task, and a study of Black American children by Williams (1976; not discussed here) used more-or-less spontaneous speech on preselected topics. These differences may confound attempts to generalize across studies. It may be the case that reading, say, is a more natural activity for some children than for others, or that more spontaneous speech will bring out different linguistic qualities in different groups. Certainly, reading and more spontaneous speech differ considerably in terms of formality. Here, we could recall the work of Joos (1967), who postulated five sociolinguistic styles ranging from the highly formal (frozen) to the very informal (intimate). He discusses the attributes of each, as well as the contexts in which each tends to be elicited. Suffice it to say here that all speakers have a range of possibilities open to them, in any situation, from which they may make a choice. Whether speakers select from their repertoire in ways which seem context-appropriate to others is, of course, another very interesting matter.

Some speakers, traditionally downgraded in speech-evaluation studies, are reported to have rich and articulate speech styles, particularly in less formal contexts. For example, the Black speakers so profoundly misunderstood by compensatory-education theorists like Bereiter and Engelmann (1966) were seen to be possessors of a vital oral culture by Labov (1973) and others. Where Bereiter and Engelmann saw Black children as lacking rudimentary forms of dialogue, as unable to recognize single words, and as viewing language as something dispensable in social life, Labov described a community 'bathed in verbal stimulation from morning to night' (p.33). He demonstrated quite effectively that changing the experimenter-child interaction from a formal and presumably intimidating one into a more relaxed, informal 'interview' vastly increased the child's verbal output. Labov's work, incidentally, was also a classic demonstration of the linguistic validity of Black English — a useful test case, since that variety was so long seen as an inferior approximation to 'proper' English. The 'non-verbal' child of Bereiter and Engelmann was thus replaced by the verbal one of Labov. The command of language in the community setting, the use of metaphor and allusion, and the proficiency at rapid-fire and demanding verbal exchanges all show that the Black speaker, far from being verbally deprived, is a talented language user and innovator (see Edwards, 1989).

Any study which involves reactions to speech must be aware of the range of styles possible, and should select from them one which seems the most appropriate for the issue at hand, or attempt to investigate how style differences may influence evaluations received. This second approach is the one taken in this study, which investigated reactions to speech samples from three groups of rural children in Nova Scotia.

The first aspect of the study was to attempt to assess differences in evaluations of different *types* of speech. As will be seen below, three degrees of speech formality were presented to judges here. The second thrust was to extend the generality of previous findings, few of which have dealt with rural populations. In this study there was a group of white children representative of the dominant English-speaking community. There were also two minority groups — children of Acadian background and Black children. Earlier work (Gillis, 1978) had found some evidence of differential reactions here; ratings of the speech of Black children were found to be less favourable than those elicited by the speech of children from the other two groups. It should be pointed out that the intent in the present work was *not* to conduct a linguistic analysis of the three groups' speech patterns, but rather to study reactions to that speech. If the reactions differ, then it is reasonable to suggest that differences exist among the speech styles, but this was not the focus here and consequently it is not possible to point to specific language features contributing to differences in evaluations; rather, the intent is to suggest more global stereotypes related to speech.

Method

For the larger investigation of which this study is a part, 107 school children supplied three tape-recorded speech samples each (see below). All children were drawn from rural populations in northeastern Nova Scotia, and all were students in English-medium schools. As noted above, three groups were involved: Black children, white children of Acadian background (hereafter referred to as Acadians), and white children from the dominant English-speaking community (referred to as Anglos). At each of three grade levels (only two of these were used for analysis here, as the number in the third was insufficient for present comparisons) in each of three communities, all of the available children participated. The numbers thus reflect real-life distributions, making provision for the small number of children for whom permission to tape was not granted by parents. From these totals, 18 children (three boys and three girls at each of the three populations) from each of Grades 3 and 5 participated in the present study. The average age of the Grade 3 children was 9 years 7 months; for the Grade 5 children it was 11 years 3 months. All 36 children were selected on the basis of their average scholastic standing.

Each child provided three types of speech sample. First, an unfamiliar English reading passage was selected for each of the two grade levels with the assistance of teachers. The Grade 3 passage was a 222-word selection about kite-flying. The Grade 5 selection, 301 words in length, told the story of a farm cat. Second, a story-retelling procedure was employed. This is a variation on a theme of Piaget (1955) and Houston (1973). In the original version, the experimenter tells one child a story, that child tells it to another, and the second child repeats it to the experimenter. In the adapted version used here (see also Edwards, 1977), the experimenter tells the child a story, and the child tells it back to the experimenter. This variant, which seems to work well, is obviously less formal than a reading passage. It has enough of a play element to hold the child's interest, and it allows some common basis of comparison across children while obviously also allowing considerable freedom of speech. The stories used here were, for the Grade 3 children, a tale about a circus elephant (approximately 650 words) and, for the Grade 5 group, a story about animals and robbers of about 700 words. The third type of speech was a still more informal one. Children were encouraged to speak freely on any topic of interest to them.

Each child was seen individually for the taping session, which took place at school, and which was conducted by a female assistant. The reading passage was recorded first, after the child was given an initial, unrecorded run-through. Second, the story-retelling was recorded; occasionally a child was prompted here if there was a lengthy pause. Finally, the child was asked to talk about something of interest and, after a topic was decided upon, the recording commenced.

All recordings were evaluated by student teachers (white, female English speakers). Three judges rated each of the Grade 3 children's speech samples, and five evaluated the Grade 5 children. Judges heard the reading and the story-retelling passages in their entirety, while the spontaneous speech samples were presented in a form cut to between 60 and 90 seconds to achieve a rough uniformity across children. Reading passage times averaged 133 seconds for the Grade 3 group and 134 seconds for the Grade 5 children; story-retelling times were, on average, 116 seconds and 129 seconds for the Grade 3 and Grade 5 groups respectively.

Raters for each of the grade-level groups attended three one-hour sessions in a language laboratory. In the first session, they heard the children reading, in the second the children were engaged in the spontaneous speech and, on the third occasion, judges listened to story-retelling samples. Although the variable *type of speech* represents a replicated measure here, the judges were not told that they would be hearing the same children in each of the three sessions.

Each rater was given a booklet for each session containing the same number of pages as there were children to be evaluated. Each page comprised 15 seven-point scales, drawn from previous work (see Edwards, 1989). Nine of these scales reflected the three broad personality dimensions mentioned above; thus scales relating to intelligence, ambition, and confidence all reflect speaker *competence*; those relating to sincerity, generosity, and reliability reflect speaker *integrity*; scales dealing with likeability, cooperativeness, and warmth reflect *social attractiveness*. In addition, there were six other scales, dealing with school and school-related matters: social status, pronunciation, likely school success, vocabulary, fluency, and degree of disadvantage. Judges were told only the children's grade level, not their sex (see below).

The ratings of judges were totalled so that, on each scale (and, consequently, on each of the three broad dimensions which the first nine scales represented), children received one score for each type of speech sample. In short, the design was a three-way analysis: group (Black, Anglo, Acadian); by sex of child (an important variable, since much previous work has demonstrated the unequal school performance of girls and boys; see the Discussion, below); and by type of speech (reading, story-retelling, spontaneous speech). The last measure here is a repeated one within subjects (children). Separate analyses were performed at each grade level, for each of the three personality dimensions and six 'other' scales.

Results

In this section, technical details of the analyses, including cell totals and significance levels are omitted; they are, however, available upon request from the author. Generally, the analyses performed allow us to see how ratings received on the 15 scales relate to the three main variables in the study (group, sex, and type of speech), and to interactions among them. The word 'significant' refers here to differences which are statistically meaningful, while a 'trend' indicates a difference of lesser import; it should be noted, though, that statistically non-significant trends may still have some illuminative value. We will note, first, the results pertaining to the main variables, and then proceed to interesting interactions.

(a) *The Student-Sex Factor*
The first main variable is perhaps of the least direct interest for this study but, as noted above, is of broader concern in all educational investigations. On the personality dimensions, at both grade levels, the girls received more favourable ratings than did the boys. This was significant in two cases (Grade 3 *attractiveness* and Grade 5 *competence*) and approached significance in the other instances. On all six of the other, scholastically oriented scales, girls were rated significantly more positively than boys, at both grade levels.

(b) *The Group Factor*
This factor was significant only on the *competence* dimension at the Grade 5 level (when we consider the three broad personality dimensions). Here the Anglo children were evaluated more positively than the Acadians who, in turn, were viewed more favourably than the Black children. In the other five analyses here, no significant group differences were detected; however, it is worth noting that the *trend* in every case was the same — Black children were rated least positively and Anglo and Acadian children most positively.

This trend can also be seen when we turn to the six remaining dimensions. Here the Anglo children always received the most positive evaluations, followed by the Acadians, with the Black children in third place. The trend was significant on all six scales at the Grade 5 level, and non-significant on the scales at the lower grade level.

(c) *The Speech Type Factor*
With regard to *competence*, *integrity*, and *attractiveness*, there was a clear trend here. At both grade levels, spontaneous speech provoked the highest ratings. In four cases, reading was next most favourable; in the other two, story-retelling was in second place. Results were significant here on three of the six analyses — the *competence* dimension at both grade levels and the *attractiveness* dimension at the Grade 3 level.

Spontaneous speech always elicited the most positive evaluations on the other six dimensions as well. This trend, although entirely consistent, only reached significance on the Grade 3 *school success* dimension.

(d) *Significant Interactions*
Among the analyses of the three personality dimensions, there was a significant group by speech type interaction on two of the Grade 3 dimensions, those of *integrity* and *competence*. In each case, inspection of ratings revealed that Black children were profiting most, as it were, from the spontaneous speech

evaluations. Or, to put it another way, the differences in evaluations between Black children's reading/story-retelling and spontaneous speech productions were much more marked than were those pertaining to the other two groups of children. There was a trend here for the remaining Grade 5 dimension too, as well as for the three Grade 3 dimensions.

Among the other six dimensions, significant group by speech type interactions were found on all Grade 5 dimensions except that of *disadvantage*, where there was, nevertheless, a trend in this direction. As with the results just noted, it was among the Black children that the spontaneous speech evaluations were most differentiated from the other two speech types.

On two dimensions at the Grade 3 level, *integrity* and *pronunciation*, there was a significant sex by speech type interaction. This indicated that while boys consistently received higher ratings for spontaneous speech, girls fared better in reading. There was also a tendency to this result on the Grade 3 dimensions of *vocabulary*, *fluency*, and *disadvantage*, and on the Grade 5 dimensions of *pronunciation*, *school success*, and *disadvantage*.

Finally here, on the Grade 3 dimensions of *status*, *pronunciation*, *vocabulary*, and *fluency*, there was found a significant sex by group interaction. This reflected the fact that girls among the Black group actually fared more poorly than boys, unlike their counterparts in the other two groups. There was a tendency for this to be the case on the remaining two of the six scholastically oriented scales at this grade level as well, though not on the three personality dimensions of *attractiveness*, *integrity*, and *competence*.

Discussion and Conclusions

To begin again with the sex factor, a large number of studies have demonstrated more favourable evaluations of girls than of boys in academic settings. This may be related to the preponderance of female teachers in elementary schooling, at least in North America, and may also be related to certain personality characteristics of girls which make academic acceptance easier (see Edwards, 1989). The present study's findings tend to support this earlier work, especially with regard to the dimensions relating primarily to school-oriented characteristics. Generally, the findings regarding student sex are consistent across the other variables, although there were some significant sex by speech type interactions. These, if anything, tend to confirm the school-related superiority perceived of girls over boys inasmuch as, on scales relating mainly to school success, girls were perceived more favourably at the formal and school-oriented task of reading, while boys were rated more positively on the more informal spontaneous speech task. There were also found, at the Grade 5 level, significant interactions between student sex and group, showing that Black girls were rated more poorly than boys. This clearly goes against the general trend. It may be related to the fact that the judges here were white and made numerous errors of sex-identification of Black girls at the Grade 5 level. That is, it is quite possible here that girls did more poorly than boys because their sex was not clearly identified; hence, the sex-stereotypes operating in tasks of this kind became confused (see, on this point, Edwards, 1979b).

When we turn to consider the results of the group factor, we can note some obvious differences in evaluations given to Black, Anglo, and Acadian children. On the three broad personality dimensions, the group factor was significant only on *competence* at the Grade 5 level, although Black children were consistently rated less favourably than the other two groups. In fact, the general trend is for little difference between Anglo and Acadian children, but noticeable, if not significant, differences between these two groups and the Black children. These differences are more marked at the Grade 5 level than among the younger children and it is worth speculating here that, with regard to the latter, differences may not be as expected as they might among older children, where scholastic achievement has become more important (it *is* only a speculation, of course, since there were different children involved here). This speculation is supported by the findings relating to group differences on the six school-related scales. Here, in every case at both grades, Anglo children received the most favourable ratings, followed by the Acadian children, and then the Black children. Significance was achieved here on all six scales at the higher grade level.

Overall, then, with regard to the group factor, it appears as if the familiar results of earlier studies are essentially confirmed here. Black children are evaluated least positively and Anglo children most favourably. Two things remain to be explained. First, why was significance not found on *all* scales, as was the case, for example, in the Edwards (1979a) study? Second, why did Acadian children actually fare better, in some cases, than the Anglo children?

As regards the first point, it is probable that the clear urban trends found in Edwards (1979a) and in other studies are not replicable among rural children where distinctions between standard and nonstandard are not, perhaps, so clearcut (see Edwards & Jacobsen, 1987). That is, were a comparison to be done between rural white and urban white children, the former would probably be judged as less standard. Work with white rural children in the United States (e.g., Appalachian populations) tends to support this. To put it another way, the present 'standard' Anglo population and the more nonstandard Acadian population are probably not so far apart as these labels would suggest.

With regard to the second point, the younger Acadian children especially are, therefore, probably not so different from the Anglo group as first might be supposed. Also here we should bear in mind that the older Acadian children are more French in their speech than the younger ones. That is, the community in which they live is following the usual patterns of increasing assimilation to the English-speaking milieu. Consequently, the amount of French used in the home is decreasing and the younger children are becoming less linguistically distinguishable from their Anglo counterparts. This probably explains why the Anglo-Acadian differences are generally smaller at the lower grade level than at the Grade 5 level (but see the earlier caution about speculation).

Finally, we come to the effects of the type of speech sample. Here the general tendency is clear — less formal speech produces more favourable ratings (especially among boys; see above). It must be admitted, of course, that significance was only reached here in four cases: grade 3 *attractiveness*, *competence*, and *school success*, and Grade 5 *competence*. Yet the trend is uniform elsewhere and the order of importance (in terms of provoking favourable reactions) of the three speech types does not vary randomly. The interactions of group and speech type are very interesting here since they reveal that Black children profit most from less formal speech situations. This was a general trend throughout, which proved significant mainly at the upper grade level.

A main focus of this study was, of course, upon the effects of varying speech styles. Here it has been possible to demonstrate that more informal speech generally provokes the most positive reactions, in terms of overall personality assessments as well as on more school-oriented dimensions. This surely has implications for all whose work involves children and speech samples. At the very least, it brings to mind the cautions of Goffman (1972) and others that to neglect the situation in which speech is assessed is to neglect something of great importance. In this study, the speech situation was manipulated; in others, it may be possible to study more naturally occurring situations. In either case, investigators should be aware that favourableness of impressions may vary with situation type. There was some indication here that this will be more salient for boys, since girls in this study showed a tendency to fare better under more formal (one might say school-like) conditions. It is interesting to note, further, that the big differences occurred between spontaneous speech and reading/story-retelling. That is, the latter two, although introduced as occupying different positions on the formality continuum, seem not to do so, so far as present results are concerned. It may simply be that story-retelling is better considered as a close approximation to reading rather than as occupying a more middling position between reading and spontaneous speech. In any event, the results here show that story-retelling and reading alternate in the second and third ranks of favourability ratings.

The significant speech type by group interactions are worthy of some further comment, since they show that, among older children especially, Black children profit most from the spontaneous speech situation. This certainly relates to previous work (cited above) on the orally rich culture of Black children and adults, for it is not unreasonable to suppose that such a culture flourishes best in relatively informal conditions. The interactions found here support the writings of Labov and others, and tend to further discount those of earlier researchers who had made blanket and negative assumptions about Black children's language. Further work might focus specifically upon the speech of Black children and elucidate those areas in which they will show up most favourably. As well, the use of larger numbers (of both speakers and judges), the refinement of speech type samples, and the introduction of different evaluative scales would be worthwhile in any extensions to the present study. However, for all its limitations, this chapter has demonstrated consistent, if not always statistically significant trends. There are implications here for the study of speech in general, as well as for cross-cultural and cross-subcultural investigations.

References

Bereiter, C., & Engelmann, S. (1966). *Teaching disadvantaged children in the pre-school*. Englewood Cliffs: Prentice-Hall.

Dusek, J., & Joseph, G. (1983). The bases of teacher expectancies: A meta-analysis. *Journal of educational psychology*, *75*, 327-46.

Edwards, J. (1989). *Language and disadvantage*. 2nd ed. London: Cole & Whurr.

———. (1983). Review of *The language trap* (Honey). *Journal of language and social psychology*, *2*, 67-76.

———. (1979a). Judgements and confidence in reactions to disadvantaged speech. In H. Giles & R. St. Clair (Eds.), *Language and social psychology*. Oxford: Blackwell.

———. (1979b). Social class differences and the identification of sex in children's speech. *Journal of child language*, *6*, 121-27.

———. (1977). The speech of disadvantaged Dublin children. *Language problems and language planning*, *1*, 65-72.

Edwards, J., & Jacobsen, M. (1987). Standard and regional standard speech. *Language in society*, *16*, 369-80.

Edwards, J., & McKinnon, M. (1987). The continuing appeal of disadvantage as deficit. *Canadian journal of education*, *12*, 330-49.

Giles, H. (1973). Communicative effectiveness as a function of accented speech. *Speech monographs*, *40*, 330-31.

———. (1971). Patterns of evaluation to R.P., south Welsh and Somerset accented speech. *British journal of social and clinical psychology*, *10*, 280-81.

Giles, H., Bourhis, R., & Davies, A. (1975). Prestige speech styles: The imposed norm and inherent value hypotheses. In W. McCormack & S. Wurm (Eds.), *Language in many ways*. The Hague: Mouton.

Giles, H., Bourhis, R., Trudgill, P., & Lewis, A. (1974). The imposed norm hypothesis: A validation. *Quarterly journal of speech*, *60*, 405-10.

Gillis, S. (1978). Teachers' evaluations of the speech of black, white, and French Canadian children's voices. Unpublished BA thesis, Department of Psychology, St. Francis Xavier University, Antigonish, NS.

Gleitman, L., & Gleitman, H. (1970). *Phrase and paraphrase*. New York: Norton.

Goffman, E. (1972). The neglected situation. In P. Giglioli, (Ed.), *Language and social context*. Harmondsworth: Penguin.

Guy, A. (1988). Language and social class. In F. Newmeyer, (Ed.), *Language: The sociocultural context*. Cambridge: Cambridge University Press.

Honey, J. (1983). *The language trap*. Kenton, Middlesex: National Council for Educational Standards.

Houston, S. (1973). Syntactic complexity and informational transmission in first-graders: A cross-cultural study. *Journal of psycholinguistic research*, *2*, 99-114.

Joos, M. (1967). *The five clocks*. New York: Harcourt, Brace & World.

Kochman, T. (1972). *Rappin' and stylin' out: Communication in urban black America*. Chicago: University of Illinois Press.

Labov, W. (1973; 1969). The logic of nonstandard English. In N. Keddie, (Ed.), *Tinker, tailor ... The myth of cultural deprivation*. Harmondsworth: Penguin.

Lambert, W. (1967). A social psychology of bilingualism. *Journal of social issues*, *23*, 91-109.

Lenneberg, E. (1967). *Biological foundations of language*. New York: Wiley.

Piaget, J. (1955). *The language and thought of the child*. Cleveland: Meridian.

Rist, R. (1970). Student social class and teacher expectations: The self-fulfilling prophecy in ghetto education. *Harvard educational review*, *40*, 411-51.

Rosenthal, R., & Jacobson, L. (1968). *Pygmalion in the classroom*. New York: Holt, Rinehart & Winston.

Seligman, C., Tucker, G., & Lambert, W. (1972). The effects of speech style and other attributes on teachers' attitudes toward students. *Language in society*, *1*, 131-42.

Trudgill, P. (1975). *Accent, dialect and the school*. London: Edward Arnold.

Waterman, J. (1966). *A history of the German language*. Seattle: University of Washington Press.

Williams, F. (1976). *Explorations of the linguistic attitudes of teachers*. Rowley, MA: Newbury.

Chapter Eight

The Career of Black English: A Literary Sketch

George Elliott Clarke

Editors' Introduction

When a language variety is used by a smaller group within a larger population, certain notions may arise with regard to its nature and history, and its use. These notions usually include the view that the smaller group's dialect is inferior to the majority dialect in its grammatical structure and in its vocabulary resources, that historically it is no more than a deviation from the standard dialect, and that its use by the minority indicates an irrational stubbornness in clinging to an impoverished and faulty vernacular. Ideas like these, mostly based on misconceptions, are quite often shared by insiders and outsiders alike. Yet members of the inside group also feel that the vernacular offers them a richness of nuances and that it is uniquely suited for expressing their life experiences; the very sound of it can be a source of pleasure; and so speakers within the group and outsiders, too, are inclined to conclude that the unique qualities of the dialect outweigh the perceived faults.

However, the notions of 'inferiority' do not hold up in the face of linguistic reality. In matters of grammar, for instance, it is well known that different languages have different grammatical systems. In Russian an expression like 'he very smart' shows correct grammatical construction; whereas the omission of copula-verb 'to be' in English dialects is viewed as a sign of grammatical inferiority. The view that vocabulary resources are depleted is also indefensible, if only on the grounds that all speakers, of all language varieties, use only a small fraction of the available vocabulary resources (how many of us use the words *ambage*, *loment*, or *whorl*, and how often?) The notion of 'deviation from standard' does not jibe with historical evidence: many dialects are very old and quite conservative, while standard dialects undergo constant change. (For example, North American English has kept the old expressions *I guess* 'I think,' *fall* 'autumn,' and *druggist* 'pharmacist,' which in England have been replaced by other words.) To deviate from standard would imply, somehow, that a minority dialect is being re-invented in each generation, on the basis of a calculated 'deviation.'

Still, even mistaken notions have a tenacity which is not easily disturbed, especially when results of objective research are not readily available.

Until recently, information about Black English was scarce. H. L. Mencken, whose book *The American Language* (4th ed., 1936) offers valuable information in many areas, discusses also Black English but comments that 'Negro speech has been little investigated by philologians' (p.363). Mencken lists some dozen relevant titles, mostly of articles published in journals such as *American Speech* and *Dialect Notes*. He was inclined to accept the dominant opinion of his time; namely, that Black English had evolved from English dialects, rather than from African pidgins. Mencken's views come under stern criticism in J. L. Dillard's book *Black English* (1972) on grounds of inconsistency and bias.

While studies of Black English before the second half of the twentieth century were indeed few, literary representations of Black English started appearing in the works of various authors. The best known of these are 'The Gold Bug' (1843) by Edgar Allan Poe, *Uncle Tom's Cabin* (1851-2) by Harriet Beecher Stowe, *Uncle Remus* (1881) by Joel Chandler Harris, and *The Adventures of Huckleberry Finn* (1884) by Mark Twain.

Literary use of dialect, interesting and instructive as it may be, poses questions of accuracy, not only with regard to the authors' ability to observe and transmit, but also with regard to the readers' ability to read dialect correctly; even when an author's work is very careful, such features as intonation, word-stress, tempo of speech, and quality of voice are left to readers' imaginations. Nonetheless, literary uses of Black dialect in the past, and in more recent literature, play a significant part in popular perception, and have been used as sources of information for developing a historical view of Black English.

Still, even with the advent of serious sociolinguistic research by such linguists as William Labov (1969), and a comprehensive study such as Dillard's *Black English* (1972), what the general public could gather was limited to an investigation of Black speech in the United States only. Readers wishing to find out anything about the history of Black English in Nova Scotia would be left without resources — at least, until the publication of a separate article by Dillard, entitled 'The History of Black English in Nova Scotia — A First Step' (1971, Rpt. 1973). The paper was aptly titled — for indeed it attempted what had not been attempted before: a scholarly account of the sources and development of Black English in Nova Scotia — and it became the forerunner of other investigations. Dillard's 'History' forms the point of departure of the chapter which follows here and it also figures in an extensive research project by Shana Poplack and Sali Tagliamonte, though Poplack and Tagliamonte disagree with Dillard's conclusion that Black English in Nova Scotia is derived from Pidgin English, and that it is similar in this respect to other varieties of African American English. Partial results of this project have been published as 'African American English in the Diaspora: Evidence from Old-Line Nova Scotians' (1991). Poplack and Tagliamonte obtained their data-base by conducting a series of well-planned interviews.

Their aim is to arrive at a historical perspective with regard to the earlier stages of Black English by comparing several varieties of Black English; that is, rather than merely describing the features found in the varieties under investigation, they draw historical conclusions from comparing Black Nova Scotian English, the English of Black speakers in Samaná (in the Dominican Republic), and a collection of interviews with former slaves recorded in the US in the 1930s. The study determines statistically not only the presence of certain features, but also the conditions under which they occur, such as, for instance, the fact that the copula form of *to be* in the present is significantly more likely to be omitted after the subjects *we/you/they* (1991, p.28) than after the subject *I*. For Poplack and Tagliamonte, Black Nova Scotian English constitutes a crucial element in the historical study they have undertaken.

While their investigation is sure to make a significant contribution to the general understanding of Black English and its history, there are other aspects of the use of Black English in Nova Scotia, which are of interest to Blacks and non-Blacks alike, and which are the subject of the following chapter.

In this chapter, George Elliott Clarke recapitulates the main elements of the history of Black English in Nova Scotia from the point of view of a continuing struggle against oppression, and of perseverance in the use of this vernacular despite the social disadvantages associated with it, or the ridicule persistently heaped on it by non-Black writers, and then proceeds to discuss the revival of Black English as a language of the cultural renaissance among gifted young Black writers. Clarke even compiles a short glossary of specific Black Nova Scotian words. And, even more importantly, he coins a new word to refer to the speech of Black Nova Scotians: he calls it *Africadian*, and with this new name, we may feel, new interest and new attitudes will take root with respect to a dialect much too long left unexplored and unappreciated. *(LF & MH)*

***

The Career of Black English: A Literary Sketch
by George Elliott Clarke

Like so many minority tongues around the world, the speech of the majority of Black Nova Scotians (I prefer to call them 'Africadians,' a word I formed from the union of 'African' and 'Acadian') has been 'buked and scorned, repressed and suppressed, and labelled 'dialect,' 'lingo,' 'jargon,' 'bad English,' 'broken English,' and 'patois.' Their 'accent' has been called 'American' and 'Southern.' Their tongue has been treated as foreign, alien, and deviant. However, their speech is as Nova Scotian as standard Nova Scotian speech, and it has been a common language in the province for at least two centuries. Most importantly, this speech, popularly referred to as 'Black English,' is slowly emerging as a valid and vital literary and performance form as a result of the efforts of writers and performers connected with the Africadian Cultural Renaissance which began in the province around 1983.

I would argue, in fact, that one cannot separate the reception of Black English in Nova Scotia from the treatment of Africadians by the majority culture. Whenever a people is oppressed, their tongue likewise suffers. Wherever a people experience liberation or improvement in self-confidence, their tongue likewise flourishes.

To understand the career of Black English in Nova Scotia, that is to say, its two-century-long ascent from a position of utter disparagement to one of incipient respectability, one must examine its origins. Associated, first, with the slave trade, it was later treated as a comic deviance by white authors and performers in Nova Scotia. Due, in part, to these parodies, the tongue was generally eschewed by educated, middle-class Africadians. Instead, it became the sole province of the poor and uneducated, who gave it succour in their folklore. Still, some middle-class Africadians retained a working knowledge of the tongue to maintain their own sense of racial solidarity. The language is presently enjoying a 'Second Coming' as an important artistic device for Africadian performers and writers.

The Genealogy of Black English

The variety of Black English spoken in Nova Scotia is descended from a tongue which was forged and shaped in the fiery furnace of the slave trade. Distinguished linguist and scholar J. L. Dillard states that 'American Black English can be traced to a creolized version of English based upon a pidgin spoken by slaves; it probably came from the West Coast of Africa' (1972, p.6). This variety of Black English is the immediate ancestral tongue of Africadians, for the majority of them are descendants of African Americans who came to the province en masse in the two major migrations of 1783 and 1815. Dillard also asserts that 'African languages survived in the New World for a time,' and he mentions that scholar David Dalby 'has documented the widespread use of Wolof, which seems to have a special *lingua franca* status among West African languages, in the [original] thirteen [American] colonies' (1972, p.74).

This common African language allowed slaves taken directly from polyglot West Africa to the Caribbean islands and the Americas to communicate with each other while, at the same time, learning the rudiments of their European masters' tongues, mainly Portuguese, French, Spanish, and, of course, English. Though based on European languages, then, these pidgin varieties were established, says Dillard, 'through African resources' (p.83). In fact, the English version, which Dillard calls 'West African Pidgin English' (p.83), was likely used not only in the Thirteen Colonies (New England and the South), but throughout British North America, wherever slavery was practised, including in Nova Scotia and New Brunswick.

This hybrid language was born amid violence. American slaves were compelled to learn a basic version of English to increase their 'value' for their masters and their ability to perform a variety of tasks. Canadian poet Marlene Nourbese Philip describes this 'education' in the following passage:

> To speak another language is to enter another consciousness. Africans in the New World were forced to enter another consciousness, that of their masters, while simultaneously being excluded from their own.... [L]anguage was one of the most important sites of struggle between the Old World and the New World. The outcome of this struggle was the almost absolute destruction and obliteration of African languages. (1989, p.15)

However, as Dillard emphasizes, Africans in British America did not simply adopt the speech of their masters. They transformed it; they Africanized it; they made it their own. They used it as a means to negotiate their way through a hostile white society and to construct a degree of protective community with each other. Nourbese Philip acknowledges this fact:

> In the vortex of New World slavery, the African forged new and different words, developed strategies to impress her experience on the language. The formal standard language was subverted, turned upside down, inside out, and even sometimes erased. Nouns became strangers to verbs and vice versa; tonal accentuation took the place of several words at a time; rhythms held sway.... The havoc that the African wreaked upon the English language is, in fact, the metaphorical equivalent of the havoc that coming to the New World represented for the African. (1989, pp.17-18)

The shotgun wedding between West African languages and English (and other European tongues) resulted in the birth of a distinctive English, namely,

Black English. Dillard reports that early Black English took two forms: West African Pidgin English and 'Plantation Creole,' the actual Anglicized language spoken by the masses of slaves on plantations and farms, both of which were in use at the same time (1972, p.85).

Black English among the Bluenoses

The situation was no different in Nova Scotia. Dillard observes that 'with its long seacoast, Nova Scotia has been a more likely place for the use of the [West African] Pidgin English of the maritime slave trade … than inland Canada' (1973, p.508). For one thing, '[s]laves were transferred from one place to another, as from Nova Scotia to Surinam … quite freely in the eighteenth century' (p.513). Probably, too, slaves were traded up and down the Atlantic coast, for '[t]he literary evidence … provides a clear picture of a continuum of eighteenth, nineteenth and twentieth century Black English from the American South to Nova Scotia, with no great break in such places as New York City, Boston and Connecticut' (p.517). C. Bruce Fergusson, former Nova Scotia Provincial Archivist, reports the presence of sixteen Black slaves in Halifax in 1750 (1948, p.1) who, in all likelihood, spoke a version of Black English.

The use of West African day-names for slaves yields further evidence of the historical presence of Black English in Nova Scotia. Dillard reports the prevalence of such names as '*Quaco* 'male born on Wednesday" and *Quashee* "male born on Sunday"' in records published by Fergusson (1971, p.258). 'Pheobe,' a female slave name that also appears in the work of Fergusson, is an English corruption of 'Phibba,' a day-name for a female born on a Friday (p.259). Such distortions fostered further creativity on the part of the slavemasters. 'Believing that some of the slave women were named for the goddess of the moon,' Dillard writes, 'the whites apparently proceeded to the next logical step (to them) and gave names like *Caesar* … and *Scipio*' (1971, p.259). Such Romanized names were commonplace for Africadians. In fact, the nineteenth-century Nova Scotian author, Thomas Chandler Haliburton, includes an Africadian character named 'Scip,' presumably a short form of Scipio, and uses similar names, such as Cato and Pompey, in his sketch entitled 'Slavery' (1838).

The presence of the day-names, like Black English in general, underscores 'the great amount of African culture which remains, iceberg-like, below the surface of the Europeanized Americas' (Dillard, 1971, p.260). For instance, the day-name 'Quasheba,' denoting a female born on a Sunday (p.259), probably survives in Black Nova Scotia or Africadia as 'Sheba.' Moreover, while 'the African use of reduplicated names' lives on in America in such forms as "Bus Bus" for "Boston," "She She" for "Sheila," and "Leelee" for "Lisa"' (pp.260-61), Africadians use similar names. I have heard the names 'Bun Bun' (for a man) and 'Leelee.' The persistence of such naming practices proves as well the rootedness of Black or, rather, Africanized

English in Nova Scotia.

By the time of the 1783, post-American Revolutionary War arrival, then, of the 3500 Black Loyalists, many of whom had Southern United States roots, Africanized English was already an established fact in Nova Scotia. Certainly, though, their arrival boosted the career of Black English in Nova Scotia, for they surely brought with them a complex oral culture, both secular and religious. Rev. David George, the leader of Baptist Black Loyalists, in his 1793 memoir, recalls learning 'a hymn of that great writing man, [Isaac] Watts' (p.476). Moreover, Black Loyalist songs and dances, both of which involved, presumably, the use of Black English, were common enough to receive censure. In 1789, for instance, the government of the Loyalist settlement of Shelburne passed an ordinance 'forbidding negro dances and frolicks' (Smith, 1888, p.77). Given its long history in the province, Black English is as Nova Scotian as blueberry grunt.

Black English, White Mischief

While the Black Loyalist colonization of Nova Scotia cemented the use of Black English as a common tongue in the Africadian community, the arrivals in 1815 of Black refugees (following the War of 1812) and, before 1861, of fugitive slaves via the Underground Railway did not, assuredly, weaken the language's popularity. However, the presence of this visibly distinct group of settlers, many of whom had come indigent and illiterate to 'Nova Scarcity,' and who had suffered further discrimination once settled, served to make the tongue the butt of racist humour. Much of the evidence of the language's use in Nova Scotia in the nineteenth century is found, then, in the pages of authors who abused it for 'comic' purposes.

These authors, such as Haliburton, were following a custom which, even in the early nineteenth century, was a well established tradition. African American critic Henry Louis Gates states that 'the *spoken* language of black people had become an object of parody at least since 1769 when *The Padlock* appeared on the American stage, including among its cast of characters a West Indian slave called Mungo,' whose language was 'represented by a caricature that signifies the difference that separated white from black' (1987, p.6). African American writer Gayl Jones, in her study, *Liberating Voices: Oral Tradition in African American Literature* (1991), points out that 'the containment [that is to say, the restriction to dialect] of the black voice seems the prerequisite of parallel freeings of voice in European American literary traditions' (p.164). In other words, white writers — Nova Scotian, British, and American alike — often employed a bastardized Black English, signified by a reliance on mere changes in orthography, to highlight the supposed superiority of their own speech and writing. In her critical work, *Playing in the Dark: Whiteness and the Literary Imagination* (1992), African American novelist Toni Morrison emphasizes 'how the dialogue of black characters [in white-authored texts] is construed as an alien, estranging dialect made deliberately unintelligible by spellings contrived to disfamiliarize it' (p.52). Frantz Fanon also emphasizes the estranging usage of 'dialect,' observing that 'to make [a Black] talk pidgin is to fasten him to the effigy of him, to snare him, to imprison him, the eternal victim of an essence, of an *appearance* for which he is not responsible' (1967, p.35).

White distortion of Black English served another purpose, however. It permitted white writers to pretend to be African, thereby permitting the discussion of risqué and outré subjects. In effect, the white use of Africanized English constituted a kind of literary blackface. Morrison agrees:

> In minstrelsy, a layer of blackness applied to a white face released it from law. Just as entertainers, through or by association with blackface, could render permissible topics that otherwise would have been taboo, so American writers were able to employ an imagined African persona to articulate and imaginatively act out the forbidden in American culture. (1992, p.66)

Not surprisingly, the careers of writers such as Haliburton coincided with the rise of blackface minstrelsy. According to folklorist Neil V. Rosenberg, this early form of pop culture 'began in the 1840s with white American performers who carefully studied black performing arts,' which they then 'endeavoured to present as authentically as they could' (1988, p.142). Songs, in particular, enjoyed a wide currency. V. L. O. Chittick suggests that the minstrel songs that appear in Haliburton's work 'were carried to his attention ... [by] the spring-time Nova Scotian visitations of the travelling American circus, with its coloured entertainers' (1958, p.177). The minstrel show, 'with its blend of eccentric costumes, blackface makeup, and a musical ensemble that included fiddles, banjos, tambourines, and bones' (Abrahams, 1992, p.131), was as influential an entertainment form as is television today. In adulterated guise, it survives in country and western music (which has retained the African-originated banjo and some dance steps and instrumental techniques created by slaves) (Cantwell, 1984, pp.125, 255-65; Abrahams, 1992, p.102). In blackface form, it has maintained its popularity in rural parts of the Maritimes to the present (Hornby, 1991, p.85). Of course, 150 years ago, too, a ready audience existed for this type of comedy — even in literature.

Robert Cantwell stresses that 'the racial attitudes symbolized by blackface placed the performer, whatever his background or temperament, among his audiences, not among the people he parodied' (1984, p.265). That is to say, a white performer — or writer — could demonstrate his or her kinship *with other whites* by imitating the speech of persons of African heritage. He or she became a kind of ideological tar baby, who absorbed and cancelled within his or her identity, the possibility for positive recognition of African difference. Haliburton falls into this camp, for he spent his career as a kind of satirical Socrates, promoting 'the greater empire of the British peoples, a world-wide Anglo-Saxon unity' (Logan, 1989, p.25). Hence, while his use of Africanized English is often related to some issue of importance to his Anglo-American readers, he generally affirms a negative view of Africanness.

Still, Haliburton is the most important nineteenth-century Nova Scotian recorder of Black English. Dillard cites Haliburton's writings as evidence of 'the existence of Black English all the way from the American South, by way of Boston and Connecticut, to Halifax, Nova Scotia' (1972, p.103). In 1850, a French reviewer, Emile Montegut, praised Haliburton's books, 'badly composed yet full of excellent pages, made colourful with American dialect, provincial English, and the jargon of Negroes, fishermen and seamen' (p.72). In her 1956 study of Haliburton's use of various types of English, including 'Negro Lingo,' Swedish scholar Elna Bengtsson observes that 'America is a conglomeration of different nationalities, all mangling the English language in different ways. Haliburton … would not have been Haliburton, had he not utilized this to create comic effects' (p.45). Haliburton's work showcases the minstrelization of Black English.

A typical example of Haliburtonian Black English appears in 'Slavery,' the aforementioned 'Second Series' (1838) sketch in Haliburton's *The Clockmaker; or, The Sayings and Doings of Samuel Slick, of Slickville*, a work which appeared in three separate and different 'Series' between 1836 and 1840. In the following excerpt, Haliburton's hero, Sam Slick, stopping at an inn between Kentville and Wilmot, meets Scip, an escaped slave who yearns, incredibly, to return to slavery:

> Oh, Massa Sammy! Massa Sammy! Oh, my Gor! — only tink old Scippy see you once more? How you do, Massa Sammy? Gor Ormighty bless you! How you do? … Oh Massa Sam, you no recollect Old Scip, — Massa 'Siah's nigger boy? How's Massa Sy, and Missey Sy, and all our children, and all our folks to our house to home? De dear little lily, de sweet little booty, de little missy baby. Oh, how I do lub 'em all! … How is dat black villain, dat Cato? … I hope dey cowskin him well — I grad of dat, — oh Gor! dat is good. (1838, pp.97-98)

Scip's speech contains items that descend from West African Pidgin English, including *Massa*, *Gor* (*Gar* in Dillard's list of 'characteristic structures of Pidgin English' (1973, pp.508-9)), and negation with *no* ('you no recollect'). Even so, his speech is as distorted as the notion that he would want to return to slavery.

In a 'Third Series' *Clockmaker* sketch, 'The Black Brother' (1840), Haliburton's presentation of a minister's speech includes snatches of song which, Chittick states (1958, pp.178-79), descend from minstrel shows:

> De Raccoon ginn to scratch and bite,
> I hitty once wid all my might,
> I bungy eye and spile his sight,
> Oh, *Ise* de child to fight.
>
> But I is a new man now wid de ingenerate heart, and only fight old Scratch, old Adam, or old sin, but not a brudder in de flesh—no naber I ain't goin' get mad no more.
>
> For little childer neber let
> De angry passions rise,
> Your little hands were neber made
> To tear each oder's eyes.
>
> Nothin' else save him from catchin' it, for I is de boy dat could do it.... Temper, him werry trong, and say cuss him, bung up both he eye, and put in de dead lite.... (Haliburton, 1840, p.49)

Chittick argues that Sam Slick's 'repertoire in song was acquired mainly from what he could have heard on the contemporary vaudeville stage, so-called music-hall "ballads" of the sort featured in "black-face" minstrel shows' (1958, p.177). Nevertheless, I would also suggest, given Haliburton's employment for many years as a circuit-judge, a position in which he was certain to meet Africadian servants, witnesses, and accused persons, he surely gleaned some of his knowledge of Black English from these sources.

Another mid-nineteenth-century white writer who had occasion to transcribe Africadian English was Frederick S. Cozzens, an American writer who spent a month touring the province. In *Acadia; or, A Month with the Blue Noses* (1859), Cozzens holds forth on the condition of the Africadians he encounters in his travels. To him, they are figures of pity and of comedy; indeed, their 'very language was pregnant with mirth' (p.43). Here is Cozzens's account of an exchange between himself and Mrs. William Deer, who, with her husband, kept an inn near Preston:

> 'And which place do you like the best — this or Maryland?'
>
> 'Why, I never had no such work to do at home as I have to do here, grubbin' up old stumps and stones; dem isn't women's work. When I was home, I had only to wait on misses, and work was light and easy.'
>
> ... 'But why,' said I, 'do you prefer Nova Scotia to Maryland? ...'
>
> 'Oh!' replied Mrs. Deer, 'de difference is, dat when I work here, I work for myself, and when I was working at home, I was working for other people.' (1859, pp.64-5)

Though Cozzens attempts to make Mrs. Deer sound ridiculous, she makes him sound silly instead: her reply is sensible, and it implies her opposition to slavery.

White writers like Haliburton and Cozzens were not the only authors to ink works in Africanized English, however. At least one fugitive slave, namely, John William Robertson, who had escaped from the slaveholding South to Nova Scotia by boat, utilized it in his pamphlet, *The Book of the Bible against Slavery* (1854). Robertson was one of the many escaped slaves who, though barely literate because they had been denied formal education by law, published slave narratives. These narratives were important weapons in the struggle against slavery which, though abolished throughout the British Empire in 1833, continued legally in the United States until 1865. If their language was occasionally rough, it served merely to authenticate their authors' experiences. This point is exemplified in the case of Robertson, who was illiterate when he landed in Halifax in 1852.

While it is true that such 'fugitive slaves did not leave their plantation dialects behind them' (Dillard, 1973, p.515), I would further argue that they retained an innate sense of the structures of their dialects. For instance, even though Robertson's narrative reflects a superficial knowledge of Standard English, his grammar exhibits his deeper, original schooling in Black English. To be precise, his syntax seems to follow his speech rather than some literary model:

> … but I knowed one thing that God has declared unto all men, I desire the righteousness which is of the law…. Under divine Providence I proceeded to the sea side, and I saw the sky was darkened and clouded for rain, but I felt that heaven was shining in my heart, saying away, and I made up my mind…. The wind being light, was not twenty miles from home when the day broke, and wind rose to a hurricane, but as the sun rose the wind blowing very hard indeed. (1854, p.4)

Robertson's use of the grammar of Africanized English inaugurated a tradition which continues to this day.

Despite Robertson's powerful work, however, Black English in Nova Scotia became associated with the 'blackface' English of writers like Haliburton and Cozzens. These writers of Black 'dialect' failed to produce works that could be described as '"revelatory of interior lives" as well as society, history, landscape, and language' (Jones, 1991, p.32), but they did succeed in creating negative stereotypes. Haliburton reveals nothing profound about his Scip, for instance, but he does create a handy caricature.

Mass versus Class

The effect of such stereotypes was to force Black English to go underground, in a sense, in Nova Scotia. While it remained the public tongue of most Africadians, it was likely frowned upon by the elite, a group consisting mainly of teachers and ministers of the African Baptist Association, an Africadian religious organization which was formally constituted at Granville Mountain in 1854. Two small collections of church-sung hymns and spirituals, published respectively by Rev. F. R. Langford and Rev. W. N. States in 1882 and 1903, attest to this fact, for the spirituals are all printed in Standard English. Yet the ministers' congregations could not have sung these songs in Standard English, for, as is recounted in detail by historian/biographer Colin A. Thomson (1986, pp.8-9), Africadians did not receive extensive formal schooling/indoctrination in Standard English until well into the twentieth century. Furthermore, spirituals epitomized oral art. Blyden Jackson terms them 'the epic verse of black America' through which 'an African ethnicity speaks ... in their incremental leading lines, their choral iterations, and their call-and-response chants' (1989, p.314). Their inherent orality would have worked against renditions in Standard English.

The ministers' decisions to print their booklets in Standard English highlights Dillard's insight that social class membership is the greatest determinant of whether an Africadian or African American will speak Black English or Standard English. Generally, the more educated or, rather, the more assimilated into white society one is, the less likely one is to speak Black English, the tongue of the mass of African North Americans, a collectivity defined by economic as well as racial discrimination. Dillard emphasizes that 'it is true that the economically disadvantaged Blacks of today are primarily members of the unassimilated group.... It is the members of this undervalued culture who are the basic population for a study of Black English' (1972, pp.231-32). This class division in black community speech was surely exacerbated by the nineteenth-century clownish use of Black English by white writers, but it had always existed.

Dillard points out that 'there were three language groups among the slaves': 'Those who learned the English of their masters' (a *relatively* 'good' English); 'the great mass of native-born field workers, who spoke Plantation Creole' (or early modern Black English); and 'recent imports from Africa,' who spoke West African Pidgin English (1972, p.98). Consequently, Dillard notes, 'The differentiation of varieties of English used by Black speakers [was] based most probably upon social factors within the slave community' (1972, p.86). Because Black English is not a geographically determined dialect, but rather a sociolect or social dialect (Dillard, 1973, p.507), that is to say, the language of a specific, class-constructed group, the class distinction in its use continues.

This division between folk and elite speakers is pronounced in any marginal or colonized community. Commenting on this phenomenon as it affected Blacks in colonized Martinique, Fanon remarks that 'the Negro of the Antilles will be proportionately whiter — that is, he will come closer to being a real human being — in direct ratio to his mastery of the French language' (1967, p.18). A colonized or marginalized person pursues this sort of psychological and linguistic 'lactification' (p.47) because of his or her sense of inferiority 'created by the death and burial of [his or her] local cultural originality.... The colonized is elevated above his jungle status in proportion to his adoption of the mother country's cultural standards. He becomes whiter as he renounces his blackness, his jungle' (p.18). For some Africadians, then, rejection of Black English and mastery of Standard English provided a means of assimilating into mainstream society. E. Franklin Frazier's remarks on the education of the African American middle class are just as relevant to its Africadian counterpart: 'students were taught to speak English correctly and thus avoid the ungrammatical speech and dialect of the Negro masses' (1965, p.71). The Africadian vernacular, in the minds of the elite, was associated with the vulgar and the uncouth.

This association had repercussions for the career of literary Black English in Nova Scotia: essentially, it disappeared for several generations, not to re-emerge until the 1970s. The reason was that, as I have written elsewhere, 'the progenitors of [early twentieth-century] Africadian literature were mainly ministers. Indeed, they produced and propagated all the literature that mattered — petitions, songs, newsletters, histories, speeches, and sermons' (Clarke, 1991, p.17). Combined with 'Africadian culture's puritanical streak (a natural feature of an ecclesiastical community),' this fact 'militated against the publication of tales that could be considered lewd, rude, or crude' (p.16). In brief, the Africadian religious elite was not about to propagate Africanized English even if some of its members used the tongue.

The Survival of Black English

Accordingly, most Africadian literature published between the turn of the century and the mid-1970s was written in Standard English. One major exception was, though, the publication in 1931 of *Folklore from Nova Scotia*, a compendium of lore collected, mainly from blacks, from around the province. The compiler, Arthur Huff Fauset, was a pioneering African American anthropologist who would later achieve fame as the author of a class study of urban African American religion, *Black Gods of the Metropolis* (1944). As I note in my introduction to *Fire on the Water: An Anthology of Black Nova Scotian Writing* (1991), Fauset seems not to have understood the strong bowdlerizing effect of the African Baptist faith upon the recounting of folklore, and 'was exasperated by the refusal of some of his informants to recite material that they felt was beneath their dignity' (p.16). Nevertheless, his collection is a treasure trove of circa 1920s Africadian English and lore.

Fauset's collection is rich with material. His informants demonstrate an inimitable authenticity. Here is a portion of a version of 'Cinderella' told by Caroline Reddick, then aged 87, of New Glasgow:

> There was a rich Lord's son at the party an' he fell in love with her. He danced mostly with her. He wouldn't pay any attention t'others. She had a foot about six inches long, an' glass slippers. 'Twasn't no

> other lady there with glass slippers. He laughed an' talked, an' squashed with her. All the others jealous, wonder why he stay with that strange girl. The music was so sweet that Cindy forgot, an' she stayed overtime. (1931, p.5)

The following trickster tale was related by Ned Brown, then aged 60, of Dartmouth:

> Rabbit came in man's house of a bluff to warm himself. The man knowed what he was up to, an' said to him, 'If you come in to warm yourself, when the cold comes I'll throw you out into the snow.' Rabbit said, 'Oh, don't do dat.' Man said, 'I will.' … Den de man got mad, an' he throwed him out, Rabbit all the time hollerin', 'For God's sake, whatever you do, don't put me out of a frosty night.' After he throwed him out, Rabbit said, 'Ho, ho, I was bred an' born in de snow, didn' you know dat?' (p.46)

These excerpts demonstrate some of the persistent features of Africadian English: the use of repetition ('glass slipper,' 'snow,' 'don't'); the omission of linking verbs ('others [were] jealous') and articles ('t[o the] others,' 'in [the] man's'); and indulgence in verbal experimentation ('squashed'). Brown's story also provides proof that such forms as 'dat' have had a long history in Africadia, for this word also occurs in the texts of Haliburton and Cozzens.

The Renaissance of Black English

The type of folk speech surveyed by Fauset is the basis for all of the innovative literature which characterizes the contemporary Africadian Cultural Renaissance. Although they likely do not know Fauset's work, such writers as Frederick Ward (1937-), Walter Borden (1942-), Charles R. Saunders (1946), Gloria Wesley-Desmond (1948-), Maxine Tynes (1949-), George Boyd (1952-), and David Woods (1959-) certainly utilize the vitality of folk speech, of Africadian English, in their works. These writers are, in a sense, 'bilingual,' for they use both Standard English and Black English.

Previous Africadian writers, by privileging Standard English, gave voice mainly, as did early African American writers, to the 'literate elite, whereas folklore is the expression of the mass,' Donald A. Petesch declares (1989, p.130). In this tradition, to become a writer was 'a way of leaving the black mass' (p.130). The present generation of writers differs. While they have been described as forming 'part of the indigenous Black Nova Scotian middle class' (Mannette, 1990, p.4), these writers, for the most part, unlike some of their forebears, embrace Africanized English.

Their recuperation of the tongue can be related, in fact, to the revolutionary use of oral traditions in emergent, once marginalized literatures. G. Jones believes that contemporary African American literature demonstrated the movement from the restrictive forms (inheritors of self-doubt, self-repudiation, and the minstrel tradition) to the liberation of voice and freer personalities in more intricate texts' (1991, p.178). The same process is underway in Africadian literature. This literary assertion of the vitality of Africadian English is necessary for, to cite Jones again, 'the foundation of every literary tradition is oral,' whether it is audible or inaudible in the text (p.3). The specific experience of Africadians cannot be named completely until it is named in their unique tongue. The return of Africadian writers to the vernacular, then, reflects the 'nation's need to name its own songs, themes, and character in its own distinct language' (p.7). This measure also represents an effort to reclaim the collective memory of history, for the 'lack of history and literature … is a result of the "amnésie culturelle" which,' says Sylvia Soderlind, 'is symptomatic of the experience of colonization' (1991, p.92) and, I would add, of marginalization.

If 'the revolutionary's difficult task' is to restore memory and language 'to the people' (Soderlind, 1991, p.92), *Riverlisp: Black Memories* (1974), a collection of stories and poems by Ward, exemplifies this process. Based in part on conversations that Ward had with exiles from Africville, the 150-year-old, North End Halifax, Africadian village which the city bulldozed into ruins between 1964 and 1970, the text builds on the original orality of writers like Robertson and the Africadians interviewed by Fauset:

> When Grandma Snooks spoken'd you see'd
>
> a sleeping bee
> cuddled in a tear drop
> *hidden hind a elephant's ear*
>
> … cause she talk'd in them parable kind of vissions [*sic*] to show her meanings: 'Fuss is round all beautifull-ness. When you's in trouble boy, you just seeks that inner place you got it! we all's got it!
>
> But Micah Koch's *inner place* was all fuss too. He'd seen Miss Purella Munificance.
>
> Dear sweet Purella Munificance the huckster man on his produce wagon, put light to your meaning so we can understand huckster man be thinking on your continence he sing the painter's brush strokes of your mouth; a low soft soothing: ahhhh sound of the sea bird, leaning on the air! … (1974, p.36)

Ward is a consummate artist in Black English. In him, the language becomes not only poetry but music. He even challenges the expected placement of contractions: where one might expect to read 'we's all,' Ward offers 'we all's.'

While Ward's work achieves a kind of aural surrealism, Saunders's rendition of the speech of Africvillers is true to life, even sweetly poetic. After conducting extensive interviews with former Africville residents, Saunders decided not to speak in his own voice, but in a blend of the voices he had heard:

> It was as though all the voices I had listened to on tape and in interviews had combined into one. And that one voice decided to speak through me. (*Africville*, 1989, p.3)

His 1989 narrative, 'A Visit to Africville: Summer 1959,' resonates with realism:

> We used to get coal that fell off the hoppers and the tender. In the wintertime, you need every piece of coal you can get to heat your house. No more of that, with these growlin' diesel engines. Steam engines sounded friendly; these diesels sound like they want to kill you. And they go too doggone fast.
>
> Can't complain too much about the trains, though. Plenty of our menfolk worked as Pullman porters. Travelled all over Canada and down in the States, they did. Kept those sleepin' cars cleaner than the Sheraton hotel. They'd come home in their uniforms with the shiny brass buttons, and they'd be like heroes comin' back from a war. Best job a coloured man could get in the old days. Not so bad now either, if you want to know the truth. (*Africville*, 1989, p.5)

Read in its entirety, Saunders's text accumulates terrific power. Note his use of the standard Africadian technique of repetition ('coal,' 'diesel/steam engines' 'diesels').

Tynes is a more liberal, that is to say, a more universalist writer than Ward and Saunders, for she prefers to write primarily in Standard English. However, the grammatical structure of her texts is often in Black English, and actual fragments of the speech occur in stories such as 'For Tea and Not for Service' (1990):

> Celie doesn't remember the afternoon ending, or how she got out of there. But she does remember the warm and secret hug from Dora as she put Celie into her coat; and that hot, breathy whisper into Celie's collar, 'I knows 'em, child. I knows 'em too well.' (p.88)

Tynes's Africadian English is reserved for expressions of secret wisdom, private knowledge.

Another example of the contemporary flowering of Africadian English is 'Voices,' a section of poems in Woods's first book of poems, *Native Song* (1990). Influenced by Ward, they are yet fine, original, song-like poems, especially the succinct but sweet 'Love':

> 'I love that girl so much,
> My hair getting kinkier.' (p.51)

A final instance of the Renaissance of Africadian English is taken from Borden's play-in-poetry, 'Tightrope Time' (1986). Borden is an expert in rhythm, diction, and imagery, all vital elements in the effective writing of Africadian English:

> … and don't go blabbin' about your father;
> he was walkin' in the devil's shoes
> before he left his mama's tit,
> and be the time that he was twelve years old,
> every girl in this here country
> knowed the colour of his drawers.
>
> and that same old fool come in my face
> and had the nerve to say:
> my boy will be a real man;
> *yeah — steady, fast and deadly;*
> and true's i'm sittin' in this chair,
> a chill went through my bones —
>
> well Doodle Boy roared down that road
> and drove hisself to hell.
> and wrapped hisself around that tree
> and took some young folks with his. (pp.39-40)

Borden writes with a deep sense of orality. His use of 'knowed' echoes its occurrence in the texts of Brown and Robertson.

For Borden, Woods, Ward, Saunders, and several other Africadian writers, Africadian English has become a vital element of their self-expression. They are writers who are 'easy in their bones, at home … with the black mass, the traditional source of black strength' (Petesch, 1989, p.131). They manage to combine literate expression and folk grammar and diction. They seek 'to keep the deep structure, the movement, the kinetic energy, the tone and pitch, the slides and glissandos of the demotic within a tradition that is primarily page-bound' (Nourbese Philip, 1989, p.23).

For one thing, orality influences the rhythms of their texts, which are often written to sustain public presentation and performance. Indeed, 'the *righteous* recital of a poem or story, the *proper* enactment of a play, the *soulful* utterance of speech or song' are crucial to the Africadian sensibility (Clarke, 1991, p.25). For this reason, 'Africadian writers share a similar rhetorical style based not so much on language as on rhythm' (p.25). This rhythm, often marked by long, rolling sentences, also features such devices as parallelism and the catalogue. However, Africadian texts also exhibit such characteristics as the 'multiple-voice, complex metrical patterns' that Abrahams identifies in classical African American culture in general (p.xviii). They also feature a high degree of repetition, a signal figure in black culture.

Conclusion

Black English has had a long career in Nova Scotia. Though it first arrived in chains and suffered persecution for its difference, it survived and flowered in the utterance of those who had no hope of, and perhaps even less interest in, assimilating into the white Nova Scotian middle class. It will continue to flourish given that the Black community remains substantially unassimilated into the Nova Scotian mainstream. As Dillard observes, 'Black English thrives in Nova Scotia ... perhaps because of the aloofness of the white population from the Black' (1972, p.114). Given this 'aloofness,' Africanized English is certain to remain a tongue in its own right. Even so, its users ought not to be subjected to the economic discrimination which has often been their lot.

While we Africadians will continue, in increasing numbers, to learn Standard English, that education should not be won at the expense of our own native, strange, beautiful, and musical tongue. Even as we enter academia and scale corporate ladders, we should seek to further the career of Black English in Nova Scotia. We should always remember the special voice of our people. We should always remember the old Africadian proverb, 'All I gotta do is stay black and die.' Amen.

Further Sources of Africadian English

For the works of other writers, please consult my anthology, *Fire on the Water: An Anthology of Black Nova Scotian Writing*, Vol. 2 (1992). See, especially, the work of Raymond L. Parker (1936-) and, in Volume 1, of Grace May Lawrence (1928-), whose work, though ostensibly in Standard English, shows a Black English grammatical structure. For further examples of oral Africanized English, see the two-volume collection, *Traditional Lifetime Stories: A Collection of Black Memories* (1987-1990). Two recent films also feature Africadian English. See the National Film Board (NFB) production *Black Mother, Black Daughter* (1990), directed by Claire Prieto and Sylvia Hamilton, and another NFB production, *Remember Africville* (1991), directed by Shelagh Mackenzie. For Africadian English put to music, listen to The Gospel Heirs' recording, *in the light* (1991), especially the track, 'God Brought His People Out.'

Appendix: Toward a Glossary of Africadian English

More research is necessary to prepare a thorough glossary of Black Nova Scotian or 'Africadian' English. However, a few terms can be mentioned. This glossary does not include such commonly used English words as *banjo*, *bozo*, *buckaroo*, *gumbo*, *jazz*, *juba*, *juke*, *okay*, *okra*, *tabby*, *tote*, and *voodoo*, all of which are of definite or strongly suspected African origin (see Dillard, 1972, pp.118-9). I have also attempted to avoid slang. Many of the words and phrases listed here have been in use (in rural areas at least) for several generations.

Ashy	Describes dry, dark skin.
Association	The annual August gathering of members of the African United Baptist Association and their families and friends to worship God, enjoy fellowship, and celebrate homecomings.
Aunt Jemima	A Black female who acts 'white' or who curries favour with whites.
Aya	Sugar. (Gerald Taylor, a former executive director of the Black United Front of Nova Scotia, told me, in 1986, of a Dartmouth couple who used this word.)
Big-feeling	Proud, vain.
Black	Used as an intensifier, as in *Mind your own Black business!*
Blue(-black)	Describes a dark-skinned Black person.
Buried	To be totally immersed in water during baptism. The term arises from the phrase, 'buried in the likeness of Christ.'
Clip	To strike or hit; to cut (hair).
Crack	To strike or hit.
Cream and molasses	Describes a person of Black-white ancestry. See Marion Robertson, *The Chestnut Pipe* (1991, p.213).
Cross-eyed	Angry.
Crying doll	An infant.
Cut (one's) eyes	To cast a quick, mean look.
Day work	Cleaning and cooking in other people's houses.
Derasifying	Good, tasty, delicious.
Dirty (one's) knees	To kneel and pray.
Drag	A horse-drawn, plank-platform on wooden runners. See Raymond L. Parker, *Beyond the Dark Horizon* (1987, p.62).
Dried up; dry	Describes a person who is boring or old or strict and unpleasant. Can also apply to things and places.

Exhorters	Lay preachers. See Willard Parker Clayton, *Whatever Your Will, Lord* (1984, p.48).
Good-fisted	A good fighter.
Greens	Vegetables.
Hamhocks	Hog portions.
Heavy-natured	Lustful.
Hotcomb	A heated, steel comb used to straighten negroid hair.
In service	Working as a cook or maid in a stranger's home.
Lick and lap	To make love.
Little house	An outhouse.
Lucifer	A male lover. See Grace May Lawrence et al, *Reflections to the Third Power* (1989, p.45).
Making pictures	Telling stories; making someone believe something that isn't true. See Fauset, *Folklore from Nova Scotia* (1931, p.11).
Mean-minded	Mean, nasty.
Miserable	Describes a *mean-minded, no-'count* person, who's probably full of *piss and vinegar*.
Money	Bubbles that appear in stirred tea. The term refers to a good-luck game in which one tries to spoon up the bubbles. If one succeeds, one should receive money.
Nappy	Describes supposedly unkempt negroid hair.
New Road	An area of Preston.
Niggerish	Devilish.
Nigger rig	A plain and simple invention.
No-'count	No good.
Oreo	A Black who ignores other Blacks or who sides with or acts 'white.'
Out home	Usually used by an urban Black to refer to the family homestead, generally in a rural community. Can also be *back home* or *down home* (especially if one is in Montreal, Upper Canada, or even further west).
Padana	Bread pudding. See Marie Nightingale, *Out of Old Nova Scotia Kitchens* (1970, p.23).
Pasty-faced	A white person or a light-skinned Black person.
Picky	Describes supposedly unkempt negroid hair.
Piss-ass	A nasty person.
Piss and vinegar	What a *mean-minded* person is full of.
Pullin' (on)	Accosting or grabbing a woman to try to coax her into intimacies.
Pup	An upstart.
Queen of Sheba	A vain girl or woman.

Receive the Right Hand of Fellowship	To be formally welcomed by a minister into membership in a church.
Rubber-lipped	Describes supposedly too fleshy lips.
Run	To sleep around; to sleep with someone; to commit adultery.
Seekers' bench	A place set aside in church, following the invitational hymn, for those seeking salvation. See Clayton (1984, p.33).
Shakes	Sex.
Showoff	A vain person who boasts of or brashly displays his or her looks, talents, achievements, or possessions.
Shuck	To sham; to shirk or avoid labour or duty.
Slack ass	A negative term for caucasoid buttocks.
Slow as cold molasses	Describes a slow-moving person.
Steel wool	A negative term for negroid hair.
Stringy	A negative term for caucasoid hair.
Stuck-up	Proud, vain, *big-feeling*.
Suck (one's) teeth	To make a noise with the tongue and the teeth to express displeasure or anger.
Sugar bowl	Vagina.
Sugar diabetes	Diabetes.
Sweet man	A male lover.
Take the water	To experience baptism.
Talk black, sleep white	Describes a Black person who espouses the cause of Blacks, but whose lover or spouse is white.
Teehee	To laugh.
Testify	To speak; to tell the truth; to bear witness.
Two-faced	Describes a back-stabber or hypocrite.
Uncle Tom	A Black male who acts 'white' or who curries favour with whites.
Uppity	Proud, uncompromising, resistant.
Upside (one's) head	The spot where a parent or elder *clips* a disobedient youth.
Vanilla fudge (cookie)	A white person who hangs out with, sides with, or acts 'Black.' Opposite to *oreo*.
What's (his/her) face?	What's (his/her) name?
Womanish	Describes a girl who sasses or who boldly or brashly pays others, including adults, no mind.
Yellow	A light complexion. A *high yellow* Black person has very light- coloured skin.
Yellow and white earth	Cash. The term probably derives from yellow and white gold. See Lewis J. Poteet, *The Second South Shore Phrase Book* (1985, p.44).

References

Abrahams, R. D. (1992). *Singing the master: The emergence of African American culture in the Plantation South.* New York, Pantheon.

Bengtsson, E. (1956). *The language and vocabulary of Sam Slick I.* Upsala Canadian Studies V. Ed. S. B. Liljegren. Copenhagen: Ejnar Munksgaard; Upsala: A.-B. Lundequistska Bokhandeln.

Black mother, black daughter. (1990). Dir. C. Prieto and S. Hamilton. National Film Board.

Borden, W. (1986, Sept.). Tightrope time: Ain't nothin' more than some itty bitty madness between twilight & dawn. *Callboard, 34 (2)*, 8-81.

Cantwell, R. (1984) *Bluegrass breakdown: The making of the old Southern sound.* Urbana: University of Illinois Press.

Chesnutt, C. W. (1969; 1900). *The house behind the cedars.* New York: Collier-Macmillan.

Chittick, V. L. O. (1958). Books and music in Haliburton. *The Dalhousie review, 38 (Summer)*, 207-21. Rpt. in R. A. Davies (Ed.), (1979), *On Thomas Chandler Haliburton: Selected criticism.* Ottawa: Tecumseh.

Clarke, G. E. (1991). Introduction. *Fire on the water: An anthology of Black Nova Scotian writing.* Vol. 1. Early and Modern Writers 1785-1935. Lawrencetown Beach, NS: Pottersfield.

Clayton, W. P. (1984). *Whatever your will, Lord: A brief history written in commemoration of the 139th anniversary of Emmanuel Baptist Church, Upper Hammonds Plains, Nova Scotia.* Hantsport, NS: Lancelot.

Cozzens, F. S. (1859). *Acadia; or, A month with the Blue Noses.* New York: Derby & Jackson.

Dalby, D. (1972). The African element in Black American English. In C. Cazden, V. John-Steiner, & D. Hymes (Eds.), *The function of language in the classroom.* New York: Teachers College-Columbia University Press.

Dillard, J. L. (1973). The history of Black English in Nova Scotia — A first step. *Revista interamericana review, 2 (4)*, 507-20.

———. (1972). *Black English: Its history and usage in the United States.* New York: Vintage- Random.

———. (1971). The West African day-names in Nova-Scotia. *Names, 19*, 257-61.

Fanon, F. (1967). *Black skin, white masks.* Trans. C. L. Markmann. New York: Grove. Trans. of *Peau noire, masques blancs.* (1952). Paris: Editions de Seuil.

Fauset, A. H. (1931). *Folklore from Nova Scotia.* Memoirs of the American Folk-Lore Society 24. New York: American Folk-Lore Society.

Fergusson, C. B. (1948). *A documentary study of the establishment of Negroes in Nova Scotia between the War of 1812 and the winning of responsible government.* Publication No. 8. Halifax: The Public Archives of Nova Scotia.

Frazier, E. F. (1965). *Black bourgeoisie: The rise of a new middle class in the United States.* 1957. New York: Collier-Macmillan.

Gates, H. L., Jr. (1987). *Figures in black: Words, signs, and the 'racial' self.* New York: Oxford University Press.

George, D. (1790-1793). An account of the life of David George [as told to Brother John Rippon of London and Brother Pearce of Birmingham]. *Baptist annual register, 1*, 473-84.

The Gospel Heirs. (1991). *in the light.* Atlantica Music.

Haliburton, T. C. (1838). *The clockmaker; or, The sayings and doings of Samuel Slick, of Slickville*. Second series. London: Richard Bentley; Halifax: Joseph Howe.

———. (1840). *The clockmaker; or, The sayings and doings of Samuel Slick, of Slickville*. Third series. London: Richard Bentley; Halifax: Joseph Howe.

Hornby, J. (1991). *Black Islanders: Prince Edward Island's historical black community*. Charlottetown: Institute of Island Studies.

Jackson, B. (1989). *A history of Afro-American literature, volume 1, The long beginning, 1746- 1895*. Baton Rouge: Louisiana State University Press.

Jones, G. (1991). *Liberating voices: Oral tradition in African American Literature*. Cambridge: Harvard University Press.

Labov, W. (1969; 1973). The logic of nonstandard English. In N. Keddie (Ed.), *Tinker, tailor ... The myth of cultural deprivation*. Harmondsworth: Penguin.

Langford, F. R. (1882). *A call from Zion: Jubilee songs and old revival hymns*. Weymouth, NS.

Lawrence, G. M., et al. (1989). *Reflections to the third power*. Conway, NS: Grace May Lawrence, et al.

Logan, J. D. (1989). *Thomas Chandler Haliburton*. Makers of Canadian literature. L. A. Pierce, (ed.). Toronto: Ryerson.

McKerrow, P. E. (1976). *A brief history of the coloured Baptists of Nova Scotia, and their first organization as Churches, A. D. 1832*. 1895. Rpt. as *McKerrow: A brief history of the coloured Baptists of Nova Scotia—1783-1895*. F. S. Boyd, Jr., (ed.). Halifax: Afro-Nova Scotian Enterprises.

Mannette, J. A. (1990). 'Revelation, revolution, or both': Black art as cultural politics. Paper. 400 Years: African Canadian History. Multicultural History Society of Ontario. Toronto.

Mencken, H. L. (1936). *The American language*. 4th ed. New York: A. A. Knopf.

Montegut, E. (1850). Un humoriste Anglo-Americain. Haliburton. *Revue des deux mondes*, *5*, 731-48. Rpt. in R. A. Davies (Ed.), (1979), *On Thomas Chandler Haliburton: Selected criticism*, Extracts from selected contemporary reviews/ critical essays, trans. F. Ledwidge, Ottawa: Tecumseh.

Morrison, T. (1992). *Playing in the dark: Whiteness and the literary imagination*. The William E. Massey Sr. lectures in the history of American civilization 1990. Cambridge: Harvard University Press.

Nightingale, M. (1970). *Out of old Nova Scotia kitchens: A collection of traditional recipes of Nova Scotia and the story of the people who cooked them*. Halifax: Petheric.

Nourbese Philip, M. (1989). The absence of writing or How I almost became a spy. In *She tries her tongue, her silence softly breaks*. Charlottetown: Ragweed.

Parker, R. L. (1987). *Beyond the dark horizon*. Cherrybrook, NS: The Black Cultural Centre for Nova Scotia.

Petesch, D. A. (1989). *A spy in the enemy country: The emergence of modern Black literature*. Iowa City: University of Iowa Press.

Poplack, S., & Tagliamonte, S. (1991). African American English in the diaspora: Evidence from old-line Nova Scotians. *Language variation and change*, *3 (3)*,

Poteet, L. J. (1985). *The second South Shore phrase book: A Nova Scotia dictionary*. Hantsport, NS: Lancelot.

Remember Africville. (1991). Dir. S. Mackenzie. National Film Board.

Robertson, J. W. (1854). *The Book of the Bible against slavery*. Halifax.

Robertson, M. (1991). *The chestnut pipe: Folklore of Shelburne County*. Halifax: Nimbus.

Rosenberg, N. V. (1988). Ethnicity and class: Black country musicians in the Maritimes. *Journal of Canadian studies/Revue d'études canadiennes, 23 (1 & 2)*, 138-56.
Saunders, C. R. (1989). *Africville: A spirit that lives on.* Catalogue. Halifax: The Art Gallery, Mount Saint Vincent University; The Africville Genealogy Society; The National Film Board, Atlantic Centre; Cherrybrook, NS: The Black Cultural Centre for Nova Scotia.
Smith, T. W. (1888). The Loyalists at Shelburne. *Collections of the Nova Scotia Historical Society, for the year 1887-88, 6*, 53-89.
Soderlind, S. (1991). *Margin/alias: Language and colonization in Canadian and Québécois fiction*. Toronto: University of Toronto Press.
States, W. N. (1903). *Hymns sung at the services*. Halifax.
Thomson, C. A. (1986). *Born with a call: A biography of Dr. William Pearly Oliver, C.M.* Cherrybrook, NS: The Black Cultural Centre for Nova Scotia.
Traditional lifetime stories: A collection of Black memories. (1987-90). Cherrybrook, NS: The Black Cultural Centre for Nova Scotia.
Tynes, M. (1990). *Woman talking woman*. Lawrencetown Beach, NS: Pottersfield.
Ward, F. (1974). *Riverlisp: Black memories*. Montreal: Tundra.
Woods, D. (1990). *Native song*. Lawrencetown Beach, NS: Pottersfield.

Chapter Nine

Written Mi'kmaq–English as Used by the Mi'kmaw Communities in Cape Breton

Stephanie Inglis

Editors' Introduction

Readers may have noted that several chapters of this book so far have dealt with aspects of Nova Scotia English in situations of language contact, even though language contact itself has not been their central topic. Where two language communities come into contact with each other over a period of time, they almost always influence each other. The many words and expressions borrowed from German in the Lunenburg dialect attest to this, as do other borrowings from French, the remnants of African modes of expression in Africadian English, and even such subtle indications as the Gaelic-influenced emphatic *great big* in the speech of Cape Bretoners.

Throughout most of its history, English has been very open to the possibilities of borrowing from other languages, particularly in the area of vocabulary. Most new additions to the lexicon have been welcomed, especially those that refer to material objects. Unfortunately, nowadays, when 'new' expressions imply some shift in cultural concepts, they may be rejected as 'un-English,' 'unnecessary,' or, in terms of Standard English, just plain 'incorrect.'

Standard English implies not merely a stable form of the language, but also a stable cultural group. The standard language becomes the measure of correctness, and anything nonstandard is therefore by this dichotomous definition incorrect; that is, the inherent correctness of ethnic and regional dialects has no place in the standard/nonstandard dichotomy. As Chapter Seven demonstrates, the recognition of a 'standard' language therefore entails certain socio-cultural attitudes towards nonstandard forms. These are not always completely disparaging: given the general openness of English to new expressions, a regional or ethnic lexicon may be regarded as colourful, and, in the context of mixed feelings about social stratification, regional or ethnic accents may be seen as friendly and attractive. But the standard grammar, it seems, is sacred, and a lapse into regional or ethnic grammar is perceived as the sign at best of a lack of sophistication, at worst of linguistic incompetency.

In most circumstances where a second language is being acquired, the emphasis is on correctness as defined by the standard form of the language, and the learning process itself is basically imitative; that is, the student attempts to imitate the standard language, and the more accurate the imitation, the more competent the student is considered to be. This process is, of course, unobjectionable for a student who merely wishes to enter and experience the culture of a different language group, but in a genuinely bilingual situation it may not be so innocuous. For language groups never overlap cultural groups exactly, and the demands of a standard form of the second language will therefore necessarily involve rejection of at least some of the cultural concepts of the first. This is one of the reasons why languages borrow words from each other in language contact situations — they are to some extent borrowing each other's cultural concepts.

What many people do not realize is that cultural concepts may be incorporated as much in the grammar of a language as in its vocabulary. Even where the grammars of two different languages seem to be relatively similar, there may be slight differences of concept. If we take a minor change in English grammar influenced by the prolonged contact between English and Norman French in the Middle Ages, we can see that there are subtle conceptual differences. In Old English the noun was inflected, with a number of oblique cases, including the genitive. While most of the oblique cases disappeared, the genitive remained as a means of expressing the possessive relationship, although its form was simplified (to *'s* in Modern English). In French, the possessive relationship is expressed by the preposition *de*. We thus have the parallel English/French expressions *Mary's friend* / *(l')ami de Marie*, which are usually regarded as having the same meaning.

In many of its uses, the French preposition *de* could be translated by English *of* (originally meaning 'from,' cf. Modern English *out of*). By using *of* in a possessive function (where it does *not* mean 'from'), English speakers could avoid the ambiguity of such pairs as *the wall's length/the walls' length* by replacing them with the French forms *the length of the wall/the length of the walls*. The result is that in English the two grammatical structures came to exist side by side. But this is not just a useful technique for resolving a possible ambiguity. The existence of the two grammatical structures has permitted further developments in English, so that we now have the multiple possibilities:

Mary's friend
a (the) friend of Mary
a (the) friend of Mary's
one of Mary's friends.

In this case, the influence of a French grammatical structure on English has resulted in an expansion of English concepts.

English and French are not identical culturally, but they are fairly close. The relationship between English and the Celtic languages and cultures is more distant, despite their geographical proximity. Yet the lengthy contact between English and the Celtic languages in bilingual situations has resulted in many borrowings, including grammatical borrowings, in the subsequent Celtic regional dialects of English. This is particularly true of Irish English, whose main development as a distinctive regional dialect during the late eighteenth and nineteenth centuries occurred without much interference from Standard English speakers. Indeed, as the Irish scholar P. L. Henry commented, in a discussion of Irish English sentences judged by more 'competent' speakers to be so incorrect as to be amusing:

> from a linguistic point of view [such sentences] are vastly more interesting than the ordinary conventional kind which is learned or acquired by imitation; because they show the creative spirit at work forging an instrument for personal use, rather than adopting it ready-made from others. (1977, p.24)

The point he makes is that these speakers, rather than passively accepting Standard English and a consequent suppression of their own culture, have succeeded in creating Anglo-Irish, 'a vastly more stimulating and worthwhile achievement' (p.24).

Many Irish Gaelic words have, of course, been adopted into Standard English, but it is not often recognized how much the grammar of Irish Gaelic has influenced English, especially in North America. A few examples will suffice. The Celtic languages in general lack direct positive and negative answers to questions (English *yes/no*), and so circumlocutions are frequent. In Irish, there exists also a practice of making positive statements by means of negative syntax, so that the answer to a simple question can become logically most complex: 'Would you like to dance?' '*I don't mind if I do*.' This kind of negative-positive statement has actually entered Standard English, along with others, such as: 'How did it go?' '*Not bad*,' and '*That's not too good*.' While purists may still dislike the placement of the Irish negative, rejecting statements such as, 'He *isn't* expected to win' in favour of the more traditional 'He's expected *not* to win,' or, preferably, 'He's expected to lose,' in which the negative is eliminated altogether, the form *isn't expected to* is showing every sign of establishing itself in Standard English.

Taking another example, the tenses of the Irish verb are not the same as those of Standard English. In particular, Irish lacks a perfect tense, so that a question like 'Has Donna arrived yet?' would be impossible in Irish, where the simple preterite suffices. Recently, the simple preterite in this situation has begun to appear more and more frequently in English, probably as a result of reinforcement from Irish English, as well as other dialects (as M. B. Emeneau noted, as early as 1935, 'The Lunenburg dialect shows a tendency to use the preterite … rather than the perfect …' (see p.46 above)). The common form of the question among younger Nova Scotians, and many other North

Americans, is now: 'Did Donna arrive yet?' This is still not accepted as Standard English, but Halifax young people find the standard form old-fashioned — *you'd have to be at least thirty to say it.*

This is not an argument against learning a second language properly, but a caution. Cultural concepts differ, sometimes very widely indeed, and it often may be that second-language speakers coming from a bilingual situation, far from being 'incompetent,' or, more technically, 'noncompetent' in the second language, may actually be showing, in P. L. Henry's words, 'the creative spirit at work.' The Mi'kmaq-English speakers in the following chapter may not in the long run have much effect on Standard English, although it is a great deal more likely that they *are* actively involved in the process of developing a Mi'kmaq-English dialect. However, as Stephanie Inglis shows, in her analysis of their writing in terms of Mi'kmaq, rather than English grammar, many of their 'mistakes' show a willingness to grapple most creatively with the inability of Standard English to express quite ordinary Mi'kmaw concepts. *(LF & MH)*

***

Written Mi'kmaq-English as Used by the Mi'kmaw Communities in Cape Breton

by Stephanie Inglis

Written Mi'kmaq-English has become of much interest to many Nova Scotians, particularly non-Mi'kmaw educators who teach Mi'kmaw students. As Danesi and Dipietro (1991), Odlin (1989) and others point out, much of the original emphasis for the concept of language transfer, the idea that second language learners would transfer grammatical concepts from their first language into their second language, came from the work of Charles Fries and Robert Lado in the 1940s and 1950s. Odlin, in his book *Language Transfer* (1989), points out:

> … much of the empirical research in the 1970s and 1980s has led to new and ever more persuasive evidence for the importance of transfer in all [linguistic] subsystems. (p.24)

What one often sees in the written English of many Mi'kmaw university students whose first language is Mi'kmaq is the use of Mi'kmaw semantic categories with English language structure rules. The students exhibit in their writing a form of substratum borrowing (Odlin, 1989): they utilize Mi'kmaw semantic categories with English syntax.

Understanding Written Mi'kmaq-English

The following analysis comes from work with Mi'kmaw high-school and university students in Cape Breton, Nova Scotia. Almost all of the students had Mi'kmaq as a first language. An analysis of the written English of these students gives us some insight into the interesting dynamics of the interplay of meaning systems across languages in contact situations. On Cape Breton Island the majority of individuals speak English as a first language. There are, however, five Mi'kmaw communities on Cape Breton: Membertou, Eskasoni, Chapel Island, Whycocomagh, and Wagmatcook. The largest of these communities, Eskasoni, has a population of approximately 2500 people. In several of these communities the Mi'kmaw language is still spoken as a first language.

A contrastive analysis of the two languages, Mi'kmaq and English, was carried out and used as a tool for analysing the samples of written Mi'kmaq-English. However, it is important to note that not all first-language Mi'kmaq-speaking students write using Mi'kmaq-English; many write using Standard English. The use of contrastive analysis as an analytical tool gives an interesting perspective on discussions of variations of standard written English, for as Odlin (1989) points out:

> We must remember that what we are discussing are 'cross linguistic influences' which often affect second language (L2) production … by interacting with other influences be they social, economic or linguistic. (p.24)

Because of the difficulty in choosing criteria for cross-linguistic comparisons and because structurally Mi'kmaq and English are so different, a contrastive analysis based on semantic categories was done. Various meaning categories, or language functions were chosen, and it was then determined how each of these meaning categories was expressed grammatically, both in the English language and in the Mi'kmaw language.

Use of Prepositions in Written Mi'kmaq-English: The Concepts of Direction, Location, and Position

The meaning frameworks used by writers of Mi'kmaq-English are usually reflective of Mi'kmaw meaning paradigms, not English meaning paradigms. For instance, a student whose first language was Mi'kmaq, when writing using the dialect of Mi'kmaq-English, would use English prepositions as in the following examples:

(1) It refers to the island which was beautiful *with* flowers blooming and the growing palm trees.
(2) *In* the island there is no hatred, very peaceful and no enemies.
(3) Before the boys entered *into* the island it was idyllic *to* the garden of Eden.
(4) Idyllic suggests *to* the garden where Adam and Eve first lived.
(5) *From* the end of the novel the boys who were originally peaceful became animal like creatures.

In sentences (1) through (5) above we see the prepositions *with*, *in*, *into*, *to*, and *from* located correctly before a noun or noun phrase, but conveying nonstandard meanings.

(1) *with* occurring before the noun *flowers*;
(2) *in* occurring before the noun phrase *the island*;
(3) *into* occurring before the noun phrase *the island*;
(4) *to* occurring before the noun phrase *the garden*;
(5) *from* occurring before the noun phrase *the end*.

What we see in the above samples of written Mi'kmaq-English is an application of preposition usage which though nonstandard is *consistent* in that the prepositions are positioned within the sentence as in Standard English; that is, the prepositions come before nouns. However, the prepositions chosen express meanings which would be considered nonstandard.

The Mi'kmaw student writer has focused more on the 'action' involved, rather than on the 'thing' involved as conveyed by the English preposition, which denotes a concept of direction, location or position. For example, when I discussed the last sentence, number (5), with the student who wrote the essay and suggested the Standard English form *At the end of the novel …*, the student explained that what she meant was *From the end …*, i.e., *From now and forever into the future time the boys became animal like*. This is a focus on process, whereas in Standard English we focus on things, as in *At the end of the novel*, i.e., the end of the thing, or the novel. The Mi'kmaw student had applied a Mi'kmaw semantic concept of process orientation to her presentation of English prepositional usage in order to come up with the concept of *From the end of the novel*. Of note is the choice of the preposition itself. Many Standard English writers would perceive this use of the phrase *From the end of the novel …* as being nonstandard; yet, if we discuss what the Mi'kmaw student meant when she wrote the line *From the end of the novel*, we are led by the answer through a mental door into the world of *ilnuita'simk*.

The Expression of Direction/Location and Position Concepts in the Mi'kmaw Language

Ilnuita'simk means 'to think as a Mi'kmaq.' The Mi'kmaw language is a member of the Algonquian language family. Mi'kmaq is related to such languages as Cree and Ojibwa and is very similar in structure to these languages:

Ojibwa	nibaa	S/he sleeps/is sleeping
Mi'kmaq	nepat	S/he sleeps/is sleeping
Cree	nipaw	S/he sleeps/is sleeping

The structure of the languages of the Algonquian family is polysynthetic. *Polysynthetic* languages are those which often have one word as a sentence. In such languages the various word parts inside a word indicate who does what to whom. In languages which are polysynthetic, it is the structure of the word which is often more important than the structure of the sentence. Compare this to the family of Germanic languages, which includes English. In English, it is the structure of the sentence which takes precedence over the structure of the word. In English speakers can make mistakes in the structuring of a word, yet still be understood as long as they have organized the sentence correctly. However, in a language such as Mi'kmaq, the opposite is true. Speakers can order words in a sentence in a variety of ways, but they must correctly order the word parts inside the individual word if a clear meaning is to be achieved.

For example, the English sentence *You are sleeping* is conveyed in Mi'kmaq by one word, *Nepan*. The Mi'kmaw word part *Nep-* means 'sleep,' the Mi'kmaw word part *a-* means 'state,' and the Mi'kmaw word part *-n* means 'you' (singular). By changing the last element of the word *Nepan* to *-t*, speakers are able to say *Nepat*, which means 's/he is sleeping.' The final *-t* in Mi'kmaq stands for 's/he' (present indicative).

We see that in Mi'kmaq one word is used to convey what in English takes many words to express. This is possible because each word in Mi'kmaq is made up of several meaningful parts. To change the meaning of what is communicated, Mi'kmaq speakers change the word parts found inside of the word.

MI'KMAQ			**ENGLISH**
nepay	*nep -a -y*		'I am sleeping'
		Sleep State I	
nepan	*nep -a -n*		'You (singular) are sleeping'
		Sleep State YOU	
nepat	*nep -a -t*		'S/he is sleeping'
		Sleep State S/HE	

It is from the perspective of the structural characteristics of the Mi'kmaw language that we must come to understand the meaning frameworks of Mi'kmaq-English. In English, the group of words known as prepositions are used to convey the concepts of direction, location, and position. Prepositions include words such as *like*, *to*, *from*, *under*, *over*, *by*, *at*, and so on. In Mi'kmaq, *no prepositional-type word is used*. The concepts of direction, location, and position in the Mi'kmaw language are indicated by the first word part or morpheme of the Mi'kmaw verb. To change the concept of direction/location/ position in Mi'kmaq, speakers change the initial morpheme of the verb. Thus, the concepts of direction/location and position in Mi'kmaq form a meaning category which is verb-focused. The following Mi'kmaw examples give some insight into this:

***asikom**-ukkw-al-k*	'I follow him/her across …'
***toqju**-ukkw-al-k*	'I follow him/her up …'
***el**-ukkw-al-k*	'I follow him/her toward …'
***pisk**-ukkw-al-k*	'I follow him/her in/into/to …'
***al**-ukkw-al-k*	'I follow him/her around/about …'
***tew**-ukkw-al-k*	'I follow him/her out of/outside of….'

In the above examples *asikom-* means 'across,' *toqju-* means 'up,' *el-* means 'toward,' *pisk-* means 'in/into/to,' *al-* means 'around/about,' and *tew-* means 'out of/outside of.'

In Mi'kmaq, the primary focus in conveying the concept of *across* is to indicate not that one is 'across-ing' *something*, as in English when one goes *across a river* or *across a bridge*, but that one is 'across-ing' in a certain way, that is, *following across*, *running across*, or *jumping across*. If an English-speaking person were to ask a Mi'kmaq speaker to tell him or her how to say *across* in Mi'kmaq, the Mi'kmaq speaker would ask first, 'Well, what do you mean *across*? There are many different words for *across*,' or, 'It depends on *how* you are going across.' We note that the Mi'kmaq speaker does not say, 'It depends on *what* you are going or placing across.'

In English, the use of prepositions is frequently explained in terms of their systematic *positioning* within the English sentence. Explanations are given that prepositions always introduce a phrase, or that prepositions always precede a noun. For example, in English, we would expect sentences such as 'Mary walked on the road,' with the preposition *on* preceding the noun phrase *the road*.

Because of the effects of language transfer, samples of written Mi'kmaq-English exhibit a variation of standard prepositional usage characterized by nonstandard prepositional choice. What this means is that the choice of the preposition being used is nonstandard. The meaning of the preposition is often utilized in written Mi'kmaq-English in a more process-oriented sense. Consequently, we find examples such as in sentences (6) through (9) below, where the prepositions *for*, *in*, *on*, and *of* respectively are not connected semantically to any great degree to the noun or noun phrase which follows them. The prepositions are being used in a more process-oriented manner. An extreme example of this is found in sentence (8): 'She put me *on*,' which is the Mi'kmaq-English way of indicating 'to give someone a drive in your car,' and which is a direct translation of the Mi'kmaw verb *nasalik*, meaning 'to put something onto something so that one may move that thing along or transport it to another place or position.'

(6) She stands out well *for* the native students [who] attended all the academic institutions …
(7) The only problem is trying to get others to help *in* and maybe come up; [sic] with more reasonable ways to make improvements…
(8) She put me *on* … [This means 'She gave me a drive in her car.']
(9) The people will always have a more positive attitude *of* where they are living.

Use of Pronouns in Written Mi'kmaq-English

The application of Mi'kmaw meaning frameworks in the use of English prepositions is one systematic pattern characteristic of written Mi'kmaq-English. Another characteristic pattern is the nonstandard use of English pronouns. In standard written English, a noun or pronoun is required as subject or object of the verb. Pronouns such as *he*, *she*, *we*, *me*, or *I* can be used either by themselves or to replace a noun which has been previously mentioned in the text. The noun which the pronoun refers to is known as its antecedent. For example, in the following sentences *she* and *it* of sentence (11) refer, respectively, to the antecedent nouns *Jane* and *ball* of sentence (10).

(10) Jane saw the ball.
(11) She kicked it.

In Mi'kmaq there are words which act as pronouns, such as *ni'n*, which means 'I' or 'me,' and *ki'l*, which means 'you' (singular). However, these words are optional in writing or speaking Mi'kmaq. Pronouns such as *ni'n* or *ki'l* are used in Mi'kmaq only for emphasis. Consequently, we may translate the following English sentences into Mi'kmaq by using only one word — a Mi'kmaw verb. No separate pronoun word is needed.

(12) 'I see him.'	*Nemi'k.*
(13) 'I see her.'	*Nemi'k.*
(14) 'They see me.'	*Nemi'jik.*
(15) 'He sees you.'	*Nemi'sk.*
(16) 'She sees you.'	*Nemi'sk.*
(17) 'You see me.'	*Nemi'n.*

There are two things to note about the Mi'kmaw sentences in examples (12) through (17) above:

i. It is the inflection or the ending of the Mi'kmaw verb which tells a listener or reader who does what to whom in any Mi'kmaw sentence. Thus, the Mi'kmaw verb *nemi'k* may be broken down as *nem-* meaning 'see,' *i'-* indicating transitivity with an animate object, and *-k* indicating a present indicative relationship between 'I' and 'him/her' (see sentences (12) and (13) above).

ii. The Mi'kmaw language does not code for gender in either the subject or the object, so we note that the Mi'kmaw sentences (12) and (13) are translated using the *same* verb form, and the same applies to (15) and (16). In the Mi'kmaw language there is only one third person entity *nekm*, which may be translated into English as either 'she' or 'he.' What is of importance to the Mi'kmaw consciousness is not gender but the distinction between animate, that is, having spirit or essence, and inanimate, that is, without spirit or essence. In Mi'kmaq, speakers cannot choose a correct plural ending or choose a correct possessive marker without first knowing whether a noun is inanimate or animate.

As a result of these meaning differences between the Mi'kmaw and the English languages we often see in written Mi'kmaq-English examples of English pronouns incorrectly matched for gender or number. The occurrence of incorrect pronoun reference in this variation of standard written English shows evidence of Mi'kmaw language categories being applied to the English pronoun system.

> (18) It is fair to say that the freedom of speech is essential to every nation, so that *they* may thrive and prosper with the help of *its* people.

Both *they* and *its* in sentence (18) refer to the singular noun phrase *every nation*. Similarly:

> (19) Those nations that permit their peoples right to speech, and listens to *it*, find that there is co-operation and unity.

It in sentence (19) is meant to refer to the plural noun *peoples*.

As we examine the above samples of personal pronoun usage we are reminded that as groups of individuals who share a common language come into contact with groups who speak a different language, instances of language contact occur, resulting in the occurrence of cross-linguistic influences and the creation of language variation and dialects.

Conclusion

The difference between dialect and language as described by Crystal 'is fairly clear cut … all languages [may] be analysed into a range of dialects, which reflect the regional and social backgrounds of their speakers' (1987, 284/24). One should add to the above description the observation that regional dialects of Standard English, such as written and spoken Mi'kmaq-English, reflect the cultural consciousness framed by the first language of the speakers of the dialect. Language analysis gives insight into a people's framework of reality. Often society makes adverse judgments about dialectal English, and often these judgments stem from a lack of understanding of the systematic characteristics of an individual's language patterns and how language contact can affect them.

Variations of any language are simply that — systematic variations of grammar, be they syntactic, lexical or semantic, which are linked to groups of people who have group markers identifying them as collectives. These group markers may be ones of geography, or of cultural or ethnic affiliation.

Mi'kmaq-English, and more specifically written Mi'kmaq-English, is a variation of standard written English which gives us some insight into the interesting dynamics of the interplay of categories of meaning across languages. An analysis of this variation of Standard English lets us examine what has happened as a consequence of over 200 years of language contact between two very diverse languages, Mi'kmaq and English, on the island of Cape Breton in Eastern Nova Scotia.

References

Bartelt, G., Jasper, S. P., & Hoffer, B. (Eds.). (1982.) *Essays in Native American English.* San Antonio: Trinity University.

Brewer, J., & Brewer, R. W. (1982.) Tokens in the Pocosin: Lumbee English in North Carolina. *American speech, 57 (2)*, 108-120.

Crystal, D. (1987.) *The Cambridge encyclopedia of language*. New York: Cambridge University Press.

Danesi, M., & DiPietro, R. J. (1990). *Contrastive analysis for the contemporary second language classroom.* Toronto: OISE Press.

DeBlois, D., & Metallic, A. (1984). *Micmac lexicon.* Canadian Ethnology Service paper no. 91. Ottawa: National Museums of Canada.

Fleisher, M. S. (1982.) Educational implications of American Indians' English. In R. Clair & W. Leap (Eds.), *Language and renewal among American Indian tribes: Issues, problems and perspectives*. National Clearing House of Bilingual Education.

Henry, P. L. (1977). Anglo-Irish and its Irish background. In D. Ó Muirithe (Ed.), *The English language in Ireland.* The Thomas Davis lecture series. Dublin: Radio Telefís Éireann & The Mercier Press.

Inglis, S. (1987). *The fundamentals of Mi'kmaq word formation.* Unpublished MA thesis. St. John's: Memorial University of Newfoundland.

Kroskrity, P. V. (1982.) Language contact and linguistic diffusion: The Arizona Tewa speech community. In F. Barkin, E. A. Brandt, & J. Ornstein-Galicia (Eds.), *Bilinguals and language contact: Spanish, English and Native American languages*. New York: Teachers College Press.

Leap, W. (1982). The study of Indian English in the U.S. Southwest: Retrospect and prospect. In F. Barkin, E. A. Brandt, & J. Ornstein-Galicia (Eds.), *Bilinguals and language contact: Spanish, English and Native American languages*. New York: Teachers College Press.

Odlin, T. (1989). *Language transfer*. Cambridge: Cambridge University Press.

Wolfram, W. (1984). Unmarked tense in American Indian English. *American speech, 59 (1)*, 31-50.

Chapter Ten

Incorporations from English in Nova Scotia Acadian French

Karin Flikeid

Editors' Introduction

One of the most significant features of the language situation in Nova Scotia is the widespread phenomenon of language contact. Not only in the past, but also in the present groups of people speaking different languages at home come in close contact with each other at school, at work, in offices, shopping centres, on various formal and informal occasions. Although English is obviously dominant in Nova Scotia, there is enough leeway for both official and unofficial bilingualism to continue as a part of the Nova Scotian linguistic picture. This situation offers a rich background for the study of such aspects of language contact as are treated in the present chapter, especially under the headings of borrowing and code-switching in Acadian French.

Both borrowing and code-switching have great significance for the understanding of the development of English, a language with a history dominated by 'waves' of borrowing from other languages. Standard textbooks on the history of English assign lengthy chapters to tracing the influx of vocabulary items from Scandinavian, Norman French, and subsequently also from other languages, ranging from Arabic to Yiddish. 'By 1400, the entire nature of the English lexicon had been transformed by the flood of loan-words from French' begins the section on French Influence in C. M. Millward's *A Biography of the English Language* (p.171).

A careful examination of the social context which forms the background for borrowing and code-switching helps us to understand the process of borrowing, and to picture the conditions under which it takes place. While most textbooks and reference works necessarily focus on the results of the borrowing process, a *fait accompli* of the incorporation of thousands of words which now function as an integral part of the English language, the present chapter examines and analyses the process itself. We are shown what items are more or less likely to be borrowed, when they are likely to be borrowed, and by whom. We are also shown how speakers feel about borrowing from another language, something that is difficult to reconstruct in detail from the known facts about the history of English, but which goes a long way towards illuminating the process.

Most importantly, we are shown that borrowing is a natural consequence of the language contact situation, and that it tends to occur even in situations where the speakers are seen to be making an effort to avoid it. The sociolinguistic methodology which is refined in the course of the present study brings to bear all relevant factors, such as the size of the Acadian communities whose speech patterns are under investigation, their proximity to larger English-speaking centres, the age of the speakers, the age and social position of the person to whom they were speaking, the effect of a third person being present during an interview, and even the speakers' awareness of the fact that they were introducing English words in the course of a conversation.

The present study is highly instructive in focusing on borrowing as an ongoing process, instead of looking at the results of borrowing, as is more common in studies of linguistic history. What emerges very clearly is the fact that much of the borrowing is ephemeral in nature. Words borrowed by a few speakers on occasion, or even on many occasions, do not necessarily become permanent features of the language. It is possible to borrow a word or expression without much ceremony, and then, with as little ceremony, to let it go again. This observation confirms that linguistic borrowing, gaining, losing, and adjusting are ordinary features of all language contact situations, past and present.

The chapter examines, side by side, two complementary processes, the process of borrowing, in which foreign lexical material is adapted according the requirements of the recipient language, and the process of code-switching, in which foreign material becomes juxtaposed with native elements, but remains consistent with the grammatical patterns of the language of origin. Flikeid has analysed a large corpus of data obtained from carefully controlled interviews with French-speaking Acadians living in Nova Scotia, and in interpreting the data evaluates the relative importance of a variety of sociolinguistic factors. It emerges from this study that borrowing and code-switching are complex and multi-dimensional social phenomena, which, studied in the Acadian context, can also throw light on similar phenomena in other societies and in other times.

The relative isolation and small size of Nova Scotia's Acadian communities has helped them maintain conservative traits reminiscent of the parent-dialect of those regions of France from which the ancestors of present-day Acadians once hailed. As in Nova Scotian English, side by side with the conservative features, innovations can also be seen. The many examples of Acadian speech analysed in this chapter provide an opportunity to become acquainted with a dialect which is rooted in the past and at the same time also open to ongoing innovation. *(LF & MH)*

***

Incorporations from English in Nova Scotia Acadian French

by Karin Flikeid

In the language contact situation experienced by the Francophone minority in Nova Scotia, the use of English is inherent in daily life. As a consequence, elements drawn from English have become a part of the French spoken locally. Linguistic stereotypes have arisen, invoked both by members of the group itself and by others, which characterize Acadian French as 'half English, half French.' The present study, originating in a corpus-based sociolinguistic inquiry into the current Acadian language situation, evaluates the reality behind this 'quantitative' perception.

Linguistic Background

Overall, the Acadian group forms only a small minority in Nova Scotia: only 5% of the total provincial population has French as its mother tongue. Moreover, the geographical distribution is such that there is no area of Nova Scotia where the Acadians form a regional majority. This is the result of historical circumstances. The massive expulsions of the Acadians by the British during the period 1755-63 scattered the existing population outside the borders of Nova Scotia. The subsequent partial return, authorized after the British-

Map 1
Map of the Atlantic provinces, indicating the five Nova Scotia Acadian communities studied

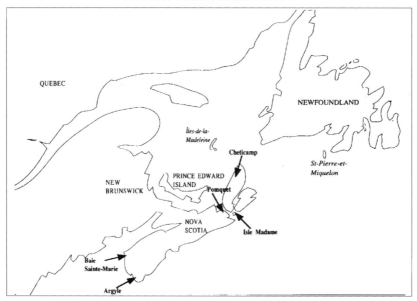

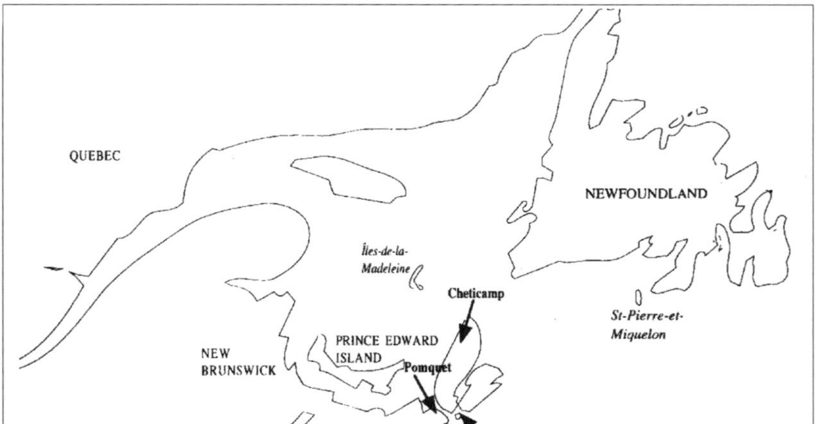

French peace treaty of 1763, was subject to stringent requirements which led the Acadians to regroup as smaller units in different parts of the province, creating a series of linguistic enclaves. On Map 1 are shown the major areas of current Acadian concentration, where there is substantial language maintenance. Cities, such as Halifax and Sydney, where the Acadian component is entirely due to recent in-migration, have not been considered here. In other parts of the province, although population segments of French ethnic origin exist, assimilation has led to language loss. The regions shown on Map 1 are the ones included in the present study. In order of decreasing population size (based on the number of inhabitants whose mother tongue is French, according to the 1991 census), these areas are Baie Sainte-Marie (6895), Argyle (5265), Isle Madame (3635), Cheticamp (3230), and Pomquet (865). All are characterized by relative linguistic isolation, both in terms of contact with each other and with outside Francophones. They also have in common their strong internal cohesion and homogeneity, factors which have contributed to the preservation of the French language. As part of this heritage, there is a tendency towards shared linguistic attitudes and norms within the individual communities.

Relationships with the dominant language group may take different forms in each region, determined in part by the original settlement patterns. In some areas, French and English-speaking settlers received land grants side by side, and their descendants now find themselves intermingled. Elsewhere, greater homogeneity dominated the initial settlement process, with the result that today's population forms a well defined Francophone enclave (Ross & Deveau 1992). The contrast is obvious in terms of the subsequent level of interaction between the two language groups, and in the choice of language in institutional settings. Mixed populations have tended to accept unilingual English services more readily than have the others, as have the smaller groups more generally (Comeau et al. 1987). In particular, the degree to which French has been used in the school setting often reflects the numerical balance of power in a particular area. The French-language content at a given point in time again determines the mastery of written French of that generation of school children (Rawlyk & Hafter 1970). Further factors which influence levels of bilingualism include occupational pressures, which lead to out-migration towards English-speaking areas. The subsequent return of whole families whose children have not been brought up in French can have a significant impact on these small local communities. The circumstances outlined here combine to varying degrees in shaping the bilingual patterns of each community and account for the regional differences in linguistic behaviour.

Methodology and Data Base

The present study is drawn from a research project on Acadian French which was designed to carry out systematic comparisons among the major Nova Scotian communities, and which has been made possible by funding from the

Social Sciences and Humanities Research Council of Canada since 1984. Through a corpus of recorded oral interviews, collected in each of the five areas using an identical protocol, sociolinguistic and dialectal contrasts can be delineated. The present data base has proved useful in conducting both synchronic and diachronic studies.

In order to obtain well differentiated registers, a two-phase approach to the interview process was adopted: informants were first interviewed by a member of their own community, and subsequently by an outside Francophone. The well established familiarity of the local interviewers, combined with the strong local cohesion, resulted in a spontaneous and relaxed register in the first series of interviews, which contrasts with the more formal register elicited by the outside interviewer. The data base used for the present study is made up of 120 of these double interviews, which have been transcribed and computerized, and which contain over 800 000 words of text. During the transcription process, English-language elements were identified and tagged, making an automatic extraction process possible. A total of 34 300 such tagged elements form the basis of the following analysis.

Overall Quantitative Comparisons among Regions

An initial assessment of the extent of language contact phenomena in the various Acadian regions studied can be drawn from Figure 1, which shows the relative incidence of English-origin elements of all types. The two interview situations described above are distinguished, as are three age groups. Before examining the regional contrasts, several overall tendencies can be pointed out. One is the systematic reduction in the proportion of English-language elements when speaking to an outside Francophone. This can be taken to indicate that the driving force behind these incorporations is not lexical need, but community norms. Another clear-cut pattern is the age related increase in use of these elements: the youngest age group displays higher levels across both registers and in all the regions studied, which parallels the increasing

Figure 1

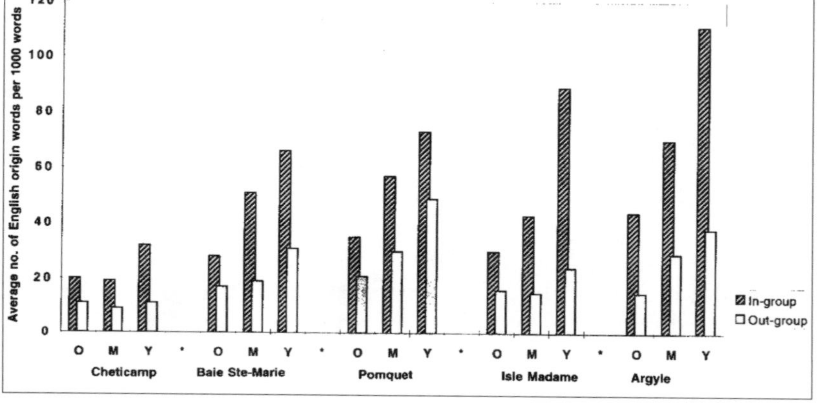

exposure to English over time.

What factors can explain the differences among the communities studied? A complex model emerges, combining the effects of circumstances outlined in the section 'Linguistic Background' above (p.160-161). Some factors act together, reinforcing each other; others have opposing effects, cancelling each other out. Contrasts in settlement patterns would lead us to expect the communities of Cheticamp and Baie Sainte-Marie, with their marked geographic homogeneity, to differ from Argyle and Isle Madame, with their checkerboard settlement pattern. This does indeed correspond to the results illustrated in Figure 1. Considerations of population size seem to be overridden, however, in that Baie Sainte-Marie and Pomquet, the largest and the smallest communities studied, have very similar profiles. As for the French language component in the education system, it would lead us to group Isle Madame and Pomquet, the least favoured in this respect, in contrast to the other three. Such a grouping, however, goes against the findings for Argyle. Yet these may well be accounted for by the factor of Argyle's proximity to Yarmouth. Large urban centres, which in Nova Scotia are Anglophone by definition, play an increasingly important role, as villages cease to offer services that can now be found in the towns. In a vicious circle, this again leads to the necessity of visiting the towns more often. Yarmouth thus serves as a pole of attraction for Argyle, and to a lesser extent, for Baie Sainte-Marie, as does Antigonish in the case of Pomquet. From this perspective, Cheticamp appears 'favoured,' in being relatively distant from any such urban centre. A unique advantage of Cheticamp, with regard to linguistic influences, is also the absence of immediately neighbouring English-speaking communities in all directions but the south, as a result of topographical barriers and the Cape Breton National Park. Obviously, as Figure 1 shows, the remoteness and cohesion of this community carry more weight than the numerical strength and institutional infrastructure of the Baie Sainte-Marie area.

A questionnaire exploring day-to-day language use was administered during the interview sessions. Two individual indices were extracted from the results, one combining the questions on language use in different contexts of communication, the other on reading, listening, and viewing preferences. These were labelled 'active' and 'passive' indices respectively, and cover a scale from 1 to 5, where 1 corresponds to 'always in French' and 5 to 'always in English.' The community means are shown in Table 1. Here again, a comparison with the ranking of Figure 1 shows that the factor of language use does not by itself suffice to explain the degree of penetration of English-origin forms into the language. The fit for Cheticamp is excellent, but we would expect to find Pomquet at the other extreme, which is far from being the case.

Overall, the figures in Table 1 give an indication of how advanced the results of language contact are in Nova Scotia, in terms of the intimate presence of English in day-to-day life. Although there is only one community, Pomquet, where informants do not claim that French outweighs English in active use, the massive predominance of English media is reflected in the high figures obtained for the second index in all communities.

Table 1
Language Use Indices by Region

	Active language use	Passive language use
Cheticamp	1.52	3.83
Baie Ste-Marie	1.59	4.59
Argyle	1.63	4.34
Isle Madame	2.37	4.46
Pomquet	3.02	4.70

Statistical analyses, using the technique of multiple regression, have been carried out on the individual rates of English-language incorporation, combining the explanatory factors discussed above. (A more detailed account can be found in Flikeid (1989).) First of all, the reduction in contact elements from the informal context to the more formal one is found to be highly significant. Because the social variables turn out to have different effects in the two contexts, separate analyses were done for each. To take the informal, or vernacular speech context first, we find that community membership accounts for 25% of the observed variation, while individual factors account for a further 38%, the largest effect being that of age. Interestingly, the level of schooling and the language use indices had only negligible explanatory power.

In the more formal context, the relative weights of the factors shift dramatically: here, the language use indices are the best predictors of the incidence of bilingual phenomena, together accounting for 22% of the variation, with other individual factors coming second, and regional affiliation last. Age does not have a significant effect, and the level of schooling is negatively correlated. The latter finding may in part reflect the fact that the higher a student advances in the education system, the greater is the role of English.

A comparison between the two registers leads to several observations. Not only is the ordering and selection of significant factors different, but the overall level of variation accounted for is lower in the formal register (34% as opposed to 63%). A common explanation can be advanced for both findings: the factors measured in our study primarily involve group membership (this includes age groups), and though these do come into play in the vernacular speech situation, in the formal situation it is likely that individual factors not targeted by our investigation play a greater role. Interaction with an outside interlocutor does seem to be guided by elements of the individual experience, such as degree of bilingualism, type of occupation, and practice in accommodating to speakers of other varieties. While in-group communication is directed by pressures to conform to community norms, interaction with someone from outside the community is characterized by the desire to speak 'good French,' that is, to avoid anglicisms, as shown in the example in (1) below. When the two influences are in conflict, for instance, when group members witness an exchange with an outsider, tensions may arise due to conflicting loyalties. (We preferred one-to-one interviews for this very reason.) The success of this strategy of accommodation will of course be limited by the speakers' repertoire and by force of habit. Thus there may well be cases where access to French-language vocabulary equivalents is more limited both in individuals and community-wide (as demonstrated by the case of Pomquet, for example, where there is less of a shift between interview contexts than in the other communities).

(1) — Des fois, quand qu'on va en promenade de même, on rencontre des différentes personnes avec des français pis....
— Qu'est-ce qui est différent?
— Nous-autres on a plus ... comme on use ça ... on parle avec des mots anglais, on mêle.
— Quand vous parlez avec les gens du Québec, est-ce que vous changez votre... ?
— Non. (Rire). Peut-être si on était par là avec eux, on serait pas si honteux, *but* par ici, si on parlait différent, le monde, hein, ils trouvont ça curieux, hein. Pis là ils disent, 'Elle est faraude.' Faraude ... on dit faraude, sais pas comment-ce que vous diriez ... fier. (IM 190:024b)

Types of Language Contact Phenomena

An established distinction in the literature on language contact is that between borrowing and code-switching (Weinreich 1953; Poplack 1985, 1992; Romaine 1989; Heller 1988; Myers-Scotton 1993). Poplack (1992) stresses the fundamentally different function of these two strategies, where borrowing is characterized as 'the *adaptation* of lexical material to the morphological and syntactic ... patterns of the recipient language,' and code-switching as 'the *juxtaposition* of sentences or sentence fragments, each of which is internally consistent with the morphological and syntactic ... rules of the language of its provenance' (pp.255-6). Operationally, then, an initial division will be between single, integrated, lexical items on the one hand, and multi-word segments, whose internal morphology and syntax are English, on the other. Further refinements on this categorization will be to exclude from the first group words which have one of the specific functions associated with code-switching, examining these in conjunction with the multi-word segments having the same functions. A second adjustment will be to extend the notion of single lexical items to cover phrases which function as a single unit. This has been general practice with regard to compound nouns, but here a variety of other grammatical categories are envisaged. Multi-word colloquialisms will be the object of a separate analysis (see pp.175ff below), because the semantic cohesion which characterizes these sequences militates against a straightforward analysis of them as code-switches. Formally, the classification is further complicated by occurrences of partial integration or translation of elements of the English-origin colloquialism.

The classification of English-origin elements in our corpus benefits from comparisons with the growing number of articles and monographs dealing with this aspect in the French-Canadian situation. Work on the English borrowings in the French of Atlantic Canada includes King (1991), Péronnet (1989), Roy (1979), and Perrot (1995a & b). Other French-speaking areas of Canada are studied in Beauchemin et al. (1992), Mougeon & Beniak (1991), Poplack (1985), and Poplack et al. (1988). Groups studied in the United States with regard to contact phenomena include the Cajuns (Brown 1986, Picone 1994), and the Franco-Americans of New England (Fox & Charbonneau 1995). Particularly close to the sociolinguistic, quantitative approach of the present chapter is the work of Poplack on Ottawa-Hull French, and specific comparisons with Poplack's data will be included.

(a) Lexical Borrowing

A further distinction within the category of single-word elements is that between established, widespread loan-words and one-time or 'nonce' incorporations (Poplack et al. 1988). Based on a given corpus, an observed frequency of *one* occurrence cannot tell us whether this is indeed a nonce phenomenon or whether it is only a single occurrence of a widespread one. Thus the distinction must again be operational, based on our observed frequencies. The examples below correspond to a frequency-based contrast, in that those in (2) were only attested once, whereas those in (3) were used by more than 10 speakers in a given community. The former also represent what we might intuitively expect in terms of a one-time, idiosyncratic borrowing. The proportion of one-time occurrences is quite large, and relatively stable from community to community, for example, 52% in Cheticamp and 53% in Argyle, to take the two extremes of the Nova Scotia continuum (with regard to overall incidence of contact). If we add words which were used more than once, but by only one speaker, the percentages rise to 67% and 69% respectively.

(2) Ça fait ils ont été obligés de grandir le trou. Y avait un *abutment* dans le milieu, ils ont vouté c'te *abutment*-là. (POM 12:519)

C'est pas curieux qu'ils *recuperat*iont pas, n'a longtemps assez qu'ils étiont au lit, ils saviont pas quoi faudrait qu'ils faisiont. (PUB 6:896)

Quand t'allais à Co-op, du maquereau, n'en veux-tu, n'en voilà, y en avait si tant, ça me ressemble.... Ah, le poisson était unreal. (IM 5:616)

(3) Moi, j'aurais ben eu aimé d'avoir une belle maison neuve pis des beaux grands rooms quand je m'ai marié, mais je pouvais pas. (CH 19:191)

C'est que j'arrivions là pis j'avions point nos guitares, faurait je furent les qu'ri et ça, tu sais, le monde enjoyait ça. (BSM 5:488)

Y avait quatre, cinq enfants encore chez nous, pis ils étiont busy à travailler au foin. (POM 22:009)

The distribution by grammatical category has a special significance in view of the literature on borrowing, which has included numerous attempts to establish scales of 'borrowability' (Haugen 1950; Singh 1981; Muysken 1984; van Hout & Muysken 1994), i.e., the relative ease with which different grammatical categories tend to be drawn upon. These may be correlated with the intensity of language contact (cf. Thomason & Kaufman 1988). Here, it is interesting to compare the Nova Scotian communities with each other as well as with language-contact situations described elsewhere. Table 2 gives the breakdown for two of the Nova Scotian communities, representing the highest and lowest levels of incorporations from English respectively.

Table 2
Word-class distribution of lexical borrowing types, for two regions (in-group register)

	Argyle	Cheticamp
Nouns	61%	67%
Verbs	19%	18%
Adjectives	9%	9%
Interjections	2.5%	3.5%
Adverbs	6%	2%
Prepositions	1.5%	<1%
Pronouns	1%	<1%
Conjunctions	1%	<1%

Closed-class forms or function words, such as prepositions, pronouns, and conjunctions, are rarely borrowed from one language to another, and, when borrowed, are therefore seen to be indicative of more intense language pressures. From Table 2, which shows the grammatical distribution in the informal stylistic context, we see that borrowings in these categories are most frequent in Argyle, which is the community with the greatest overall incidence of English-language incorporations, as we have seen above. The small number of lexical types must be interpreted in the light of the fact that these grammatical words form a limited set in each language, in contrast to the open-class categories such as nouns or verbs. The prepositions attested in our corpus include *for*, *from*, *by*, *down*, *around*, *about*, *outside*, and *alongside*. Examples are given in (4). Borrowed pronouns, essentially indefinite pronouns, quantifiers, or *wh*-words, include *anyone*, *anything*, *anybody*, *everything*, *whoever*, *whatever*, and *which*. Their use is illustrated in (5). Conjunctions, in addition to those exemplified in (6), include *but*, *so*, *or*, *though*, *either*, and *whether*.

(4) Je crois pas qu'ils avont rien *against* de l'église, pas yun de zeux. (PUB 15:840)
J'ai marché *across* la cimetière. (POM 5:517)

Je nous en venions comme le devant derrière *like* pour le havre de Louisbourg. (IM 23:086)

(5) Ah, ben n'importe quel groupe ethnique ou racial ou *whatever* que t'as, c'est important de rester ensemble. (CH 1:278)

Je crois pas n'a *anyone* de la famille qui tient de lui. (PUB 12:568)

Anybody peut avoir du *ham* à c'te heure. (POM 7:501)

(6) C'était pas de quoi de grave, là, tu sais, *unless* que tu voles ou que tu tues. (IM 7:463)

Ben je trouve à c'te heure c'est meilleur *because* tu peux suire la messe si c'est en français. (POM 11:337)

Je l'avons attrapée de bonne humeur *although*, tu sais, a' savait quand l'a réveillée et toute ça. (BSM 11:424)

Adverbs are also low on the scale of borrowability, although some subcategories, such as sentence adverbs, are more easily borrowed, particularly if they also function as loosely attached discourse markers (*now*, *then*, *anyway*, *anyhow*). Adverbs in *-ly* (exemplified in (7)) are less commonly incorporated. Other adverbs are illustrated in (8); further examples of borrowed adverbs in this category are *again*, *ago*, *below*, *never*, *only*, *somehow*, and *somewhere*. Several of these require adroitness in the insertion process because word order and other syntactic constraints differ in the two languages. Indications that borrowing results from direct contact with local English can be seen in the adverbial usage of *right*, *some*, and *good*, illustrated in (9).

(7) Je l'achetons *individually* parce que tout le monde aime point la même affaire. (BSM 4:123)

Oh, ben quand tu fais ton ouvrage, *usually* tu travailles pas mal avec ta tête en bas. (IM 8:358)

Il arrivit un *car* là pis c'était de Manitoba. *Automatically* moi je pensais qu'ils étiont anglais. (CH 10:744)

(8) Il allait plus vite *backwards* qu'il allait en avant. (POM 8:465)

T'as ben des affaires aujourd'hui pis le monde est *still* pas content. (IM 19:544)

C'est sale dans la cave pis ça monte en haut *even*, la poussière. (BSM 19:762)

(9) Ben j'étions loin de chez nous itou, mais c'était *some* beau. (BSM 4:448)

Ils alliont aux maisons pis ils chantiont au ras la porte, comme ils chantiont *right* fort. (POM 9:247)

Ils le mettont sus une guénille, mais je veux dire ils colliont *good* dessus. (IM 14:429)

If we take the more unusual borrowing categories just exemplified and compare them to the more readily borrowed ones, i.e., content words such as nouns, verbs, and adjectives, we see that nonce loans are more frequent in the latter group (72%) than in the former (32%). Thus these more unusual borrowings tend to be shared by the whole community.

A comparison with quantitative findings for five Francophone communities in the area of Ottawa-Hull (Poplack et al. 1988) shows the function-word categories to be less prevalent overall than in our Nova Scotia corpus. Pronouns and conjunctions made up less than 1% each and no prepositions were attested. Further, Poplack found adverbs to be extremely rare in the Ottawa-Hull corpus, and those in *-ly* absent entirely.

There appears to be a correlation between the intensity of language contact at the community level and the extent to which loan-words are drawn from categories low on the scale of borrowability. It can be seen in the contrasts among the Nova Scotian communities, as well as in the higher levels found in Nova Scotia overall, in comparison with other French-Canadian situations where contact is less intense. An obvious reason for this is that in order to manipulate borrowed elements which are directly involved in the organization of sentence grammar, such as prepositions or adverbs, a great deal of mastery of the two systems is necessarily implied, as well as practice in insertion. The substitution of a borrowed noun for a native one requires little such skill, as does the adoptions of interjections, discourse markers, and other peripheral elements.

(b) Code-Switching

When a sequence of several words maintains its internal English syntax and morphology, it is a candidate for classification as a code-switch. Single words and compounds may also be code-switches: one way in which this is discernible is through their marked function. A classification of the discourse functions of such multi-word and single-word segments is given in Table 3, following Poplack (1985).

Table 3
Code-switches by discourse function, for two regions (in-group register)

	Argyle	Cheticamp
Metalinguistic commentary	0.4%	0.1%
English bracketing	0.8%	6.0%
Translation / Explanation	1.1%	3.5%
False start / Hesitation	0.1%	14.5%
Other discourse functions	2.3%	7.0%
Fixed expression / colloquialism	46.0%	30.0%
Nominal group	12.5%	34.0%
Other unflagged switches	36.8%	4.9%

A series of functions that may advantageously be grouped together for consideration are those where the speaker signals awareness of making a switch. These include in particular the first three categories of Table 3. Metalinguistic commentary is exemplified in (10), bracketing in (11), and translation/explanation in (12). Poplack's (1985) study showed that the speaker's need to signal awareness in this manner was greater in French-majority communities in Hull (where 59.1% of all switches fell into these categories) than in the minority settings of Ottawa (34.5%). Table 3 shows that in Nova Scotia this function is far less prevalent, ranging from 2.3% in Argyle to 9.6% in Cheticamp. In the formal interview context, the proportion does rise considerably, from 2.3% to 37.8% in Argyle, for example. (See the next section (p.174 below) for further discussion of the in-group/outsider contrast. With regard to the comparability of the two French-Canadian corpora in this respect, see Flikeid 1989.)

(10) *But* les vieux parlerait pas comme ça, je veux dire, pis '*back*er le *car*,' les vieux dit, 'il recule.' (IM 12:32)

Even des Anglais, ils *catch*eront *up* vite à cause que y a beaucoup de mots anglais, tu sais. Des fois on dira comme j'ai dit '*catch*er *up* vite' ou ben donc je dis 'ils attrapont vite.' (BSM 6:500)

On dirait un tambour, nous autres, pour un *porch*. Zeux, un tambour c'est un *drum*. (PUB 147:035b)

(11) J'ai des petits *great grandchildren* qu'ils appelont pis j'aime ça, ah mon Dieu! (IM 26:238)

Mais tu sais, sus ça, tu sais, comme qu'ils diseriont, *knock on wood*, on est pas trop malchanceux. (CH 7:268)

Y avait eu ça qu'ils appellent un espèce de *victory parade* là. (BSM 20:202)

(12) J'avions tout le temps un ... *a trash collecting day*, là, tu ramassais tout le ... les *trash*. (PUB 3:445)

Si ils avaient trente dans une classe, ils araient aimé avoir trente *A students*, tu sais, des étudiants toutes nombre un. (CH 8:404)

Ben quand mon mari s'en a été, il s'en a été parce j'avions un *home* à payer, une maison à payer. (IM 27:122)

A special case of translation found in the Nova Scotian communities is illustrated in (13), where the informant translates a French term into English, for the benefit of the interviewer, generally belonging to a younger generation. A further potential case of signaling is the case of the false start/hesitation (14). This group is again more prevalent in Cheticamp (14.5%) than in Argyle (less than 0.1%), which may well indicate that it is related to the first three, in terms of consciousness.

(13) Ben tu ramassais toutes les petites cerises rouges, les *choke-cherries*. (POM 16:479)

Le lendemain je sortirent pis je perdirent le canot, le treize de décembre, *Friday the thirteenth*. (IM 23:47)

Ils bouchiont les cheminées avec euh … de la moutarde. Quoi-ce qu'est de la moutarde, c'est euh … l'herbe du hâvre qui se ramassait l'automne … ça qu'ils appellent de la *eel-grass* en anglais. (POM 18:263)

(14) J'aime à parler anglais, du moins que la personne croie pas que je parle de yelle ou que … *I want to make* … que je veule … comme je veux dire, je vas … *I make fun of her*. (IM 23:114b)

Je te dis que ç'a changé. Tu peux point euh … *you can't turn back the clock*, hein. (BSM 20:527)

C'est familial, hein, ça se donne. C'est dans tes…. C'est ton *genetic* euh … *make-up*. (BSM 8:482)

Switches which are not explicitly flagged constitute by far the largest group in all the Nova Scotian communities. Of these, a large proportion is made up of colloquialisms or idiomatic expressions. These are readily distinguishable from the essentially unpredictable sequences that constitue the archetypal code-switch, as illustrated in (15), both by their semantic cohesion and by the fact that they are often recurrent. Examples are given in (16). (17) gives a list of other expressions which are similar in nature: in (a) are found units which appear only once; (b) is a list of those which recur with some frequency. Switches which occur within idiomatic expressions will be examined below.

(15) Ils faisiont le savon. T'avais pas le … *Tide or all that kind of soap they have now*. (PUB 22:269)

Je crois *if I had to live my life over again*, je crois je serais une soeur. (POM 20:513)

Comme, si t'as pas travaillé pour quatre mois, là, *and you got no practice*, tu vas pas le faire. (IM 3:915)

(16) Je peux point dire qu'ils m'ont plus mal servi qu'un autre, hein, parce que *it's give and take*, tu sais, faut que tu pouves pleyer pour zeux. (BSM 14:501)

Je savions quíls veniont *in* et j'allions au quai guetter et, tu sais, c'était *first come, first serve*. (PUB 2:187)

Ça fait j'ai attrapé une punition pour ça, *as a matter of fact*, dix coups de *strap* chaque main. (IM 10:486)

(17)(a) *away you go*
bag and baggage
best in the world
honest to God
I bet you any money
it was done and forgotten
That's a good question.
You name it, they had it.

(17)(b) *as far as I know*
back and forth
in other words
most of the time
on the go
once in a while
That was it.
That's for sure.

Another category of units which are whole constituents are the nominal groups. Those which are idiomatic expressions as well were included in the previous category. Here we consider those of the type illustrated in (18). Just as the noun is the easiest single-word category to integrate, so too is the noun phrase. Its status as a code-switch is sometimes contested. Also, the boundary between compounds and noun phrases is difficult to determine. These phrases often have a referential function, comprising technical terms or cultural concepts habitually designated in English. Certain areas are particularly well represented: fashion, food, sports, medicine, work, and so on.

(18) Moi, c'est obligé être de la *easy listening music*. (POM 5:389)

Pis nous autres, je sons les *small woodlot owners* qui sont sous deux cents arpents. (BSM 21:365)

Leurs hommes sont morts mais zeux automatiquement restent, tu sais, comme *honorary members*. (CH 7:405)

Sociolinguistic Patterns in Code-Switching and Borrowing

(a) Flagged versus Unflagged Code-Switches

We have already mentioned briefly above that the proportion of flagged switches, those where the speakers signal in one way or another that they are aware of moving from one language to the other, rises in the interview context where the interviewer is a Francophone from outside the community. Here we will take a closer look at this phenomenon, relating it to age differences as well, for the community which has the greatest incidence of code-switches of all types, Argyle. Figure 2 shows the results of the breakdown by age-group and interview context. First of all, we can see that the increased use of flagging in the more formal context is a characteristic of all age groups. Second, comparing the age groups within each context, we see that the older the speaker, the more he or she will tend to be aware of engaging in switching practices, and feel the need to signal the switch. Conversely, younger speakers feel this need far less—perhaps because the code-switching is becoming so much a part of the community norm that consciousness of it is decreasing.

The generational difference between the interviewers and informants must also be taken into account, particularly to explain the results in the in-group

Figure 2

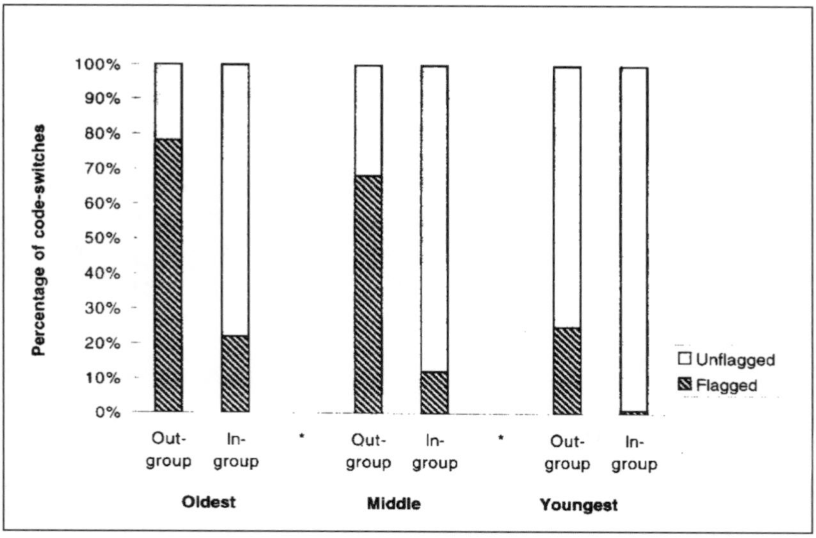

interview context. The total lack of manifestations of self-consciousness characteristic of the exchanges between two speakers of the same age, both young, contrasts with the somewhat greater incidence in the middle and older groups, who may well feel that their status as elders confers on them a role of some detachment vis-à-vis the internal community norm of unflagged switching.

(b) Gender and Age-Related Patterns in Lexical Borrowing

The same type of multiple regression as was done for overall quantitative comparisons between regions (pp.164-165 above) was applied to the occurrences of borrowing. Age again appears as a major explanatory factor in the informal context. In the case of Argyle, it accounts for 51% of the total variation. The second most important factor there is gender (6% of the total variation), with men borrowing more than women. Figure 3 shows the combined effects of these two dimensions. We see that there is also interaction between the two, in that the gap is greater as age decreases, with practically no difference between the sexes in the oldest group.

Figure 3

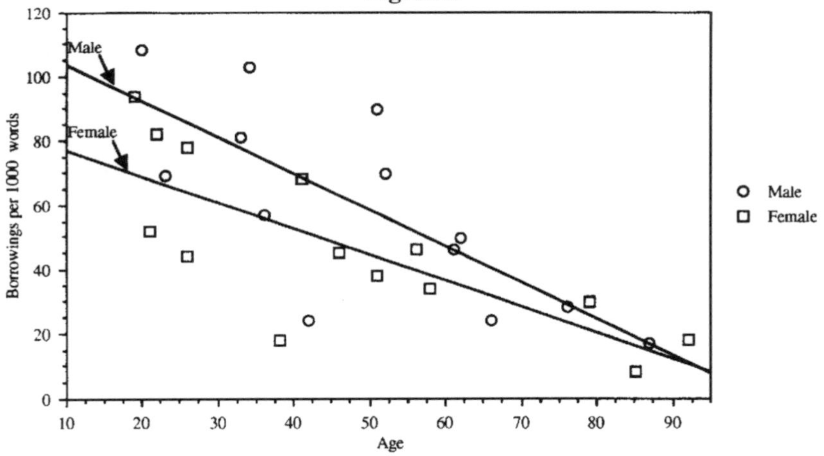

Incorporation of Semantically Cohesive Multi-Word Units

There is, in our view, not a polarity, but a continuum between the single, integrated word and the multi-word sequence within which English morphology and syntax remains intact (i.e., code-switches, by the accepted operational definition), at least in the case of the category of fixed expressions and colloquialisms. Extending the reasoning that leads to considering compound nouns as single lexical items (i.e., functioning as a single unit), special consideration must be given to complex prepositions (*as for*, *in spite of*) and conjunctions (*so that*, *as long as*), as well as phrasal verbs (*keep on*, *take over*), etc. Multi-word discourse markers such as *you know* and *I mean* also come into consideration here.

Idiomatic expressions per se, such as *right off the bat* and *all for the best*, could conceivably also be treated as single units. When they are incorporated as a whole (cf. (16)), such an analysis would be clear-cut. However, if we look at the full range of contact phenomena that occur in the context of such English-origin colloquialisms, intermediate cases appear. For example, sequences nested within the semantic unit constituted by the idiomatic expression may in themselves technically be code-switches, as in (19), the remaining part being translated or calqued. Traditionally, this situation would be treated separately from the case where only one word of such a unit of this type appears in English (20), yet the process is similar. What both have in common could be characterized as a strategy of translating or calquing as much as possible of the idiomatic expression, leaving an irreducible core, be it one-word or multi-word, which remains in the originating language.

(19) Je pense que je suis aussi bon comme le *next one* pis j'suis pas pire. (IM 19:580) [< as good as the next one]

Mais moi, y avait *no way* que je savais quoi-ce qu'il parlait *about*. (BSM 15:516) [< there was no way]

Ils disiont que j'était trop gros pour ça, mais j'allais yinque pour la *fun of it*. (POM 1:120) [< for the fun of it]

(20) C'est surtout … la qualité du poisson qu'est *processé*, tu sais, si c'est *fit* à manger. (BSM 20:256) [< fit to + infinitive]

Sa *birthday*, al avait une couple de petites filles venir *over*. (POM 11:393) [< to have X come over]

Je peux pas te dire bonnement … s'il va s'en m'nir pour *good*. (IM 23:321) [< come back for good]

A related form of partial adaptation involves a sequence of individual words, integrated one by one, such as in (21). A further blurring of boundaries occurs when the initial or final word of a semantically cohesive sequence is morphologically and syntactically integrated, while the remaining part remains unmodified (22). This is a difficult case for the borrowing/code-switching dichotomy, although it would logically be classed as a multi-word switch — the problem lies in the status of the transitional integrated word. Even more intricate is the case where the full expression is made up of only two words (23) and where the traditional view only allows us to identify two separate borrowings, which is contradictory to the intuition that these are incorporated as a unit. On the surface, some boundary words appear to be non-integrated, in particular where verbs are in tenses which have zero inflections in French. Thus, if the first example (22) had been in the affirmative, *feel out of place* would surface as a fully monolingual English sequence. It is only in comparison with the habitual treatment of such verbal groups that we see that *feel* must be classified as integrated, but with a zero French inflection.

(21) J'ai fini dans *grade* dix et je finis avec mon *average* de *overall* avec soixante et douze et je me décidis j'allais. (BSM 5:301) [< overall average]

C'était point loin, mais c'est ça, tu sais, une fois que tu fessais dans du *traffic bumper* à *bumper* comme d'icitte à Meteghan-River, ç'allait point vite. (BSM 16:51) [< bumper-to-bumper traffic]

As far que moi j'suis *concern*[*ed*], ils ariont dû avoir le français. (POM 8:306) [< As far as I'm concerned]

(22) Tu *feel* point *out of place* en *bathing-suit* dans des endroits de même. (BSM 4:230)

Ils se mariont à neuf heures, je crois, le matin pis ça *runn*ait *right through*. (POM 11:308)

Ça me plairait ben d'être yun de zeux là, comme aller *somewhere* dans un *boat* là et *end*er *up* dans un *new world*, là, tu sais. (PUB 16:305)

(23) Pis là j'ai parlé à une femme *indirectly involv*ée.... (BSM 11:319)

Y en a zeux qui tient rien que la rod dans le milieu pis quitte un *puddle form*er. (IM 3:914)

Comme *usually* ils *call*iont à *shore* et à quelques logis là. (PUB 2:185)

A distinct subgroup of the preceding category is the verb + particle sequence, or phrasal verb (24), which is morphologically and syntactically integrated, i.e., the verb is conjugated according to French morphology and elements such as the negative particle, pronouns, or noun phrase objects can be inserted between the two parts of the expression. Often there is modification of the particle by adverbs such as *right*. Over 150 phrasal verbs were attested in the corpus, many being nonce occurrences. Some additional examples are *pry out*, *switch back*, *settle down*, *smarten up*, and *break in*. Significantly, the use of phrasal verbs is correlated with the overall degree of language contact.

Thus in Cheticamp only five different forms occurred, whereas Argyle provided the largest number of examples (over 100). As can be seen from the examples in (24), use of these expressions clearly impinges on sentence organization.

(24) *So* faudrait qu'ils *block*irent ça *off* pour presque de la moitié d'une journée. (BSM 4:536)

Zeux avont dit 'A yoù-ce que t'es?' pis moi j'ai *shaké* ma tête *away* pis là zeux ont dit 'Ben t'es à Halifax.' (POM 5:413)

Je sais point on a arraché beaucoup de mois, là, ça *add*ait point *up* beaucoup. (PUB 18:533)

The preceding verbal expressions can be contrasted with cases where the initial verb is translated or calqued rather than integrated. In (25) are examples where a multi-word monolingual English sequence still remains after this process of adaptation. In the case of the two-word verbal unit, only one word is left in English (26). Where phrasal verbs are involved, only the particle is left (27). Often partial adaptation coexists with the use of the full expression (e.g., tiendre *track* vs *keep track*; garder *around* vs *look around*) within the same community or even within the speech of the individual.

(25) Ça va *both ways*. (IM 7:243b)

J'aimerais *travel*er et aller *around the world* si je pourrais. (PUB 9:712)
Y a des *instructors* qui te montront le *right way* à le faire. (POM 11:453)

(26) Non, j'ai point été dans un accident, j'assaye de m'en tiendre *clear*. (BSM 1:211)

Il faisait *great*. (POM 5:487)

Il faut tiendre notre français, *but* je crois point que faut aller *overboard*. (PUB 23:711)

(27) J'avions au moins, moi je dirais, dix cours qu'alliont *on* en même temps. (CH 2:099)

J'aime mieux sauter *off* d'un quai moi que marcher dans l'eau. (IM 3:417)

J'allions point passer *by* c'te vache-là tout seuls. (PUB 5:145)

In our view, there are degrees of adaptation to be distinguished, ranging from the fully English units ((16) and (17)) to the fully calqued versions, passing through the intermediate treatments given in (19) to (27). There are several observations to be made about the incorporation of English-origin idiomatic expressions. Their high incidence overall is indicative of the pressure exerted in a bilingual situation by the imagery of the other language — vivid and expressive, they come easily to mind. Semantically, they operate as wholes, and are integrated globally. With regard to the ease of incorporation, there is a contrast between those that are relatively peripheral, such as *as far as I know*, or *no doubt about it*, and thus readily attached to an existing monolingual French sentence, and those where the structural coherence of the sentence is intimately involved (28). Insertion of such non-detachable expressions may require the same skill in the dovetailing of the two coexisting language codes as the integration of function words discussed above. The same observation applies to the strategy of selectively translating parts of these expressions, which necessitates going back and forth between languages with a great deal of adroitness.

(28) Si mes resultats sont moins que B, ce maudit B, mon ouvrage est <u>*on the line*</u>. (CH 8:658)

C'était le diable <u>*in a sense*</u> qu'ils disiont, vois-tu. (IM 10:022)

On pouvait porter des *nylons* ... à ce temps-la, <u>*by the time*</u> moi j'ai eu quatorze ans. (PUB 14:432)

Conclusion

A singularity of the Nova Scotia data, compared to other described contact situations, is the high incidence of incorporation of all or part of cohesive semantic units, either recurrent or potentially so, in both cases different from the clear-cut code-switches which predominate in other studies. This has led us to approach the classification from another angle: starting with these units themselves, and seeing how they are treated. Taking all the fixed or idiomatic expressions which owe their content to English, a continuum of adaptation emerges, with a clear capacity of opting for extensive integration of the various elements. At one end we have the complete translations, or calques, at the other incorporation of the full English expression.

We have looked particularly at the intermediate category which includes both English and French elements, and have found that these can be attributed to a striving towards maximum integration or translation, leaving only an irreducible core in English. If this is only one word, or a number of separate words, they will be morphologically integrated. If there is a sequence of words involved, the first element will often serve as an integrated transition, particularly in the case of verbs, while the remaining part of the sequence will keep its internal English morphology and syntax. Although many fixed expressions are only loosely attached to the sentence, others are syntactically integrated, as are the core borrowings within these units. The high level of integration practised in the Acadian communities is a reflection of bilingual mastery. It ties in with the high levels of borrowings of parts of speech which demand skill in insertion: adverbs, prepositions, pronouns, conjunctions, phrasal verbs, and verbal particles.

Another major finding to emerge from the preceding analysis is the impact of the communicative context on the incidence of each of the examined processes. For every speaker in the corpus, an overall reduction in incorporations from English is observed when she or he is interviewed by a Francophone from outside the Acadian community, after having first been interviewed by a member of his or her own community. This tendency can be discerned within each of the types of language phenomena distinguished, i.e., borrowing and code-switching. Within the latter category, the contrast between flagged and unflagged sequences reveals a further difference in the degree of consciousness being signalled with regard to the switch between languages. There is an extremely low incidence of flagged switches in the in-group interviews, whereas these rise to as many as half of the total switches in the outsider interviews.

The preceding contrast ties in with the norms governing the particular communicative exchange. Within-group exchanges are subject to internal community norms. These permit massive recourse to established loans, nonce borrowing, integration of set expressions, in whole or in part, and classical code-switches. When attention is focused on achieving the speech style characterized as linguistically putting on one's 'Sunday best' (Blanche-Benveniste et al. 1990), these practices are severely curtailed, being seen as inappropriate.

The widespread capacity to control the incidence of the incorporation process belies the belief that incomplete mastery of French is the major factor involved. However, the rising incidence of incorporated elements in younger speakers is an obvious reason for concern, and misgivings in this regard were expressed by many informants. Combined with the decline in the number of domains where French is used in day-to-day speaking, it is clear that the disuse of many vocabulary items and expressions can only lead to a raising of the threshold. This is confirmed by the correlation between the language use indices and the prevalence of English elements in the outsider interviews. Decreased use of French does seem to lead to a lesser flexibility in switching to an all-French mode. The need felt by older informants to translate certain French vocabulary items for the benefit of the younger interviewers again illustrates the reality of this tendency. On the more positive side, however, is the active involvement of the schools in familiarizing students with the French equivalents of established English loanwords and with French vocabulary in general, a process enhanced by the shift towards more and more subjects being taught in French. The time when an Acadian could say bitterly of the Nova Scotia situation that English represents the language of knowledge and French a tribal dialect (Deveau 1977) is fortunately past.

References

Beauchemin, N, Martel, P., & Théoret, M. (1992). *Dictionnaire de fréquence des mots du français parlé au Quebec*. New York: Peter Lang.

Blanche-Benveniste, C., et al. (1990). *Le français parlé: études grammaticales*. Paris: Editions du CNRS.

Brown, B. (1986). Cajun/English code switching: A test of formal models. In D. Sankoff (Ed.), *Diversity and diachrony*. Amsterdam: John Benjamins.

Comeau, J., et al. (1987). *Recherche sur les facteurs d'assimilation chez les Acadiens de la Nouvelle-Ecosse*. Rapport. Pointe de l'Eglise, NS: Institut de développement communautaire.

Deveau, D. (1977). Les Acadiens de la Nouvelle-Ecosse, réveil ou crépuscule? *L'Action nationale, 67 (3-4)*, 308-320.

Flikeid, K. (1989). 'Moitié anglais, moitié français'? Emprunts et alternances de langues dans les communautés acadiennes de la Nouvelle-Ecosse. *Revue québecoise de linguistique théorique et appliquée, 8 (2)*, 177-228.

———. (1991). Techniques of textual and quantitative analysis in a corpus-based sociolinguistic study of Acadian French. In S. Hockey & N. Ide (Eds.), *Research in humanities computing*. Vol. I. Oxford: Oxford University Press.

Fox, C, & Charbonneau, L. (1995). Le français en contact avec l'anglais: analyse des anglicismes dans le français parlé à Cohoes, New York. *Revue québecoise de linguistique théorique et appliquée, 12*, 37-63.

Haugen, E. (1950). The analysis of linguistic borrowing. *Language, 26*, 210-231.

Heller, M., et al. (1988). *Codeswitching: Anthropological and sociolinguistic approaches.* Berlin: Mouton de Gruyter.

King, R. (1991). WH-words, WH-questions and relative clauses in Prince Edward Island Acadian French. *Canadian journal of linguistics, 36*, 65-85.

Millward, C.M. (1989). *A biography of the English language*. New York: Harcourt Brace Jovanovich.

Mougeon, R., & Beniak, E. (1991). *Linguistic consequences of language contact and restriction: The case of French in Ontario, Canada.* Oxford: Oxford University Press.

Muysken, P. (1984). Linguistic dimensions of language contact: The state of the art in interlinguistics. *Revue québecoise de linguistique, 14*, 49-76.

Myers-Scotton, C. (1993). *Duelling languages: Grammatical structure in codeswitching*. Oxford: Oxford University Press.

Péronnet, L. (1989). Analyse des emprunts dans un corpus acadien. *Revue québecoise de linguistique théorique et appliquée, 8 (2)*, 229-51.

Perrot, M.-E. (1995a). Quelques aspects du métissage dans le vernaculaire chiac de Moncton. *Plurilinguismes, 9-10*, 147-67.

———. (1995b). Tu worries about ça, toi? Métissage et restructurations dans le chiac de Moncton. *LINX, 33*, 79-85.

Picone, M. (1994). Code-intermediate phenomena in Louisiana French. In Beals, et al. (Eds.), *Papers from the Thirtieth Regional Meeting of the Chicago Linguistic Society.*

Poplack, S. (1992). Variation theory and language contact. In D. Preston (Ed.), *American dialect research: An anthology celebrating the 100th anniversary of the American Dialect Society*. Amsterdam: John Benjamins.

———. (1985). Contrasting paterns of code-switching in two communities. In H. Warkentyne (Ed.), *Methods V: Papers from the fifth international conference on methods in dialectology*. Victoria: University of Victoria Press.

Poplack, S, Sankoff, D., & Miller, C. (1988). The social correlates and linguistic processes of lexical borrowing and assimilation. *Linguistics, 26 (1)*, 47-104.

Rawlyk, G. A., & Hafter, R . (1970). *Acadian education in Nova Scotia: An historical survey to 1965*. Ottawa: Royal Commission on Bilingualism and Biculturalism.

Romaine, S. (1989). *Bilingualism*. Oxford: Basil Blackwell.

Ross, S. & Deveau, A. (1993). *The Acadians of Nova Scotia: past and present*. Halifax: Nimbus.

Roy, M-M. (1979). Les conjonctions anglaises 'but' et 'so' dans le français de Moncton. MA Thesis, Université de Québec à Montréal.

Singh, R. (1981). Aspects of language borrowing: English loans in Hindi. In P. H. Neide (Ed.), *Sprachkontakt und Sprachkonflikt*. Wiesbaden: Steiner.

Thomason, S., & Kaufman, T. (1988). *Language contact, creolization, and genetic linguistics*. Berkeley: University of California Press.

van Hout, R., & Muysken, P. (1994). Modeling lexical borrowability. *Language variation and change, 6*, 39-62.

Weinreich, U. (1953). *Languages in contact: Findings and problems*. Publications of the Linguistic Circle of New York, 1. The Hague: Mouton.

Chapter Eleven

Women and Language

Deborah Poff and Lindsey Arnold

Editors' Introduction

Underlying the following study conducted by Deborah Poff and Lindsey Arnold is the question whether men and women differ in their use of language. This study was based on individual interviews and on focus groups in which the participating women gave voice to their perceptions and opinions in this matter, on the whole leaning towards the conclusion that significant differences do exist between women's and men's use of language.

Posing a question about differences in language use entails special problems for English, which may on the surface easily seem to be 'the same' when used by men and women. While French, by contrast, requires us to say *je suis heureux* or *je suis heureuse* depending on the speaker's gender, in English a long story can be narrated without giving away the narrator's sex, a fact sometimes used for literary effect, as in K. K. Richardson's *Getting Away* (1992). In this sense the language of men and women is 'the same.'

In many other ways, however, the language is different. While written narrative does not need to identify the narrator's sex, most narratives do provide a variety of clues, and spoken narrative would be distinguished by the speaker's voice, intonation, and pitch, and possibly also by choice of words. Furthermore, both writing and speech make a distinction in gender when referring to a third person, as in the use of *she* or *he*, *girl* or *boy*, *queen* or *king*.

Language use differs between the sexes in yet another way, and that is in the function of group talk. In a paper entitled 'The La Have Island General Store: Sociability and Verbal Art in a Nova Scotia Community' (1972), Richard Bauman discusses the now discontinued custom of gathering in the General Store and talking in exclusively male groups. It appears that in small Nova Scotia communities in the past, men's talk, apart from ordinary communication, served also certain special purposes of solidarity and bonding. It was common for the men gathered in the store on winter evenings to share yarns about unusual events, especially those experienced while fishing, or unusual encounters, especially with the supernatural.

Women's group talk in rural communities also has a long Maritime tradition, but it has been generally downplayed as 'gossip' and its social importance overlooked. Still, some perceptive writers saw its vital importance in community life.

In *Anne of Ingleside* (1939), L. M. Montgomery gives a deft description of the function of a quilting bee for initiation of young women. An important element of the 'gossip' was to judge the conduct of others, not necessarily in terms of existing law or prevailing morality, but rather in accordance with the merits of the case, as looked at from several points of view — an approach not altogether lost with the passing of quilting bees, for we encounter a similar view expressed by the participants in Poff and Arnold's study.

Quilting bees are no longer a regular occurrence in Nova Scotia, though they can still perform an important social function, as Donna E. Smyth demonstrates in her novel *Quilt (1982)*, which is set in a rural community in Nova Scotia's South Shore.

In the last twenty-five years significant changes have taken place both in the social fabric of Nova Scotia, and in the texture of the language used by women and about women and their activities. The generally derogatory way of referring to women, their work and their place in society has gradually been replaced by a more equitable use of language.

This change, which gathered momentum in the United States in the wake of the Civil Rights movement of the sixties, reached Canada rapidly, and Nova Scotia has followed suit, establishing guidelines on bias-free use of language at all levels of public life, including, most importantly, schools, the government and the media. The matter-of-fact attitude with which Nova Scotians now use gender-neutral terms like *chairperson* makes it hard to believe that as recently as the 1980s the term was under fire in the name of logic, purity of language, and tradition. One letter-writer to the Halifax Mail-Star (Dec. 19, 1983) complained, praising the approach then taken by The Maine Times, which banned the word *chairperson* in favour of the traditional terms *madam chairman* and *mister chairman*. At present, it is probably the latter terms which would strike us as neither logical nor pure, and as for tradition, our younger generation may no longer be aware of the particular tradition that was being invoked in the argument.

Yet the changes produced in the last twenty-five years have not altogether removed the need for women to get together in order to discuss various issues, including even the use of language itself. Even though bias-free language now prevails in public life and the media, the feeling still persists that men and women use language differently, and that some problems connected with the use of language pervade our everyday lives.

The following chapter by Poff and Arnold shows that in women's perception the two sexes make use of different vocabularies, that, in effect, women grow to become bi-dialectal, learning to speak both their own language and the language of men, that women use personal conversation for different purposes than do men, that women are still put down in some situations, and that, once these various factors are taken into account, there emerges a clear need for change, built on a better understanding of these differences. *(LF & MH)*

***

Women and Language
by Deborah Poff & Lindsey Arnold

When I was growing up in the 1960s, I remember that I heard the following joke more than once. It went: 'What are the fastest means of communication?' And the punch line was: 'Telephone, telegraph and tellawoman.' As a kid, I didn't think it was funny, but I wasn't sure why. As many psychologists, sociologists and linguists have pointed out, what a culture finds funny is telling. In this case, the joke contains the aggression or hostile features that Freud thought were an essential feature of humour. It also captures the commonly held belief at the time that women talked a great deal and were gossipy and indiscreet. During the twenty-five years since then, feminists have been busy exploring and analysing the myths and realities of women and men's use of language.

This chapter we hope will contribute in a small way to that feminist discourse. In a manner consistent with much feminist research, when I started to think about this article I quickly realized that to do this research with a feminist colleague would be more rewarding both personally and in terms of our collective reflections and analyses. Consequently, the design, interviews and chapter were jointly done by both co-investigators.

This is an exploratory study of women and language based upon individual interviews and focus groups which we conducted with a small number of women in Nova Scotia over a two-month period in 1992.

Literature Review

The feminist literature on women and language is by no means easy to summarize or analyse. Basically this is because, like other feminist research, it is undertaken partly as a contribution to learning and partly as political praxis, a complex relation made more difficult by the lack of consensus about what constitutes either learning or praxis. Furthermore, the research is situated within what is still primarily a male discourse about how women and men use language. Consequently, the studies often are contradictory in their findings or when they are consistent are seen to represent radically different meanings.

Briefly, the literature falls into five basic interpretations:

1) women have qualitatively different ways of expressing themselves, ways that are in general superior to men's use of language and these differences can be measured through qualitative and self-reflective means;
2) women have qualitatively different ways of expressing themselves, ways that are in general inferior to men's use of language;
3) women and men do not differ in their use of language; however, there is a 'folk linguistic' that women and men speak differently

and this folk linguistic has the same impact on women's and men's interpretations of language use as if it were true;
4) women and men do not speak differently and this can be empirically proven;
5) women and men do speak differently and this can be empirically proven.

Obviously, each one of these interpretations has different educational and policy implications. Depending on the perspective of the authors, recommendations range from teaching women to talk more like men to re-claiming or re-valuing women's use of language.

Since this is a large and heterogeneous literature, this review will not be exhaustive but rather provide a brief introductory backdrop for the current study. One of the earliest feminist discussions of the women and language issue was a small but influential book by R. Lakoff (1975). Lakoff argued, in a primarily anecdotal and speculative treatment, that women's language is characterized by tentativeness, qualification, the use of tag questions (where a declarative claim is ended by 'isn't it?,' 'don't you think?'), greater deference, and more use of descriptors, among other things. For the past twenty years, this book has frequently been the basis of critiques of both a positive and negative nature. It has also fostered other articles and books in the same speculative vein, as well as attempts to confirm and disconfirm Lakoff's claims through empirical experimentation.

Spender (1980) took Lakoff's book to be not only bad research but also dangerous in so far as it suggested that women's language was subordinate to men's language. Spender both cites empirical counter-evidence to Lakoff's thesis and also argues that interpretation of women's language as different from men's is merely a reflection of a male-biased culture that sees the world through male-coloured glasses. According to Spender, it is not so much that women speak differently than men but rather that what they say is treated differently.

In one of the more recent contributions to this debate, Tannen (1990) argues not only that women and men use language differently but that the purpose of language is different for women and men. Tannen argues that women use language primarily to connect with others or to share feelings and experiences. Men, on the other hand, are more goal directed in their language use and, consequently, use language to exchange information and get and give advice. Tannen's thesis is that much of the breakdown in communication between the sexes is a function of this different approach to language use. Many of Tannen's examples are about how women exchange horror stories and expect sympathetic interchange or similar sharing when they tell their stories. Men, she argues, frequently respond to such stories by giving advice, since that is what they believe is required in such a situation. Tannen further argues that men are frequently confused and hurt when their advice is rejected or ignored. Women, on the other hand, interpret such advice as illustrating both a lack of empathy and an indication that they sound incompetent and in need of advice.

Besides these feminist tracts on women and language, perhaps the most significant repeated empirical observation made in the psychological literature (Cutler & Scott, 1990; Steinem, 1992) is that both men and women believe that women dominate discussions when they speak at least 30 percent of the time. More than any other finding, this suggests the cultural stereotype of the chatty, gossipy woman which may have significant consequences for how comfortable women feel in communicating their ideas and feelings.

Methodology

Having read the literature on women and language, we decided to ask Nova Scotia women whether they observed differences in language use by women and men, whether they believed that they personally used language differently than men, and, what they thought the implications of such differences might be for broader equality issues between the sexes. Thus, our objective was to investigate the thoughts of Nova Scotia women on a number of broad issues. It was important to us that the directions of our discussion be determined by the observations and knowledge of our participants. We, therefore, wanted to maintain flexible, open-ended topics and to establish an atmosphere where diverse perspectives could emerge, develop and, perhaps, shift, thereby exposing issues we could not have originally imagined. Focus group discussions have the potential for exploring all of the complexities of our participants' experiences, so that was the chosen format for information gathering.

Sample

Our intent was to document women's experiences — our own included — and our role was to assist the flow of the conversation and ensure the comfort of our participants. Our sample was not randomly selected but rather was gathered by word-of-mouth requests. Not surprisingly, most of the women who participated in our focus groups were already interested in discussing their observations of men's and women's communication patterns. As a result, the majority of our participants were in various ways involved either in the academic community — current/former students and administrative members — or were otherwise connected with our organization, The Institute for the Study of Women.

In order to supplement this 'academic' perspective with alternative 'non-academic' perspectives, we established another focus group comprised of women outside this circle. These women came from various social and professional backgrounds — a flight-attendant, a small business owner, a dentist, a librarian, and two managers. Indeed, all of the participants involved within this project — whether 'academic' or 'non-academic' — brought forth diverse social and professional experiences and observations. Interestingly enough, many of the same issues were discussed. The greatest differences between the 'non-academic' focus group and the 'academic' group were the type of language used to express similar ideas and the understanding of, and therefore response to, the feminist position.

Three focus groups of six or more women were formed, and with the participants' permission, the conversations were taped and transcribed to ensure the accurate documentation of their words. Throughout the process, our questions remained flexible and open-ended, and our interests included insights from women with different educational levels, occupational backgrounds — those who chose female-dominated areas contrasted with those who chose a male-dominated sphere — as well as different social/familial structures and religious involvement. Within the three focus groups certain patterns emerged, many of our interests were discussed from various perspectives, and yet others — specifically, observations from women working within rigidly hierarchical male-dominated occupations — were not thoroughly addressed.

In addition to these focus groups, we conducted individual interviews with three women in senior administrative positions at our own university. These women currently worked within Canada's only predominantly female university where primarily 60 percent of faculty is female and where 80 percent of the student body is female. Since two of the three administrators had previously worked in various male-dominated fields they were in a position to compare their current and past work environments and experiences. It should be noted that while we had originally intended to treat these interviews separately in our analysis, after we had re-read all of the responses, the individual interviews fit well with the comments of focus group members. In fact, many of the comments were essentially the same. Consequently, we chose to weave those interviews into the general content analysis of the other responses.

Findings: Focus Groups and Individual Interviews

In looking at the data, we found trends in our participants' observations. On some issues there seemed clear consensus. For example, women generally thought that men saw the world more neatly in black and white, true or false, right or wrong categories.

Women's and Men's Ways of Judging

One participant said:

> The word *wrong* and *right* come into his vocabulary quite frequently.

Another adds:

> … I guess, because I don't think there are rights and wrongs that are

> all that clear. But for him everything was either….

Women, it was argued, do not organize their experience this way. A participant in group 2 said:

> I think it's the words too, behind the word we don't have to think, and when we think there's no right/wrong, everything's all rounded.

Another adds:

> The whole picture.

A third concludes:

> And isn't that part of the way we interact, we look at both people's situations, and I look at this and I understand and so that means that you can't say that one is wrong and the other is right.

Women's Use of Men's Language

An interesting consequence of the observation that women and men use language differently was that men's language was more important and so women had to learn to speak both like men and like women.

A participant in group 1 stated:

> French people do much the same thing, and there's a classist approach to French and then there's a very, uh, more fundamental style of French and speaking it and you have to know the person with whom you're speaking and the kind of language they use to fully understand all of the permutations of all the information they are trying to exchange with you.

Another responded:

> If I go to a country, and I need to learn that language to make myself understood and to understand what they're saying, I think we both … I think the masculine and the feminine … have to learn. We need to learn the other's language, but not exclusively. I don't think the answer is for all men to be like women, as well as being completely impossible. And I wouldn't want that. There is value in the way … I see values in the way that men are when it's not warped out of its natural place, which is a place of balance. I think we all have to work on a cross-cultural, cross-gender….

The first speaker elaborated:

> We learn how to speak the way men do. We learn all men's moves. We watch men very carefully. But I'm not sure there's any particular onus on men to do the same. It's what they say about slavery. If you're a slave you learn the moods of your master, because at any time he can beat you. So, you become very adept. That's why they talk about the oppressed person [...] has a very wide consciousness. They know their own experience and they know the experience of their oppressor. There's not a heck of a lot of reasons why an oppressor learns the language of the oppressed person.

Another summarized:

> If men and women both can have a better understanding of the communication barriers linguistically between the two it has got to improve and enhance working relationships and social relationships as well. I think, um, that it does tend to create barriers and to disenfranchise and disempower women as opposed to men. Men don't become disempowered and disenfranchised by it but women do, and until we can raise the level of awareness of language and of the importance of it. We speak constantly, we write constantly, we communicate constantly, and yet we don't recognize that there are these linguistic barriers between the genders, but it's really important.

Dealing with Problems

Another key area that emerged was the belief that men and women identify and deal with personal problems differently. Essentially, the claim was made that men avoid personal problems but when confronted try to deal with them quickly. Women, on the other hand, it was argued, want to look at personal problems from a number of perspectives with various input before they reach a decision.

One participant notes:

> When I discuss with my friends they listen and they brainstorm and men tend to come up with a conclusion and they say, 'Okay, let's get on with it and forget it. There's the answer....' I think women tend to enjoy communicating with women, or men if they will.

Another adds:

> When I have a problem I tend to go to my friends — my female friends. It's not that when I have a problem in my life, what I need is for someone to understand, you know, not necessarily to solve my

> problems for me, but to understand and so I find when I go to my female friends I get that. We discuss my problem and it seems to work out and I feel better, but when I go to my male friends, my partner or my father, I tend to get advice.

Who Do We Like More?

Interestingly, a fair number of the discussions revolved around the nature of women and men as people, co-workers, friends, and social beings. There was disagreement here. Some women found women hard to deal with as co-workers while others thought women made better colleagues.

As one participant put it:

> Well, one thing I know in female dominated areas in the company I worked with … [there] always seemed to be a lot of petty bickering…. Whereas that didn't happen in the areas where I working with the men….

Another adds:

> Sometimes it is very hard to work with women, which is what I do. Because there is quite a bit of back stabbing on the way up. Maybe it's because women have taken so long to get into power that they have to prove that they can be just as rotten in business as men can.

Others disagreed:

> Men aren't awfully good at including others or in stepping back to give somebody else the credit. In my experience, for example, in organizations the person at the top — invariably a man — will do all the speeches or introductions … in my view … [women] are better at sharing, developing people, bringing them along.

On socializing, one participant said:

> It's interesting that you say you prefer to work with males, I prefer to work with men and if I'm out socializing I'd rather be in the room with the males than in the room with the females. Number one because they are more interesting. Unless you find — and you find people these days, females, that are more interesting — because I've sat through many conversations where we just talked about…. Boy, women are the most uninteresting people, and I think I just can't handle this, and I go and sit with the men, and they are talking about business and the problems of the day.

And, another added:

> Yeah, I find that when you're bringing up a few conflicts of the day, and some women look at you rather strange — not always — and I find that frustrating. I feel like saying, 'Shouldn't you be listening to the radio?' 'Shouldn't you be taking an interest?' but I'm categorizing.

How They Saw Men

Perhaps, not surprisingly but a little sadly, when we got three groups of women together to talk about whether women use language and communicate differently than men, much of the time was spent talking about men. These comments outnumber the rest of the discussion by far, so only a few select comments will be included here as illustrative:

> 'Real' men don't sit and have a conversation. They'd certainly love to sit down in their own little circles, and have people talk to them, and they can't.

> … Most men are like that when talking about relationships, you know, doesn't want to talk about why do people do this, and why do they … I say to my husband, 'Haven't you thought about that?' He says, 'No.'

> … I think they just have a difficult time. I know that in my relationship right now, I mean, I often tell my partner, you know, 'What do you have to say?' you know, I talk about him not talking very much and he's aware of that, and he tells me he wants to make an effort and when we're around people, some of you know him, he talks. He talks a lot. [laughter] But the two of us together, he's aware that it has to do with intimacy. There's a difficulty because it's intimacy, you know.

Are They Really Different from Us?

Participants in all of the focus groups spent a considerable amount of time trying to figure out whether there were real differences between the sexes and, if so, how those differences manifested themselves.

One participant said:

> We give men this impossible socialization, and they've got no place to put it out, because they are working in a factory where they are just one guy and they have to take a lot of shit. So, if their socialization means they have to be the dominating, top dog, masculine guy and there is absolutely no place to be that because it's um…. The ideal is dysfunctional….

Another added:

> I think they are biologically different, and I think society adds to it, and broadens the difference, but I think there is a difference between men and women. I realize that's something not … boys are attracted to cars, love to work on cars. I think it happens early on [tells how she began to raise her sons to be active in the kitchen, but now wishes they'd stay out of her kitchen, because they are 'useless']. Get out of the kitchen. Whatever woman gets you, she can train you. I don't have the time. I'd rather have my blood-pressure down here than have it way up here trying to train him.

A third argued this way:

> Maybe the education of men and women, how to get along and how to understand begins at home. Ideally, that's where it comes from. My children, I've got three girls, they don't play with dolls, they don't like dolls, so they play with cars and trucks. You know, before I … when I was a child, I'd play with a doll and 'You don't talk like that because nice girls don't talk like that. Nobody likes a saucy little girl,' and my brother would be pounding the crap out of me and nothing would happen to him, you know. 'Don't be so mean.' Never said that nobody would like him because he's mean.

A summary statement on socialization is made in group 2:

> Don't you think it has to do with expectations? There are expectations put on each gender. There are different expectations for men in our society. Our society says this is the way you have to be and this is the way you have to communicate and we train them that way. We as mothers have raised them, invited to train them that way, because that is the status quo and so on. I don't really think that there are many, much difference…. There are differences between men and women communicating now but I think it was done by pruning expectations that we have. I think men are equally sensitive or could be but they dare not be. They don't know how to be. They've been totally trimmed out of it for God knows how many generations. The next being passed on and passed on, and so we've got this situation where they say, 'This is the way it is.' I know my own husband would say, 'But this is the way I am.' You know, 'This is kinda the way I am. There's nothing I can do about it.' It's not true. There's lots that we can do about it, but then comes the area of choices. But that's been my experience, that we are expected to communicate with each other in different ways and as a result of that we are limited somewhat when we can't transcend that.

How to Change Things

As well as discussing differences, all groups spent time talking about change. Interestingly, the common theme in these remarks was about how to make women feel better about themselves. Some comments concerned the institutions which make women feel like second-class citizens. The church was considered primary among these institutions:

> I see the hierarchy in our church reflects the hierarchy in the Bible. … And the hierarchy in our society.
> … I think [participant above] hit it on the nail when she said the hierarchy in our church is affected by the Bible, and I think that our church is such an influence on us and that's why I brought it up because it has a tremendous influence on our ways. Our laws are structured around our morality which are determined by our Bible, and our laws … your [speaking generally, not specifically] Bible creates our laws which affects me in our society, and I think that that's why it's become important that the language used everywhere … and that's why I also mentioned our business policies, and our legal policy…. I guess this is why I wanted to ask if we felt language was important in our religions, and in our business policies and our laws.

Another speaker adds a personal anecdote:

> If you have … I have a friend who's a minister — an ordained minister in the Anglican Church — and she was giving communion one day, and an individual walked in and said he was not taking communion from a woman, and instead of saying, 'No, this is an ordained minister in the church,' the senior minister said, 'Oh, well that's fine. I will serve you.' That is saying to the minister, to the woman, that she is a second-class citizen. Instead of challenging the issue up front and saying, 'Our prayers have gender inclusive language which you are behaving in a gender exclusive way and we can't do that here. If you choose to take communion from men only then perhaps you had better look for another church.' It isn't done, and it's those kinds of things that…. It's fine to rewrite the hymnals and it's fine to rewrite the prayers but how do we behave?

One woman was strongly opposed to any attempt to make religion more gender inclusive:

> I don't know religion is a very personal thing. When I was growing up … I have a strong belief in the Bible and grew up in a very strict upbringing — strong women but everything was done according to

> the Bible — over the years I've gotten out of it — To me the Bible is full of stories with points and so on. It depends. You can believe in the stories that there was a man called Adam and a woman called Eve. Adam was mankind and Eve was womankind … but it would shatter me to my very roots if all of a sudden we had a Goddess there. You know, and I've tried to come to such things today, such as [when she was growing up you had to go to church on Sunday, and today you can go to church Saturday evening instead of Sunday]. Well, how come they changed it now. You can go on Saturday now. So, it's up to the individual but I personally would not like to see 'She.' To me, God is He and Christ is his Son. God and His Son, you know? I think with religion you have to give yourself up to trust and belief on things that can't be proven. I think that if we start changing everything to generic names like 'she/he' or 'shim' not she or him, we're going to lose everything. In this day and age there are no morals out there any more. It's changed so much.

As well as the church, education was seen as critical for change. One participant notes:

> I think education is the most important thing, and I don't personally feel that strongly about inclusive language. I've been working for a long time…. Um, let's take for example the education that North America received over that situation with what's his name, the black Supreme Court justice and the sexual harassment case, [someone says 'Thomas']. Right. That was the best education that North Americans have seen. I think it got to people who normally would never have talked about sexual harassment. It got the subject front and centre in a debate. There were millions of opinions of who was right and who was wrong and what did happen and what didn't happen, but people talked about it, they discussed it at cocktail parties, they worried about it at work. It brought sexual harassment as an issue to the forefront like nothing else could possibly have done in so short a space of time.

Summary Comments and Thoughts of Hope

Interestingly, the participants in all of our groups came around finally to valuing some things female and some things male. As well, they discussed looking for ways to appreciate what was rich and diverse in their own and other cultures.

Said one:

> I think we need to examine the rules and I think we need to build on female strengths. I often tell groups I'm speaking to that the very kinds of management skills we're looking for are those that are more

> consensual, more participative, that work to develop people, where there's real accountability and responsibility, and shared decision-making, etc. These are things that women are good at. These are the things that men — by nature — are not particularly good at. So, if we could build on the best of both traits, men's and women's, we would have a stronger work-force and certainly a stronger work-place, and competitive environment for all concerned.

Another added:

> I think there are several things going on at once. As a people, as a culture we're all realizing that the old forms don't work any more. So, we're all learning a new language but we're also learning.... Somehow I see the post-modern age as the time when it's possible for the first time to talk interculturally without power. At least that's thematically possible now. We have that thought now, but whether or not we can ... to use a cliché, meet the challenge is personally very frightening to me. But I think as woman the two things I'm trying to do is one, say when I'm not comfortable within a conversation and two, leave when it doesn't change. Sometimes that's all that I can do and I'm hoping that those around me are ... men and women ... are searching their own hearts to see, 'What part did I play in that discomfort?' or 'What did I do or not do?'

Conclusion

So, what have we learned here? Does this small study add anything to the existing body of knowledge on women, men and language? We think it does. We were pleasantly surprised by the breadth and depth of understanding our participants have of the many and varied ways in which language affects our personal experience, our work place experience and even how we experience our spirituality.

The participants in our study clearly believe that there are sex differences in language communication and shared their own life experiences as evidence to support those claims. They believe that some of those sex differences have negative consequences for each gender and for communication across gender while others are mutually enhancing. Women do share their feelings more, they argue, and that is a positive attribute that at least some men wish they had. They honestly spoke of the difficulty they sometimes encountered with members of their own sex while acknowledging that it may be part of trying to achieve in a male world that leads to problems in communicating and relating.

Finally, they argued that change is possible and is coming. As our last two speakers noted, in this post-modern world, old ways of doing things no longer work. Taking the best of male and female attributes and applying them in a culturally sensitive and diverse manner may be the route to human justice and a more egalitarian way of participating in the world.

The final verdict is not in on sex differences and communication and probably will not be until our society ceases to reinforce, reward, and punish on as many sex-specific grounds as it currently does. However, as long as women continue to explore their own experience with language and communication, this debate will be furthered by the growing body of knowledge and wealth of analysis that questions male-biased views of our expressive interpretations of reality.

This study is one more small contribution to that debate.

References and Suggested Further Readings

Connor, J., Byrne, F., Mindell, J., Cohen, D., & Nixon, E. (1986). Use of the titles Ms., Miss, or Mrs.: Does it make a difference? *Sex roles, 14 (9/10)*, 545-549.

Cook, A. S., Fritz, J., McCormack, A., & Visperas, C. (1985). Early gender differences in the functional usage of language. *Sex roles, 12 (9/10)*, 909-915.

Cutler A., & Scott, D. (1990). Speaker sex and perceived apportionment of talk. *Applied psycholinguistics, 11*, 253-272.

de Klerk, V. (1990). Slang: A male domain? *Sex roles, 22 (9/10)*, 589-606.

Hamilton, M. (1988). Using masculine generics: Does generic *he* increase male bias in the user's imagery? *Sex roles, 19 (11/12)*, 785-799.

Harrigan J., & Lucic, K. (1988). Attitudes about gender bias in language: A reevaluation. *Sex roles, 19 (3/4)*, 129-140.

Lakoff, R. (1975). *Language and woman's place*. New York: Harper Colophon Books.

Lynch, C. & Strauss-Noll, M. (1987). Mauve washers: Sex differences in freshman writing. *Classroom inquiry*, 90-94.

McEdwards, M. (1985). Women's language: A positive view. *English journal*, 40-43.

O'Donnell, H. (1985). Leadership effectiveness: Do sex and communication style make a difference? *English journal*, 65-67.

Piel, J. (1990). Unmasking sex and social class differences in childhood aggression: The case for language maturity. *Journal of educational research, 84 (2)*, 100-106.

Preston, K., & Stanley, K. (1987). 'What's the worst thing... ?': Gender-directed insults. *Sex roles, 17 (3/4)*, 209-219.

Sheldon, A. (1990). 'Kings are royaler than queens': Language and socialization. *Young children*, 4-9.

Slama, K., & Slowey, B. (1988). Gender-specific common nouns: Sex differences in self-use. *Sex roles, 18 (3/4)*, 205-213.

Smeltzer, L., & Werbel, J. (1986). Gender differences in managerial communication: Fact or folk-linguistics. *The journal of business communication, 23 (2)*, 41-50.

Spender, D. (1980). *Man made language*. London: Routledge & Kegan Paul.

Tannen, D. (1990). *You just don't understand: Women and men in conversation*. New York: Ballantine Books.

Chapter Twelve

Three Nineteenth-Century Literary Representations of Nova Scotia Dialect

Lilian Falk

Editors' Introduction

When looking at English as it is spoken in Nova Scotia, we often seem to be limited more or less to the form of the language which is used in our own time, because that is all we think we have access to. However, to limit ourselves in this way is to ignore the large numbers of written records, both historical documents and others, which date from before the time of large-scale audio recording. Writers use the language that they themselves are familiar with, and they provide, therefore, valid materials for linguistic investigation.

Unfortunately, a problem with many historical documents, if they are studied for linguistic purposes, is that writers generally preferred to use the standard language rather than their own local variety. Even in diaries and personal letters, where we could expect a fairly informal use of language, we find relatively little that can be labelled specifically 'Nova Scotian.' As a result, while we may be able to learn much from such works about the day-to-day routines, and the family and social relationships of Nova Scotians in the past, we rarely learn much about the way people spoke. In fact, often the most interesting of these documents from a linguistic point of view are those written not by 'good' writers, but by diarists and correspondents whose formal education had not been sufficient to give them mastery over the standard language, and whose writing, therefore, employs phonetic, rather than conventional, spellings, and words and expressions that would normally be excluded from the standard written language.

An example of such a document is the 1815-16 diary of Louisa Collins (Conrad, et al., 1988), who was born near Cole Harbour in Halifax County. The eighteen-year-old Louisa would probably have failed any formal spelling test both nowadays and in her own time. However, her brief diary reveals an active mind, a fairly wide vocabulary, a liking for reading generally — not just for 'novils' — and some acquaintanceship with the conventions of spelling, even if the result is often confusion. For example, she knows that initial [n] can be spelled *kn*, but is not at all sure when, so we find the spelling 'know' for *know*, *no*, and *now*, and the variants 'knus,' 'nuse,' and 'news' for *news*.

On the other hand, we find that some of her 'mistakes' are consistent, and may well be regarded as phonetic spellings. She almost always spells *been* as 'bin,' and *get* as 'git,' suggesting that in her idiolect the same vowel phoneme was used in these two words, probably [ɪ], so that her pronunciations were [bɪn] and [gɪt], rather than [bin] and [gɛt]. Her consistent spelling of *just* as 'jest,' or even 'jes' suggests that her usual pronunciation of this word was [ǰɛs(t)]. If we add 'brakefast' [brekfæst] or [brekfəst] for *breakfast*, then what we have is the strong implication that Louisa Collins used pronunciations that were not only common in the late eighteenth century, but which persisted in the Yankee dialect of New England. Given Louisa's Nantucket family connections, we can therefore conclude that the speech of the Collins family probably revealed a strong Yankee influence.

In addition to her pronunciations, Louisa's diary also reveals certain grammatical constructions which are even now regarded as erroneous in the standard language. One is the use of the objective case in a multiple subject: e.g., 'Eliza and *me* sit down to sowing [i.e., sewing] …' and 'Pheby and *me* have been sitting….' A second is the use of a singular verb following a multiple subject: e.g., 'Eliza and me *has* bin rompin …' and a third the use of the preterite form in place of the past participle of an irregular verb: e.g., 'I have jes *wrote* a note….' All of these grammatical constructions are still to be found in the speech of many Nova Scotians.

Documents like Louisa Collins's diary are fruitful sources of linguistic information about Nova Scotian speech in the past, within certain limitations. It was no part of her purpose in writing her diary to provide later readers with a picture of her own dialect, and so we find that there are large gaps in the information we can learn from her. For example, while she often refers to her domestic tasks on the farm, and to picking berries and currants, she uses very few words or expressions we can identify as local, so we cannot tell very much about the vocabulary of her time. In fact, most written documents include relatively few local words or expressions, except in contexts where, for example, detailed descriptions of farming or domestic implements and techniques are presented, or in the texts of advertisements in local newspapers referring to specific local goods or services.

So where can we find the unique words and phrases of Nova Scotians before the present day? One obvious source is in the writings of travellers through the province, such as W. S. Moorsom's *Letters from Nova Scotia* (1830), or in the works of Nova Scotia residents who were interested in the language themselves. Thomas Chandler Haliburton's *An Historical and Statistical Account of Nova Scotia* (1829) contains, for example, lists of words, including the names of farm implements and other tools, birds, fish, flowers, geographic terms, and so on. Yet even such works have their limitations, for they give us only lists, and do not show us the language in action.

For a more complete picture of Nova Scotia English in the past, we need to go to the writers of fiction, or at least to those writers who wished to present the ordinary speech of their Nova Scotian characters in as realistic a mode as possible. Haliburton, when presenting a fictional analysis of life in Nova Scotia, took his passive lists of words and rewrote them into vigorous dialogue, complete with all the characteristic local turns of phrase and grammatical constructions. As the following chapter points out, literature has long been a source of information about the vocabulary of the past for the compilers of dictionaries and other scholars, and where the writers are reliable and conscientious, the language of the past may come to life in literary works in a fascinating and entertaining way.

In this final chapter, Lilian Falk takes passages from the successive fictions of Thomas McCulloch, Thomas Chandler Haliburton, and the non-Nova Scotian Israel Zangwill, and uses the work of these writers to provide a brief overview of Nova Scotia English in the nineteenth century.

The study of nineteenth-century fiction has in recent years become much easier than it was formerly, thanks to the work of the Centre for Editing Early Canadian Texts. Excellent scholarly editions of Nova Scotian authors have become available, such as *The Mephibosheth Stepsure Letters*, edited by Gwendolyn Davies in 1990, and *The Clockmaker*, series One, Two, and Three, edited by George L. Parker in 1995. Zangwill's Nova Scotian novel, *The Master,* published in 1895, can still be found in the original edition in some university libraries. *(LF & MH)*

***

Three Nineteenth-Century Literary Representations of Nova Scotia Dialect

by Lilian Falk

In describing early stages of the history of English, scholars regularly use literature as their chief source of information. Much has been learned about Elizabethan English from studying the works of Shakespeare, and knowledge about later developments has come from the study of poems, novels, and plays of later periods. Historical dictionaries, British, American, and Canadian, have made extensive use of literary works as sources of information about the development of words and their meanings.

In discussing the English language in Nova Scotia it is interesting to look at the language of the past, as reflected in earlier literature, with the intent of discovering its main characteristics — whether it had elements of specific Nova Scotian vocabulary, and to what extent it was similar to 'Yankee speech' or to British English of the time.

When selecting sources for the study of English spoken in Nova Scotia in the first half of the nineteenth century, it is probably natural to choose Thomas McCulloch (1776-1848) and Thomas Chandler Haliburton (1796-1865). These two writers lived in Nova Scotia and wrote with verve and humour about life in the province. Both used language for satirical purpose, and both were excellent observers of local speech with its many variations and nuances, so much so that Haliburton's most famous character — Sam Slick — is popularly given credit for being the originator of various witty expressions which are still in use. Thus Haliburton is widely recognized as a writer of great talent, and, as a native Nova Scotian humourist, he has long enjoyed a popularity in Nova Scotia and beyond.

Thomas McCulloch, on the other hand, was born in Scotland and did not arrive in Nova Scotia until 1803, after completing his education and obtaining his ordination as a Presbyterian minister. Still, while it is true that McCulloch was not a Nova Scotia native, he did intend his writings to be a reflection of the local speech of his time, as did colonial writers in other parts of Canada; for example, somewhat later, Susanna Moodie and Catherine Parr Traill were especially successful in recording Canadian usage because, as new settlers, they were acutely aware of differences between their own usage and that of the other settlers they encountered in the new country.

In comparison, Haliburton may be seen almost as suffering a disadvantage as a writer in being a Nova Scotia native. However, in introducing a Yankee-speaking Sam Slick, Haliburton creates opportunities for the use of distinct personal and regional styles and thus a great range of language variation. Haliburton's representation of local speech has attracted the attention of serious linguists, among whose writings Walter S. Avis's unpublished MA thesis, 'The Speech of Sam Slick' (1950), is the most comprehensive. His shorter 'A Note on the Speech of Sam Slick' (1969), in *The Sam Slick Anthology*, is familiar to readers of that anthology. In 1981, Richard A. Bailey wrote a paper entitled 'Haliburton's Eye and Ear,' which reviewed Avis's thesis and added the compelling argument that Haliburton's knowledge of local speech came not only from listening, but also, to a large extent, from reading contemporary dialect literature.

Reading most probably influenced McCulloch as well. But, whatever their sources, there is much to be learned from these two writers about English in Nova Scotia in the early 1800s, as most readers of their works would agree. First of all we notice a number of words which are no longer in common use, like *stumpage*, *frolic*, and *gumflowers*, secondly we notice words and expressions so common today that we might be surprised to see them in an 1800s context, like *produce* (noun), *superfine*, and *youngsters*, or the expression *time is money*. As we read on, we also note peculiar forms of verbs such as *catched* and *knowed*.

Looking at the many unfamiliar words and expressions found in McCulloch and Haliburton, we may wish to consult specialized dictionaries like the *Oxford English Dictionary* (*OED*) and the *Dictionary of Canadianisms* (*DC*) in order to find out not only what these words mean, but whether they are recognized as words pertaining to a particular time and place, more specifically, whether they are already recognized as Canadianisms, or perhaps even as Maritime expressions.

In consulting the *OED* as to the status of some of these words, we would find that Haliburton's works were used as sources by the compilers of the *OED* and a number of illustrative quotations were extracted from them. In their 'List of Books Quoted' in the *OED*, the editors include:

> *The Clockmaker; or the sayings and doings of Samuel Slick of Slickville* 1835 (1837) 1838, 1840
> *Nature and human nature* 1855
> Ed. *Traits of American humour* by native authors 1852 (1866).

We note, however, that this list does not include *The Old Judge*.

We may assume that in quoting Haliburton, the *OED* editors were attempting to illustrate English usage as comprehensively as possible rather than having a special interest in illustrating Canadian English or Maritime English as such, but still in using quotations from Haliburton they identify both the period and the region where the word was in use.

The same *OED* bibliography which lists Haliburton's works makes no mention of Thomas McCulloch — an omission possibly owing to the fact that no edition of McCulloch's *The Stepsure Letters* was widely available at the time of the compilation of the *OED*. *The Stepsure Letters* were printed as *Letters of Mephibosheth Stepsure* from 1821 to 1823 in the *Acadian Recorder* in Halifax, Nova Scotia, a publication which was not included among the

OED's sources. It may be added that the bibliography of the second edition of the *OED* (1989) similarly makes no reference to McCulloch.

No such omission occurred when materials were being compiled for the *DC* (1967): an edition of *The Stepsure Letters* had been brought out by McClelland and Stewart in 1960, making this important work available to the editors of the *DC*. However, the *DC*, like the *OED*, did not include *The Old Judge* — which was published by McClelland & Stewart only in 1968.

The intent of the *DC* editors was to give as much detailed information on the history of Canadian English as necessary in preparing a dictionary on historical principles; therefore, it is understandable that they appreciated the importance of both McCulloch and Haliburton and used citations from these authors to illustrate the use and meaning of certain Canadian words and expressions, among which we find citations for *lines* 'strips of settlement in the back country'; *frolic* 'a party organized to help a neighbour with a task'; and *salt hay* 'hay growing on salt marshes' from McCulloch; and *Bluenose*, 'a resident of the Maritime Provinces'; *soft sawder* 'flattery'; and *Yankee* [speech] from Haliburton.

For the editors of the *DC* these words merited the designation of Canadianisms whose regional significance was also noted in their definitions. Of course, there are also other Canadianisms in the writings of McCulloch and Haliburton which are included in the *DC* but which are illustrated by quotations taken from other publications, as, for instance, *barn raising* or *callibogus*.

All such words hold an interest for students of earlier periods of Maritime English, whether or not the *DC* definitions include quotations from Maritime writers. In the case of *barn raising*, for instance, the *DC* gives a quotation from an Ontario publication of 1886, while the word also occurs in *The Stepsure Letters*, in the story of Solomon Gosling, who, 'although not very fond of hard work,' was 'always a good neighbour …' and 'at every burial and *barn raising* … was set down as one who would be sure to be there' (1990, p.8). Had the *DC* editors decided to quote from McCulloch, the illustration would have been dated considerably earlier than their Ontario quote: 1821 rather than 1886. Their choice was probably based on the clarity of the illustrative quotation for the purposes of defining the term.

In some cases the reason why a certain word could not be illustrated by quoting McCulloch is self-evident, as when a word is used humorously as a person's name and even a full quotation would not elucidate its meaning. Such a word is *callibogus* 'a drink of rum and spruce beer,' which occurs in connection with the same improvident Solomon Gosling, who mortgaged his property to 'Callibogus, the West India merchant' (1990, p.8). While the use of *Callibogus* as a name could not provide a useful quotation for the *DC*, its satiric purpose could only have been served if the word was well known to McCulloch's intended readers. Thus McCulloch's use of this word can serve as reliable indication of its widespread use in Nova Scotia at the time.

Similarly, McCulloch's use of *Gawpus* 'silly person' as a family name does not lead to an entry in the *DC*, but testifies to its being used locally, as does *Scantocreesh*, a name McCulloch gives to an outspoken, hard-working immigrant from Scotland. Since the noun *creesh* means both 'fat' and by extension 'money' the humour in the name is doubled. Of the words *callibogus*, *gawpus*, and *scant o'creesh*, which are all listed in the *OED*, only *callibogus* was included in the *DC*.

McCulloch's use of other common words as humorous names, such as Reverend Drone, Captain Shootem, Mr. Scorem, Mr. Ledger, Deacon Scruple, Miss Sippit, Mrs. McCackle, Mrs. Grumble, Mrs. Whinge and Widow Scant, further supports the view that the satire was meant to be obvious to all readers. Looking at these names we may note in passing that many of the men's names are based on their profession or occupation while women's names are more often based on their behaviour or, in the case of the widow, on her poverty, but all are equally clear in their derivation.

McCulloch's prose is also instructive as to certain older grammatical and syntactic constructions still commonly used in his time, though destined to be replaced by new standard forms. In verbs, for instance, we find old forms of the past participle which have since been replaced, as in the following:

> ... had scarcely *arriven* (1990, p.210)
> ... they get themselves *beat* (p.155)
> ... as soon be *catched* stealing (p.95)
> ... he had just *sitten* to dinner (p.17)
> Dean Scruple ... was sure I must have *wrought* upon sunday [*sic*] (p.100)

as well as the past tense *throve* (p.100), which is still used alongside the more generally favoured *thrived*. Yet another form of some interest is the verb *capiassed* as in

> Mr. Ledger sued out the mortgage and then *capiassed* him for the balance of the account. (p.27)

The word *capias* 'a legal writ' is listed in the *OED*, but as a noun only; McCulloch's use is therefore worthy of note.

There is one adverb which shows a use now discontinued: *hardly* is used to mean 'in a hard manner, e.g. involving hard work' as in

> he was very *hardly* pushed (p.24)

and

> At first also I lived *hardly* ... and I soon found myself surrounded by

every comfort. (p.107)

In adjectives we see the form *oldest son* (p.12) where we might expect *eldest* — the latter being the generally accepted form of the comparative, while *oldest* in family relationships is marked by the *OED* as dialect or vulgar usage, and it is this form which prevails in Maritime usage today. McCulloch's humour rarely draws on malapropisms or uneducated use, but when he has Mrs. McCackle, a would-be user of 'genteel stile,' describe an assembly as *most gracefullest*, we can be sure that double superlatives were already considered unacceptable in polite speech of the time.

In the matter of grammatical constructions such as the use or absence of a definite article, we may cite:

> … *the one half* of us are obliged to pay the debts of the other … (p.98)
> *The most of my neighbours* had tried to raise an orchard … (p.105)
> *The most of his time* was spent in their houses (p.126)

where *the* would usually be absent in present-day speech; conversely, we note absence of *the* in the following:

> *in summer and fall, in spring* (p.111)

and

> *in future*. (p.23)

While McCulloch's grammar still shows traces of eighteenth-century usage, his syntax has for the most part features of early nineteenth-century educated use; that is, in word order, relative position of subject and verb in sentences, and in forming of negative and interrogative sentences, the syntax shows the characteristics of Modern English, and is similar to ours. It can be remarked, however, that conditional sentences show an older construction, as in the following examples:

> Were I to consult the credit of our town, I would stop here … (p.135)

and

> … did they meet the very best of you Halifax gentry upon the road they would stare at you … (p.134)

as well as the now prevailing construction with *if*:

> … if he had got his face blackballed … he would have been a very

good negro. (p.162)

McCulloch was evidently partial to Scottish usage: many of his words are marked in the *OED* as Scottish or Northern Dialect. Among these words we may note:

blue bonnet	'a Scottish woollen cap' (p.95)
brandering	'broiling, grilling' (p.108)
to bundle	'to sleep fully clothed with a member of the opposite sex' (p.61)
Cairngorums	'precious stones' (named for a variety of crystallized quartz found in the Cairngorms, a mountain range near Aberdeen, Scotland) (p.9)
crook	'difficulty, obstacle' (p.100)
gawpus	'silly person' (p.18)
greybeard	'a jug' (p.25)
gumflowers	'artificial flowers' (p.9)
kittle adj.	'tricky, delicate, complicated' (p.95)
limmer	'rogue, scoundrel' (p.184)
to snool	'to put down, to criticize' (p.83)
to spunk out	'to leak out, become known' (p.172).

As mentioned above, the various illustrative quotes in the *OED* for the histories of these words are not taken from McCulloch, but from a variety of other sources, so, among others, *snooled* is illustrated by a quotation from Burns, and *crook* by a quotation from Sir Walter Scott's *The Heart of Midlothian*. The 'Scottish' words which stood at McCulloch's disposal thus combined the charm of regional dialect with a growing literary acceptance.

Haliburton's works, as noted before, provided the *OED* editors with a great number of quotations, many of which reflect colloquial usage. Some examples of *OED* citations are given below:

absquotilate 'decamp'

Absquotilate it in style, you old skunk ... and show the gentleman what you can do. (Clockm. 1837)

bean-pole 'a lanky fellow'

Mr. Jehiel, a bean-pole of a lawyer. (Clockm. 1837)

churchy 'excessive in conformity to the Church'

Preacher there don't preach morals, because that's churchy. (Attache 1843)

dander 'anger, irritation'

Darn it all, it fairly makes my dander rise. (Clockm. 1837)

Ebenezer 'anger, temper'

If you go for to raise your voice at him … his Ebenezer is up in a minit. (Clockm. 1838)

funkify 'to frighten'

He might have knowed how to feel for other folks, and not funkify them so peskily. (Sam Slick in England 1844)

go-to-meeting [clothes] 'good clothes'

One of those blue-noses, with his go-to-meetin clothes on. (Clockm. 1843)

[whole] *hog* 'entirely, to the very limit'

We never fairly knew what goin the whole hog was till then. (Clockm. 1837)

jugful 'a great deal'

The last mile … took the longest time to do it by a jugfull. (Clockm. 1840)

killoch (var. of killick) 'a small anchor'

I shall up killoch and off to-morrow to the tree-mont. (Clockm. 1837)

lick 'a spurt in a race'

That are colt can beat him for a lick of a quarter mile. (Clockm. 1837)

marooning 'going on a picnic'

He used to delight to go marooning. (Footnote. Marooning differs from pic-nicing in this — the former continues several days, the other lasts but one. (Nat. and Hum. Nat. 1855))

namesake 'to name for someone'

Here's a book they've namesaked arter me. (Clockm. 1836)

oatmill 'a horse's mouth, hum.'

Hold up your old oatmill, and see if you can snuff the stable at minister's. (Clockm. 1836)

poke-loken 'a marsh'

A poke-loken is a marshy place or stagnant pool connected with a river. (Nat. & Hum. Nat. 1855)

ryled [riled] 'annoyed'

I must say I feel ryled and kinder sore. (Clockm. 1836)

sockdologer 'a kick, shove'

I'll give you a *sockdologer* in the ear with my foot. (Clockm. 1836)

streaked 'angry'

If he was in your House of Commons, I reckon he would make some of your folks look pretty *streaked*. (Clockm. 1837)

tarnation a mild expletive

Now, says he, I am in a tarnation hurry. (Clockm. 1836)

While many of the words used by McCulloch were shown to be Scottish, many of Haliburton's words are identified in the *OED* as U.S., or as U.S. slang. As such they are also illustrated by quotations from other American sources; e.g., *dander* is illustrated also by a quote from James Russell Lowell, *Ebenezer* by a quote from the Public Ledger of Philadelphia, *lick* by a quote from William Cullen Bryant, *poke-loken* and *tarnation* by quotes from Henry David Thoreau and the New England Magazine of Boston, respectively.

Instructive as the perusal of specialized dictionaries may be, there is much more that can be observed only by studying the works themselves. As in the case of McCulloch, so with Haliburton, we note additional vocabulary items, and we can become familiar with everyday sentence patterns and colloquial grammatical constructions.

A book worth examining in some detail is *The Old Judge, or, Life in a Colony*, published in London in 1849. As its title suggests, this book undertakes to describe life in a Colony for the benefit of readers who are not themselves familiar with Colonial manners, customs, and idiom. The book uses the device of introducing a British traveller as narrator and a local judge as his host and willing informant. Free from the dominance of the epigram-ready Sam Slick, the book seems to reflect a more homely idiom, and offers many comments on words, expressions, and the differences between speakers of various groups. *The Old Judge* is all the more interesting since it has not been used as source by the compilers of either the *OED* or of the *DC*.

Looking at vocabulary items in *The Old Judge* we may note *nor'wester* 'fisherman's hat,' *keeping room* 'a comfortable sitting room at an inn,' *salt lick* 'a place where deer or moose come to lick salt,' *honeypots* 'ditches,' *turnpiked* '[a road] prepared for use,' *barber* 'steam rising from a lake,' *silver frost* 'freezing rain covering trees with a shiny surface,' a great variety of *bees*, or *frolics*: raising, quilting, husking, berrying, rolling, and some political words, e.g., *American Rebellion* 'the American War of Independence,' *refugees* 'Loyalists and deserters,' *clear grit* 'outspoken Liberal,' *ginger* 'a sharp-tongued Liberal.'

Several of the above words merit a comment: *nor'wester*, for instance, is defined in the *DC* in other senses, but the sense 'fisherman's hat' is not given. Haliburton, on the other hand, in 'How Many Fins Has a Cod?' gives a characteristically detailed description as follows: 'He held in his hand what he called a nor'wester, a large, broad-brimmed, glazed hat, with a peak projecting behind to shed the water from off his club queue, which was nearly as thick as a hawser' (1968, p.15).

The *OED* gives two quotations for this sense of *nor'wester*, dated 1851 and 1853, from a British and Canadian source respectively. The Canadian quote is from Susanna Moodie. The word *keeping room* does not have an entry in the *DC*, yet from the choice of the word as title of a cluster of stories, the use of quotation marks when the word is first introduced, and Haliburton's careful definition, it appears to be a word of some importance: 'The other [large room at the inn] was called the keeping room, and generally reserved for the use of the family, but where old patrons, friends, and acquaintances were not considered as intruders' (1968, p.99). A little further in the story, the room's size, shape, and furnishings are also described in detail. The *OED* derives *keeping room* 'sitting room' from the meaning of *keep* 'dwell' and marks it as 'local' and U.S. Haliburton's use and meaning, specifically as a room at an inn, allows us to mark it also as Nova Scotian.

Elsewhere in *The Old Judge*, *silver frost* is described in such detail that the description occupies almost two pages. The language is both poetic and accurate: 'There had been, during last night ... a slight thaw, accompanied by a cold fine rain that froze, the moment it fell, into ice of the purest crystal. Every deciduous tree was covered with that glittering coating ...' (1968, p.89). *Silver frost* has no entry in the *OED*, and it is given in the *DC* with a Prince Edward Island quotation, whereas Nova Scotian references are cited under *silver thaw*. Haliburton's use gives evidence that the expression *silver frost* was in use in Nova Scotia in his time.

Admittedly, it was not possible for the editors of the *DC* to include a full coverage of words pertaining specifically to various regions of Canada. Still, it is clear that *The Old Judge*, had it been used during the compilation of the *DC*, could have become the source of useful Nova Scotian citations. On the other hand, a book, even one of modest size, offers more material than can be fully reported in a given dictionary. In *The Old Judge* we notice frequent uses of slang and ephemeral words, such as:

antifogmatic	an alcoholic liquor taken to counteract the effects of damp or wet' (1968, p.21)
crinkum-crankum	crinkled' (p.60)
I will be *upsides* with you	get even' (p.179)
[it] is *all the go now*	the fashion' (p.154)

and

she *pinked* them	'wounded or killed.' (p.245)

These cannot lay claim to either novelty or specifically Nova Scotian usage, as *antifogmatic* is marked 'jocular' in the Supplement to the *OED*, *upsides* is included in Partridge (1972/1980), and the last two in Gosse (1811).

There is a good deal of folk grammar, with constructions like *han't* (p.101), *warn't* (p.66), *ain't* '[My hands] are horrid hard, ain't they?'; past participle forms *boughten*, [I have] *seed* (p.104), [you have] *heern* tell (p.104), I never was *beat* yet (p.152); and past tense *eat* (p.138), and *knowed* (*passim*).

As mentioned above, Haliburton's subtitle *Life in a Colony* indicates his purpose with all seriousness: to describe life in a well-defined part of the British Empire; that is, in the Colony of Nova Scotia. While he describes the characters of the inhabitants and their ways, he does not neglect a description of their speech; in fact, evoking certain aspects of colonial speech constitutes an important part of his endeavour, and this is why he so often offers not only new or specialized words, but also elaborate definitions, as we have seen above in the case of *nor'wester*. His purpose as well as method is clearly expressed in the story 'Merrymakings,' in his description of the narrator coming by chance upon the preparations for an outdoor festivity and asking a young woman he meets there,

> '[W]hat was the occasion of it?'
> 'It is a pickinick [*sic*] stir, sir.'
> 'A pickinick stir!' I inquired; 'what is that?' although, from the preparations that were making, the meaning was perfectly obvious, but I wanted to hear her definition yet, as I had no doubt she would express herself in the same droll language. (p.59)

Not only is Haliburton conscientious about using interesting 'Colonial' words and expressions, he also comments on the variety of speech used, mentioning, among others, 'The slow, measured, nasal talk of the degenerate settler from Puritanical New England, the ceaseless rapid utterance of the French fisherman,' the speech of 'poor Pat' as well as the voices of Blacks and Native people (p.13); all these comments, voiced by the Old Judge, are, however, couched in terms of the prejudices of the time and as such deliver information not only on how people spoke, but also on what the judge thought of people who spoke differently from himself.

It is once more the Old Judge in 'The Schoolmaster' who comments on a newly arrived stranger: 'No one knew who or what he was, or whence he came, although from his accent, manner, and habits, it was thought probable that he was either a Nova Scotian, or a native of the New England States' (p.82), a comment which probably explains why in describing the variety of speech there was no mention of Nova Scotian speech as such — it was at the time not perceived as different from the speech of New England, otherwise known as 'Yankee.'

For the two authors, McCulloch and Haliburton, description of local language was certainly not a primary purpose, but as a secondary interest, intertwined with their moral, political, and social critique of the society they knew, it received sufficient care and attention to serve as a useful source of information on English as it was once used in Nova Scotia, with its roots both in Old England and in New England, ultimately offering as many if not more insights to readers today than they offered to their own contemporaries.

A rather unlikely heir to the literary tradition created by McCulloch and Haliburton can be found in the London-born and bred playwright, journalist and novelist Israel Zangwill (1864-1926), who, however, differs from his predecessors in that he uses Nova Scotian idiom as an integral part of a serious literary work, and not for the purpose of humour or satire. In 1895 Zangwill published *The Master*, a novel set in part in Nova Scotia. The novel tells the story of a talented youngster called Matthew Strang who grows up in a small village in Colchester County and wishes to become a painter. Although Zangwill had not visited North America prior to writing the book, he filled the first part of the novel with lively accounts of Nova Scotian village life, rich with details of everyday activities and everyday speech.

After an initial ripple of interest, *The Master* eventually sank into obscurity, escaping the notice of literary historians and linguists alike. However, at the height of Zangwill's career, his books were sufficiently popular to be included in the *OED*'s 'List of Books Quoted.' Indeed, owing to the availability of the *OED* on CD-ROM, it is now possible to ascertain that the number of quotations from his works exceeds four hundred, over fifty of them from *The Master*. While most of the *OED* quotations from Zangwill's works illustrate words relating to Jewish life (e.g., *afikoman*, *beigel*, *Chanukkah*), there are also quotations illustrating general words (*Atchoo*, *bed-sitting room, luminosity*).

The book's descriptions of Nova Scotia life and its use of local speech did not attract critical attention, as they were thought to be all a product of the author's imagination. Zangwill's reputation rested primarily on his novel *Children of the Ghetto* (1892), in which he gave a realistic portrayal of life in the poor Jewish section of London where he himself was born and raised. Compared with his knowledge of London, his knowledge of Nova Scotia was highly suspect.

Still, Zangwill's descriptions of Nova Scotian landscape, of village life and of local lore are vivid and detailed, and where they can be checked against permanent landscape features, such as the view of Five Islands in Cobequid Bay, it can be seen that they are remarkably accurate, and rendered with a precision not usually found in descriptions which are based on imagination alone.

In fact, recent investigations into the sources of Zangwill's knowledge of Nova Scotia (Falk, 1993; Barry 1996) show that Zangwill had a friend named George Hutchinson, who grew up in Great Village, Colchester County, but went to London as a young man, where he studied art and became a painter and illustrator. He illustrated several of Zangwill's works, as well as the works of other popular writers of the time.

It is evident that *The Master* is a fictionalized account of Hutchinson's own life and career, and that Zangwill's knowledge of Nova Scotia came from Hutchinson himself. In matters of local idiom Zangwill was apparently guided by Hutchinson also. Moreover, in some instances Zangwill seems to have described Hutchinson's own speech characteristics, for he refers several times to the 'nasal sound' of Nova Scotian speech, and uses the unusual exclamation *Geewiglets* which occurs also in one of Hutchinson's published cartoons (*Illustrated London News*, Jan. 1889).

For an outsider, Zangwill shows himself a competent user of Canadian vocabulary and idiom. Many of the words used in *The Master* can now be shown to be Canadianisms, for they are listed in the *DC*, though the illustrative quotations come from a variety of other sources. Understandably, Zangwill's works were not used as sources by the editors of the *DC*.

Some of the 'Canadianisms' in *The Master* were occasioned by general references to history, geography, ethnic diversity, and living conditions: '*black-jack*', *Bluenose*, *board* (used by Mi'kmaw mothers for carrying babies), *buffalo robe*, *Bushranger*, *butter-tub*, *calumet* (a pipe), *caribou*, *crooked knife*, *firewater*, *flats* (land exposed at ebb tide), *frolics*, *Great Expulsion*, *ice-cakes*, *lean-to*, *Loyalists*, *Micmac*, *musquash*, *papoose*, *pung* (a sled), *rock maple*, *snow-shoes*, *squaw*, *sugaring*, *wigwam*.

While the *DC* does not always attribute various words to specific regions, their occurrence in *The Master* can be taken as an indication that they were used in Nova Scotia in the nineteenth century. In one instance the appearance of a word in *The Master* is earlier than the *DC* quotation: 'black-jack' in the *DC* is illustrated with a quote from Sir Charles G. D. Roberts's *Camp-Fire* (1896). Zangwill's frequent inclusion of quotation marks and occasional use of explanatory phrases or informal definitions shows that he was aware of the relative novelty of these words. For example, he defines *pung* in the text: 'the coffin [led] the way in a pung, or long box-sleigh' (1895, p.29).

Even though the specific 'Canadian' and North American vocabulary was generally known to European writers who tried their hand at writing fiction with American local colour, Zangwill faced the additional challenge of rendering correctly the language as it was spoken some thirty years earlier, at the time of the hero's youth in the 1860s. Here Zangwill's correct reference to such popular songs as 'The Devil among the Tailors' and 'The Vacant Chair' shows that he was scrupulous in his choice of details. His use of vernacular speech with respect to grammar, pronunciation, and colloquial vocabulary also shows an effort to recreate earlier usage. Zangwill's use of colloquial expressions often shows similarity to Haliburton's style, a fact which reflects his familiarity with literary use of Canadian vernacular. In creating 'eye dialect' he often uses the same spellings as Haliburton; e.g., *a'most* (almost), *arter* (after), *consarn* (concern), *critter* (creature), *darter* (daughter), *feller* (fellow), *Marm* (Ma'am), *perlite* (polite), and *rael* (real).

Zangwill also tries to differentiate between the speech of the various characters according to age, occupation, and status. The speech of young Matt Strang, the novel's hero, is said to differ from that of his father, who was a sailor and had travelled away from the village; his mother shows traces of her Halifax upbringing, and the pompous Deacon Hailey, nicknamed 'Ole Hey' because he always ends his sentences with *hey*, becomes a kind of pioneer in the use of the all-Canadian shibboleth 'eh.' The village teacher, M'Tavit, is a Gaelic-speaking Cape Bretoner, whose suit is rejected by the local postmistress because he does not speak 'good English.'

Zangwill himself sums up the linguistic situation in the region as follows:

> In his little God-forsaken corner of Acadia the variously proportioned mixture of English and American, which, with local variations of Lowland and Highland Scotch, North of Ireland brogue, and French patois, loosely constitutes a Nova Scotian idiom, is further tinged with the specific peculiarities that spring from illiteracy and rusticity. (p.22)

Zangwill's representation of colloquial speech seems intended to suggest distinctions between speakers of different ages and positions:

> Girls are queer critters, thet's a fact [young Matt thinks]. (p.8).
> An' you orter be 'shamed o' yourself, I do declare, goin' home all alone in a sleigh with a young man.... [Mrs. Strang to her daughter] (p.9)
> I'm verra obleeged to you ... that's richt.... [M'Tavit, the Cape Bretoner teacher] (p.37)
> But don't you git it into your figurehead that you're goin' to London—you've jest got to stay right here and look arter the farm for mother. [Matt's father to Matt] (p.23)
> Father'd be terrible ugly if I was to settle anythin' while he was to the store. [Mrs. Cattermole to the Deacon, referring to her own husband as *Father*] (p.76)
> It's in furrin parts es the devil lurks, and the further a man goes from his family the nearer he goes to the devil, hey? [The Deacon, to Mrs. Strang] (p.15)
> And dear marm he lays in the Gulf of Mexiker kinder rapped in a shroud.... [Hosea Cuddy, mate, in a letter informing Mrs. Strang of her husband's death at sea] (p.17)

The vocabulary of anger, exaggeration, exclamations, intensifiers and racial slurs agrees in the main with Haliburton, as the following instances show: *by gum*, *everlastin'*, *gooney*, *nigger*, *pesky* (adj. and adv.), *sockdologee* (a kick, shove), *spunk up*, *streaked* (angry), *tarnal*, *tarnation*, *thunderation.* But many other expressions are simply general North American, e.g., *pumpkin-pie*, *quilting party*, and *settee*.

Not only do Zangwill's characters speak the vernacular when at home, but the differences in usage cause Matt some difficulties in his early days in London. Asked by his London cousin for a loan of a 'donkey,' Matt does not know that this slang expression means twenty-five pounds, which he can ill afford to part with, and has to have it explained to him.

The Master never gained great popularity either in Canada or in England. It has been long out of print, and is not likely to enjoy a revival, unless its importance is recognized not only as a historic document but also as a novel with dramatic power. This is more probable now that a hundred years have passed since its publication.

The literary use of Nova Scotian idiom in works of literature was destined to come into its own in the twentieth century in the writings of Hugh MacLennan, Thomas Raddall, Ernest Buckler, and their successors. In the nineteenth century, the tradition was being forged, predominantly for humourous effect, but eventually for a serious work of fiction. Our interest in nineteenth-century writers and their works is repaid when we perceive and enjoy those glimpses of nineteenth-century life which the works offer. If, in addition, we also desire to 'hear' the speech of the past, these works come as near as possible to giving us an opportunity to do so.

References

Avis, W. S. (1969). A note on the speech of Sam Slick. In R. E. Watters & W. S. Avis (Eds.), *The Sam Slick anthology*. Toronto: Clarke, Irwin.

Bailey, R. W. (1981). Haliburton's eye and ear. *The Canadian journal of linguistics, 26 (1)*, 90- 101.

Barry, S. *Elizabeth Bishop: An archival guide to her life in Nova Scotia.* For the Elizabeth Bishop Society of Nova Scotia, 1996.

Conrad, M., Laidlaw, T., & Smyth, D. (1988). *No place like home: Diaries and letters of Nova Scotia women 1771-1938*. Halifax: Formac.

Falk, L. (1994). A nineteenth century literary representation of Nova Scotia dialect. In L. Falk, K. Flikeid, & M. Harry (Eds.), *Papers from the seventeenth annual meeting of the Atlantic provinces linguistic association*, Halifax, November 5 & 6, 1993. Halifax: Saint Mary's University.

Haliburton, T. C. (1968). *The old judge, or, Life in a colony*. Toronto: McClelland & Stewart.

———. (1995) *The clockmaker: Series one, two, and three.* Ed. G. L. Parker. Ottawa: Carleton University Press.

McCulloch, T. (1990). *Letters of Mephibosheth Stepsure*. Ed. G. Davies. Ottawa: Carleton University Press.

Glossary

Affix. A part of a word such as a prefix or suffix; also defined as a bound morpheme.

Africadian. The language of Nova Scotians of African descent (*Afri-* + *Acadian*). A term coined by George Elliot Clarke.

Allophones. Different pronunciations of the same sound; e.g., a voiceless pronunciation of /d/ in the vicinity of other voiceless consonants, as in the word *stopped* [stopt].

Alveolar. A consonant produced by the tip of the tongue touching the ridge behind the upper teeth.

American English. English as used in North America, especially the United States.

Asterisk *. Symbol used to indicate a hypothetical linguistic form.

Black English. English spoken by North Americans of African descent.

British Received Pronunciation. Abbreviated *RP*, this term refers to a widely used and understood pronunciation of English in southern England. The term is neutral, and does not reflect a value judgement.

British English. English as used in Great Britain.

Canadian Raising. A variant pronunciation of the diphthongs [aʊ] and [aɪ] before voiceless consonants, as in *out* and *bite*.

Cases. Case, in grammar, is the change in the form of nouns, pronouns, and adjectives, according to their grammatical function; e.g., subject, object of verb, object of preposition.

Central vowel. A vowel pronounced when the tongue occupies a central position in the mouth, e.g., [ʌ] in *but*.

Checked vowels. Vowels which are followed by a consonant, contrasted with vowels in a free position.

Copula. A linking verb, like *to be* in 'They *are* ready.'

Creole (creolized). A language resulting from contact between two language groups. It becomes the only language of the region's population.

Dialect. A language variety marked by differences from the standard language in matters of grammar, lexicon, and phonetics.

Diphthong. A sound produced by gliding from one vowel to another within one syllable; e.g., the middle sound in *loud*. In English a diphthong is an individual phoneme.

Discourse and *Discourse analysis.* Discourse is a spoken, written, or recorded utterance. Discourse analysis takes into account, as fully as possible, all circumstances attending the production, transmission, and reception of an utterance.

Discourse markers. Words which do not affect the content of an utterance, but mark aspects of the utterance itself, such as beginning, ending, shift in topic or in point of view.

Disjuncts. Words which do not convey content, but refer to the speaker's manner or attitude, such as 'frankly,' 'briefly,' 'happily,' and 'unfortunately.'

Downtoners. Words used to diminish the force of adjectives, such as 'somewhat' in 'somewhat difficult.'

Epenthetic sound. An added sound, providing a transition between two sounds, such as [ə] in [fɪləm] *film.*

Folk Etymology. Popular explanations of the origins of words and expressions, suggested by similarity to a linguistically unrelated expression; e.g., the view that 'belfry' is derived from 'bell.'

Free vowel phonemes. Vowel phonemes in a final position, contrasted with checked vowels.

Fricative. A consonant produced by constricting the passage of air without stopping it entirely.

Gender. A grammatical category which identifies certain words (nouns, adjectives, pronouns, and in some languages also verbs) as being feminine, masculine, or neuter.

Gender inclusive language. Style of speaking and writing which includes males and females in general statements; e.g., 'our *ancestors*' rather than 'our *fathers,*' '*letter carriers*' rather than '*postmen,*' '*flight attendants*' rather than '*stewardesses.*'

General Canadian English. English as used in Canada.

Grammar. Traditionally defined as a set of written rules governing correct usage; in modern times perceived rather as a set of rules naturally acquired by all speakers of a language from childhood onwards.

Grammatical system. The set of rules governing the use of a language.

Halifax Standard. English as used both formally and informally in Halifax, NS, provincial capital of Nova Scotia. The city is important linguistically as centre of government, military, commercial, and cultural institutions.

Halifax Standard idiolect. See *Idiolect.*

Haligonian. Pertaining to, or native of Halifax, NS.

High German and *Low German.* High German is the language spoken in the mountainous southern region of Germany, and Low German is the language of the lowlands in the northern region.

High onset. Onset (i.e. the beginning of the formation of a diphthong) with the tongue in a relatively high position in the mouth.

Homonyms. Words which are alike in sound and spelling, but different in meaning and origin; e.g., *bear* 'carry' and *bear* 'an animal.'

Hyper-correction. The phenomenon of applying certain learned rules of grammar or pronunciation outside the circumstances where these rules are appropriate, such as saying 'They gave the tickets to Mary and I.'

Idiolect. The speech of an individual, as distinct from the speech of a group or region.

Indicative. The mood of verbs used in stating facts. In 'We *arrived* yesterday,' *arrived* is in the indicative mood.

Infinitive. The form of a verb which is not marked for person or tense. *To go* in 'I want *to go*' is an infinitive. The related form without *to* is called 'base,' e.g., *go* in 'We must *go*.'

Intensifiers. Words used to strengthen the force of gradable adjectives, such as *very* in '*very* good,' '*very* hot.'

Isoglosses. Boundaries on dialect maps indicating the areas where certain linguistic features can be found.

Lexical. Pertaining to vocabulary.

Lingua franca. Any language used for communication between people speaking different languages, as Latin in medieval Europe, Swahili in East Africa, and English in many parts of the world.

Loyalist settlers. Settlers who came to Canada around the time of the American Revolution (American War of Independence 1775-1783). Their speech patterns exerted an important influence on Maritime English.

Maritime English. English used in the Maritime Provinces, i.e. Nova Scotia, New Brunswick, and Prince Edward Island.

Minimal pairs. Words selected for the purpose of identifying phonemes: *pin* and *bin* constitute a minimal pair, showing that /p/ and /b/ are phonemes in English, since the difference in their sound carries the distinction in meaning between these two words.

Morpheme. A minimal meaningful unit which may be equivalent to a whole word, or part of a word, e.g., 'meaningful' has the morphemes 'mean,' '-ing,' and '-ful.'

Morphology. The structure of words, and the study of the structure of words with respect to the minimal meaningful units of which they are composed.

Objective case. In languages which distinguish cases, *objective* is the form used for objects of verbs. In English, nouns have a general case and a possessive case (*child*, *child's*). Some pronouns, however, have a different form in the nominative case (*I*, *we*, *he*, *she*, *they*), objective case (*me*, *us*, *him*, *her*, *them*), and possessive case (*my*, *our*, *his*, *her*, *their*).

Oblique case. In languages which mark distinction in the cases of nouns, pronouns, and adjectives, the subject case is called the nominative, and all other cases are called oblique.

Observer's paradox. In linguistic field work, the difficulty of obtaining information about natural speech, because the presence of an observer creates an obstacle to natural behaviour.

Palatalized. A consonant altered in pronunciation under the influence of an adjoining palatal sound, e.g., /t/ in *duty* becomes palatalized by the [y] sound that follows it.

Past participle. The verb form used in such constructions as '… has *done, seen, written, returned*,' '… was *done, seen, written, returned*.'

Perfect. Verbal construction used to signify action completed before a certain point, e.g., 'They *had left* before the others came.'

Phonemes. Distinct sounds of a language which can indicate a difference in meaning, e.g., /p/ and /b/ in English.

Phonetics. The systematic study of speech sounds.

Phonetype. A phoneme possessing a certain set of articulatory characteristics.

Phonology. The sound system of a given language, and the study of such systems.

Pidgins. Languages resulting from contact between groups speaking dissimilar languages. Unlike creole, pidgins are used as a second language for trade or commerce, but do not function as a group's only tongue.

Plantation Creole. The creole language spoken by descendants of Black African slaves on plantations and farms in the Americas.

Polysynthetic. A language which incorporates the elements of a sentence into one utterance, as distinct from *inflecting* and *agglutinating*.

Praxis. Actual behaviour or application of rules, as contrasted with the rules themselves.

Preterite. The verb form used to signify action in the past, e.g., *responded, wrote*.

Register. Style and manner of speaking, such as formal or informal, adopted by speakers according to circumstances.

Relational concepts. As defined by Edward Sapir, language elements which mark such distinctions as subject and object, singular and plural, definite and indefinite, present and past, as distinct from the concrete concepts expressed by verbs, nouns, and derivational suffixes.

Relic. A linguistic feature surviving from an earlier time or previous geographic location, in spite of changes which have taken place in the meantime. For example, *fall* used in North America to designate *autumn* is a relic of earlier British usage.

Retroflex fricative. A fricative produced by constricting the passage of air and curling the tongue tip backward behind the alveolar ridge.

Rounding. In phonetics, the rounding of a speaker's lips in pronouncing certain vowel sounds, e.g., [o].

S.V. (*Sub verbo, sub voce*) 'under this word' (Latin).

Schwa. A central low vowel, usually heard in unaccented syllables, such as the 'a' in *sofa*.

Semantic. Pertaining to the meaning of words, grammatical constructions, and syntactic patterns.

Semantic categories. Unlike grammatical categories, which distinguish nouns, adjectives, and other parts of speech on the basis of grammatical function, semantic categories distinguish concepts on the basis of meaning, such as animate or inanimate, continuing or completed action, permanent or accidental attribute.

Shibboleth. A characteristic of speech by which a dialect speaker can be recognized.

Slanted brackets / /. Symbol used to indicate phonemic, as opposed to phonetic, transcription.

Square brackets [ ]. Symbol used to indicate phonetic, as opposed to phonemic, transcription.

Standard dialect. The form of a language used in the media, in public events, in formal communications, and as a medium of teaching.

Standard idiolect. The speech of an individual considered as representative of the prevailing standard in the area where the individual is living.

Substratum. A language of a group or region which has been displaced by another language, but which has left certain influences on the new language.

Syntactic. Pertaining to the structure of sentences.

Syntax. The structure of sentences, and the study of the structure of sentences, with respect to subject, predicate, word order, and order of phrases.

Tonal accentuation. Accentuation by means of tonality, such as conveying questions, statements, hesitations, by intonation alone, without pronouncing the words clearly. Written words like *hm*, *ah*, *um* are sometimes used to represent such utterances.

Toponym. The name of a place, or a name derived from the name of a place.

Underground Railway. Called 'Underground Railroad' in the USA, it was a network of secret anti-slavery activities, organized primarily to convey people escaping from slavery into safety in Canada and the free States.

Vernacular. The common everyday language of a people in any country or place.

Voiced consonants. Consonants pronounced with vibrations of the vocal chords, e.g., [b], [d], [g], [v], [z]: opposite of voiceless consonants.

Voiceless consonants. Consonants pronounced without vibrations of the vocal chords, e.g., [p], [t], [k], [f], [s].

Index

Shortz

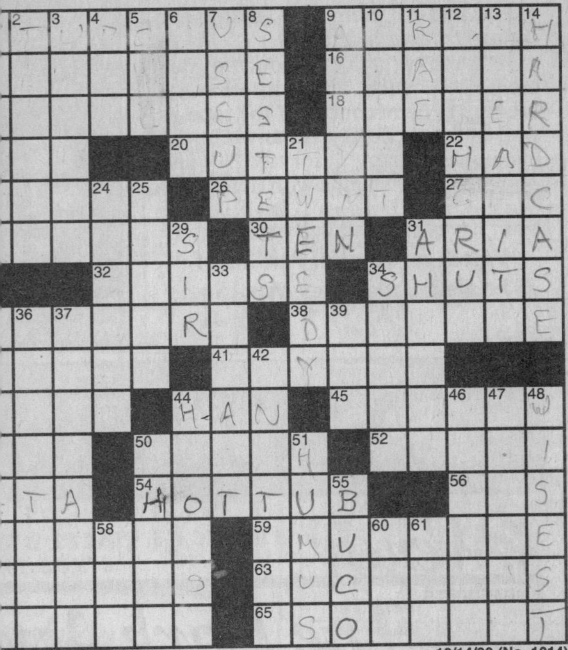

zle by Rich Norris 10/14/00 (No. 1014)

Better than average

Frank Sinatra, for one

Subs

Notable W.W. II neutral: Abbr.

Colorful fog phenomenon

Ridges on a print

One way to communicate

47 Like some salons

48 Most prudent

50 Hose

51 Woodchips, e.g.

55 Osso ___

58 Actress Lyon, who played Lolita, 1962

60 Old N.Y.C. sights

61 One of the Canterbury pilgrims

Crossword

Edited by Will

ACROSS

1 Just super
9 Over
15 Go nuts
16 Therapy subject
17 Adaptable subspecies
18 Two-hanky film
19 Ruse
20 Sacramento founder
22 Taken
23 Fun
26 Small flycatcher
27 Legendary beast
28 Accommodates, in a way
30 Venice's Council of ___
31 "Una voce poco fa," e.g.
32 Run over
34 Stops talking, with "up"
35 Forbear
38 Employee benefit, perhaps
40 Colorful fabric
41 Atlanta suburb
43 Setting for Camus's "The Stranger"
44 4th- to 6th-century Chinese dynasty
45 "When ___ is punished, its fame is exalted": Tacitus
49 Carte listing
50 Yawn
52 Medicinal plant
53 Sched. entry
54 Back porch luxury
56 Weed
57 Balancer
59 Prig
62 Many a flower
63 Blocks
64 They're pushed in alleys
65 Champion's challenge

DOWN

1 Bits
2 Show disgust
3 Stat
4 Short order?
5 Rapture
6 It may follow an omission
7 Spend
8 Sonnet parts
9 In the middle of, in dialect
10 Réunion attendee
11 19th-century Arctic explorer
12 High
13 More prone to running
14 Tough customer
21 Like some professors' suits
24 Repressed
25 Converse
29 Title of respect
31 Recherché
33 Vote out
34 Accelerating forces

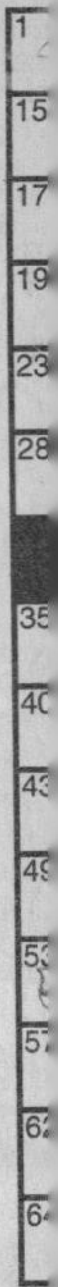

ANSWER TO PREVIOUS PUZZLE

C	L	I	M	A	X	■	I	R	A	G	L	A	S	S
R	A	R	E	F	Y	■	N	E	B	R	A	S	K	A
A	M	O	R	A	L	■	S	P	L	I	T	R	U	N
N	I	N	■	R	E	T	I	R	E	E	■	E	N	T
K	N	E	W	■	M	A	G	I	■	V	O	D	K	A
C	A	D	I	Z	■	T	H	E	R	E	F	■	■	■
A	T	O	N	E	D	■	T	V	A	■	F	O	C	I
S	O	U	N	D	E	D	■	E	N	L	I	V	E	N
E	R	T	E	■	C	O	P	■	D	O	C	E	N	T
■	■	■	R	A	K	E	I	N	■	B	E	R	T	H
A	M	A	S	S	■	S	E	E	S	■	R	H	E	E
R	O	C	■	P	E	T	R	O	C	K	■	E	R	R
T	U	R	M	E	R	I	C	■	A	L	P	A	C	A
U	S	E	R	N	A	M	E	■	R	E	S	T	U	P
R	E	S	I	S	T	E	D	■	F	E	I	S	T	Y